Nature and Natural Science
The Philosophy of F. J. E. Woodbridge

Photo courtesy of the Columbiana Library, Columbia University.

Nature and Natural Science

The Philosophy of Frederick J. E. Woodbridge

by

William Frank Jones

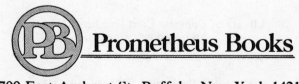

Prometheus Books

700 East Amherst St. Buffalo, New York 14215

To Donna

Published 1983 by Prometheus Books
700 East Amherst Street, Buffalo, New York 14215

Library of Congress Card Number: 82-48969
ISBN: 0-87975-183-5

Printed in the United States of America

Contents

5

Foreword

I have been much concerned for some time that the philosophy of F. J. E. Woodbridge should not become unknown, for he is still very important. I am grateful, therefore, to Professor Jones for this important and much needed book. I hope that its publication will stimulate discussion and that Woodbridge will be saved from neglect.

I am pleased to add in this Foreword some insights regarding Woodbridge's fundamental distinction between nature and the supernatural— insights growing out of my long, personal acquaintance with the man as well as his thought.

Woodbridge realized the danger of being misunderstood in using the word "supernatural," especially when used in contrast with "nature." I happened to call on F. J. E. W. at his bedside a few days before his death; he was writing "the last chapter" of *An Essay on Nature,* and he said to me (with a smile): "I'm tempted to entitle it 'Nature Suspended' instead of 'Supernatural,' but this would be even more apt to be misunderstood. I'll let it go as it stands." As Professor Jones correctly observes, Woodbridge used "supernatural" to refer to the ideal interests of persons, such as the pursuit of happiness, as distinguished from, for example, the pursuit of a scientific knowledge of nature.

Though Woodbridge's realistic knowledge developed primarily from natural sources, he used "supernatural" in connection with the creative arts, which can exploit the natural sciences for their own purposes, not because they are intellectually superior but because the arts can use the sciences for their own achievements. Drawing from examples that Woodbridge enjoyed using in expounding his philosophy, historians can improve their stories of the past by pretending to be thoroughly scientific or realistic, and religious faiths can strengthen their myths by making them historical. Thus the sciences can be used for super-science histories, when they are not used as

9

genuine sciences but are used instead to give realistic appearances to stories that are not realistic.

The greatness of F. J. E. Woodbridge — his mind, his life, and his character — is evident not only in his philosophy but also in his professional and family lives. The breadth of his life gives witness to what he called the natural and the supernatural.

At Columbia University, Dean Woodbridge was the dean of deans. He held the administrative responsibilities for all the graduate faculties, and since their subject matters varied widely his office had to act wisely in many different ways — from chemistry to charity, from the examination of "floating needles" to the study of social ethics.

To him his weekend life with family, friends, and others in the fine Woodbridge home among the hills and lakes of the upper Hudson, in contrast to his work in the city and the university, was an important part of the kind of life to which he referred as his "supernatural" existence, when he would set his scientific life and philosophy aside in order to cultivate the arts and their joys. His weekend reliefs with arts and family were genuinely "super," more significant than most of his scientific or "natural" labors. These weekend reliefs were more than reliefs from labor. He enjoyed thinking of them as a genuine "suspension" of nature.

I am confident that Professor Jones's book is an excellent exposition of Woodbridge's philosophy, as well as an accurate portrait of the mind and the man. It seems to me to be perfectly suited to honoring our good old dean.

Herbert W. Schneider
Claremont, California

Preface

Frederick J. E. Woodbridge should be much more widely known among contemporary philosophers; and it is regrettable that he is not, for he was most influential in determining the general intellectual commitments of contemporary naturalists and realists. In his "Epilogue" to *Naturalism and the Human Spirit*—a cooperative effort by fifteen of the leading spokesmen of naturalism—John Herman Randall, Jr., had this to say about the profound influence of his late teacher and colleague:

> This realistic emphasis of Woodbridge appears in a number of the essays here; for over half the contributors were students of his—he was a consummate teacher—and reveal the strong impress of his powerful intellectual personality. Much as they have learned from Dewey, it is clear to the discerning reader that most of them owe their fundamental naturalism to Woodbridge. (p. 366)

Unlike Dewey, Woodbridge was not a prolific author. Rather, his influence was exerted primarily through his gifted students at Columbia and his friends and acquaintances. Through them he influenced naturalism and realism, especially with regard to philosophical method, metaphysics, and the importance of an adequate appreciation of history, particularly the history of philosophy.

Largely because of his "realistic emphasis," for example, the methodologies of contemporary naturalists are, in their own eyes, decidedly antireductionist. His criticisms of the genetic method contributed considerably to the development of a functional or operational analysis. One of his most notable intellectual contributions, however, was his effort to revive among philosophers a concern for metaphysics and his ability to channel this concern

11

in the direction of a descriptive "first science" after the manner of Aristotle. Moreover, he greatly encouraged the development and advance of American thought by founding and co-editing with Wendell T. Bush the *Journal of Philosophy,* toward which he frequently contributed influential articles. Although Woodbridge is acknowledged by many as one of the principal figures with regard to the origin and development of both American realism and naturalism—and even pragmatism—he was critical of the views of many of the other leaders of these movements, such as Charles S. Peirce, William James, and John Dewey, for what he believed to be their lack of realism and naturalism. Woodbridge's criticisms serve as an important source commentary from inside these movements on themes of continuing interest to contemporary thought.

In spite of Woodbridge's important influence, little has been done to make his thought generally available. One reason for this neglect may be that many contemporary philosophers avoid any views that are as obviously metaphysical as those of Woodbridge. Moreover, most of his published work took the form of articles addressing specific issues rather than books that might have systematically presented his whole philosophy. In addition, Woodbridge's style is difficult. In order to communicate the qualitative richness of what he took to be Nature, his prose possessed a poetic quality. Thus while his writings are stylistically rich and poetic, their meaning is not always as clear as one would like. My attempt to render systematic what is presented less systematically in Woodbridge's published writings has been greatly aided by an extensive collection of his unpublished materials, a collection that sheds considerable new light on his position. Since he was quite deliberate in the development of a literary style that he believed would most adequately communicate his philosophy, and since he exercised great care in the composition of his written materials, close attention to the primary texts is important in understanding Woodbridge. My liberal quotations of Woodbridge's work are therefore intended to give the reader direct exposure to his style. My exposition offers a faithful clarification of his texts; for not only have I made use of the extensive unpublished collection but, also, I have been fortunate to have the expert advice of W. Gordon Ross and Herbert W. Schneider. Furthermore, given the general historical importance of Woodbridge's thought and the influence of different aspects of his philosophy, my interests here are to present, as objectively as possible, his philosophical perspective within the context of *his* intellectual concerns and to offer a thorough exposition of his whole philosophy.

My purpose is to provide an exposition of Woodbridge's total philosophy within the context of his concerns, rather than to discuss those parts of his thought that are relevant to my philosophic interests. Even so, I was attracted to Woodbridge's philosophy because I believe that it is relevant to many philosophic problems—but especially, to the growing loss of commitment to the traditional Western scientific-philosophic standard of objectivity. For as

Israel Scheffler shows in *Science and Subjectivity,* "objectivity," where all scientific statements are subject "to the test of independent and impartial criteria" (p. 1), is under attack, leading some to conclude that,

> Independent and public controls are no more, communication has failed, the common universe of things is a delusion, reality itself is made by the scientist rather than discovered by him. In place of a community, of rational men following objective procedures in the pursuit of truth, we have a set of isolated monads, within each of which belief forms without systematic constraints. [p. 19]

The radicalness with which these conclusions violate Western common sense shows how fundamental a shift in cultural perspective is this loss of objectivity. Accordingly, this loss cannot be taken lightly. Whatever the final judgment regarding our traditional commitment to objectivity, Woodbridge is a pivotal thinker: his philosophical realism is perhaps the clearest, most consistent, and most fully developed statement and defense of traditional Western objectivity. For an age concerned with the question of objectivity, therefore, Woodbridge's thought deserves careful consideration.

Many have contributed to the preparation of this book: colleagues, students, and friends. A special debt of gratitude is due Eastern Kentucky University for a research grant and sabbatical leave that provided both funds and time to complete this work. Professor Andrew J. Reck contributed in a special way, for it was he who introduced me to Woodbridge's philosophy and originally suggested the writing of a book on his thought. My colleagues in the Department of Philosophy and Religion have been constant in their support, encouragement, and intellectual stimulation — all of them important factors in helping me to maintain my enthusiasm for this project. Other members of the faculty—Charles Whitaker, Bonnie Gray, and Un Chol Shinn—have read and made helpful comments on the manuscript. A debt of gratitude is owed to Dr. Corliss Lamont, without whose encouragement and support this book would not have been possible. I would like to express my appreciation to Steven L. Mitchell, college division editor, and to Prometheus Books for preparing the final manuscript for publication and for their dedication to this project. I am grateful to Ms. Beverly McMaine, Mrs. Sandra Seithers, Mrs. Dolly Steele, and my wife, Donna, for their patience and care in typing the manuscript. For everything that is true and sound in this work, I am indebted to the encouragement, stimulation, and, in general, the skillful Socratic midwifery of W. Gordon Ross and Herbert W. Schneider. To me they will always be both professors and philosophers; they are my models of the genuine teacher and the true lover of wisdom. Without the sustenance of love and the leisure provided by the sacrifices of my parents, Dyche and Polly; my sons, Todd and Ryan; and especially my wife, Donna Thomas Jones, this venture would have been impossible. To Donna, my partner in all life's ventures, I dedicate this volume.

Eastern Kentucky University   W. F. J.
June, 1981

1

The Scope of Woodbridge's Philosophy

> The realism I would urge is one of principle rather than one of selection.[1]

> The incorporation of man into nature may well do something to man, but it must also do something to nature. It is impossible that the word "nature" can mean the same after this incorporation that it meant before.[2]

Introduction

Earlier, in the Preface, John Herman Randall, Jr., was quoted to indicate Frederick J. E. Woodbridge's influence on American realism and naturalism: in the "Epilogue" of *Naturalism and the Human Spirit,* Randall wrote,

> This realistic emphasis of Woodbridge appears in a number of the essays here; for over half the contributors were students of his—he was a consummate teacher—and reveal the strong impress of his powerful intellectual personality.[3]

One of these contributors and a former student of Woodbridge, Sterling P. Lamprecht, has also written about the influence of Woodbridge's realism:

> The Woodbridge tradition—for realization that there is a Woodbridge tradition is growing among us year by year— . . . does not consist in the continued repetition of an orthodoxy of profession and belief. The Woodbridge tradition is rather . . . a realism which finds in nature the source, the environment, and the destiny of all that occurs.[4]

15

Although the purpose of this book is to present Woodbridge's philosophy rather than an account of his influence on other philosophers, acknowledgment of his influence provides evidence for the importance of offering an exposition of Woodbridge's realism, the naturalism and humanism to which his realism led, and, more generally, his total philosophy.

His realism is fundamental to the whole of Woodbridge's philosophy, and an overview of this realism is important. This chapter is an introduction to his realism and to its implications: science is realistic and, in metaphysical inquiry, realism leads to naturalism and humanism. Here, Woodbridge's realism is discussed in a more general way; later chapters will focus upon specific issues.

Woodbridge's Realism

Woodbridge wrote, "I confess a sympathy with all realists. . . . They are evidently trying to see things as they are."[5] Not everyone, however, who claims to respect the "real" is a realist in Woodbridge's sense of the term. Within his thought a distinction is made between the "selective realist" and the "realist in principle."[6] The selective realist is one who uses the terms 'reality' or the 'real' to denote a distinction; this use does not indicate a difference in fact but, rather, "a difference in point of view, in value, in preference, in relative importance for some desire or choice."[7] On the other hand, the realist in principle, while he recognizes that all things are not equally important, accepts as his guiding principle, "all things are equally real." Since the 'real' does not denote a genuine distinction for the realist in principle, he believes that "nothing that happens can be convicted of impossibility."[8] Woodbridge claimed to be a realist in principle.[9]

Woodbridge holds that realism includes a kind of "naïveté": "what we repeatedly need is at once the most naïve and profoundest realism we can express."[10] Although the realist's selection of subject matter may be based on preference (even bias), once the selection is made, the realistic inquirer must approach his subject with an attitude of naïveté. That is, he must attempt to follow the lead of the subject matter in developing hypotheses rather than impose preconceptions on the subject.

> One should, I think, be realistic. By that I mean that one ought not to begin with definitions, and axioms and postulates which have the certain effect of controlling the argument to its conclusion. I could readily so define nature and science and mental health as to dispose of the whole question one way or the other *ab initio*. Refusing to do this is, I think, of prime importance. Too much of that sort of thing is done by both scientists and philosophers.[11]

Having initiated the inquiry, the realist will attempt to sustain his naïveté through continuing to follow the lead of the subject matter. More precisely, he will maintain the distinction between the subject matter being examined and his interpretations of it in order that the adequacy of his hypotheses can be checked in light of the subject they were constructed to clarify. For the realist, the "subject-matter of inquiry can not be called in question."[12] "It is evident that failure or success in the application [of an explanatory system or hypothesis] is due not to the system, but to the objects. The systems do not test the objects; the objects test the system."[13]

Since the realist attempts to avoid prejudice during the entire process of inquiry, according to Woodbridge, his work is scientific. The specific methods by which the realistic metaphysician practices inquiry differ from those of the special sciences. These differences, however, are not the result of differing attitudes but are the result of their different subject matters. The attitude of realism and the scientific attitudes are identical.

> The word "scientific" emphasizes that kind of intellectual integrity and disinterestedness in the pursuit of knowledge which is characteristic of those inquirers who let themselves be controlled by the subject-matter they are investigating and refuse to draw conclusions from it to suit some ulterior purpose. . . . So long as we use "science" as a noun for specified departments of knowledge and "scientific" as an adjective to indicate that the work done is done with integrity of mind and with respect for the subject-matter involved, we are on safe ground.[14]

His Contextualism

Woodbridge sometimes uses "context" to refer to the empirical subject matter of scientific inquiry.[15] There were other times, however, when he used the term to refer to the environment of objects conditioning the object under investigation: "nothing that happens in Nature is free from a context in which some sort of action and reaction is present."[16] For "context" neither refers exclusively to the subject nor to the subject's environment of conditioning objects but, rather, to both. That is, for Woodbridge, the context examined in the scientific study of any subject matter is *the way* the subject matter *behaves* within its conditioning environment. It is important to note that, while he uses the term "behavior," among others, in referring to the subject matter of inquiry, this use should not lead the reader to associate Woodbridge with the bias attributed to radical behaviorists, i.e., an exclusive emphasis on overt motor behavior. "Behavior" is, for him, any sort of "doing"—"from the movement of an ion to the thinking of a man."[17] It is equivalent in meaning to Aristotle's concept of "actuality." Woodbridge's use of the word "activity" to refer to subject matters in context is apt indeed. Accordingly, the *context* that guides the scientific examination of any subject matter is the cooperative activity of the subject in its environment.

By following the lead of the subject's activity, the inquirer can both formulate and test hypotheses stating what he believes are the ways in which the content of the subject's environment conditions its activity. If he determines *how* these factors affect the subject's activity, then he has acquired a knowledge of the "powers" that the subject possesses and can exercise when in a suitable environment of cooperating objects. Furthermore, the subject's powers comprise its "nature." According to Woodbridge, therefore, scientific inquiry seeks knowledge of the "nature" of its subjects.

Why falling bodies fall as they do and not otherwise, the physicist cannot tell us. Why oxygen reacts as it does and not otherwise, the chemist cannot tell us. Each points to a fundamental fact which he has reached and then he stops. Such fundamental facts we come upon sooner or later, such we shall always have and at them we shall always stop. Psychology is no exception to this all-embracing rule. Why a living conscious organism reacts as it does and not otherwise we cannot say. Everywhere as a last resort we are driven to the *nature* of that which reacts. *This nature is for science unfolded in the action.* Consequently, for science this *"nature" already contains the reaction which is to take place.* Thus from [a] logical point-of-view, science begs the question. To recognize this is simply to recognize one of our limitations. Not to recognize it is to reduce science in its places of last resort to an absurdity. [Italics mine][18]

Beginning his inquiry with the subject's activity, the scientist concludes with the discovery of the subject's nature. While verbs and adverbs more accurately express subject matters, nouns and adjectives more faithfully express the fruits of inquiry: knowledge of natures and kinds of natures.[19] Woodbridge summarizes his position as follows:

We understand a thing when we have discovered what it can do in relation to other things. In different relations it acts differently, but in every case with a definiteness in accord with its propriety. Its operation in specific cases is a specific operation which nonetheless illustrates its proper action.[20]

A description of Woodbridge's contextualism would not be complete without observing that he distinguishes the contexts examined by the special sciences from those he clarifies in his role as a metaphysician. Both the special scientists and metaphysicians examine their subject matters realistically and, therefore, both are scientists. The special scientist, however, seeks a knowledge of the natures of specific subject matters through an examination of specific kinds of contexts; the metaphysician, on the other hand, seeks general understanding of Nature as the all-inclusive context, that is, the generic traits of any or every activity with special regard to man's presence as a conditioning factor in every context of inquiry. The specificity of the special sciences distinguishes their subject matters from one another and from that of the metaphysician. Since the subject matters of the special sciences and the metaphysician differ, special scientists as such need not concern themselves with the broader subject matter of Nature or the discoveries of metaphysicians. When, however, special scientists lose their realistic attitude, no longer limiting their inquiry to their restricted subject matters, they may attempt to apply theories appropriate to their limited subject matters to Nature in general. Woodbridge believes that the theoretical confusion resulting from this lack of respect for difference in contexts is best corrected by realistic metaphysical inquiry that draws attention to the importance of a respect for contexts and to the richness of the variety of Nature's activities.[21]

The Method of Contextual Analysis

Throughout the process of inquiry, realistic-scientific inquirers "let themselves be controlled by the subject-matter they are investigating";[22] therefore, according to Woodbridge, the subject matter determines the kind of method the realist uses in the examination of a subject. The method of inquiry does not transform a previously unintelligible subject matter into an intelligible one; rather, knowledge is acquired through the conformation of an inquirer's theory with an already knowable, although previously unknown, subject matter.[23] In contrast, the inquirer who lacks an attitude of realism will find his inquiry to be biased, because he has forced his subject matter to conform to his method and, therefore, to conform to the preconceptions underlying the kind of method he practices.

> The subject in seeking to know an object is not bringing to bear upon it a measure already secure of what knowledge is or ought to be. He does no more than follow the lead of the suggestions which the object makes to him, does his best to organize them in a manner consonant with the object, and names the result knowledge. A fish, but not the knower of it, except in terms of the latter's natural equipment for examining it, determines what knowledge of the fish is. Even the knower's method of organization has no antecedent rules to constrain him, for such rules as he finds necessary to employ are found in intercourse with what he is seeking to know.[24]

The methods of the various sciences differ because their subject matters differ.

Even so, Woodbridge believes that because the procedures of realistic-scientific inquirers are under the authority of their subject matters, their methods of inquiry share common characteristics. These common characteristics therefore compose an essential identity of realistic method. He frequently uses phrases such as "the subject-matter of inquiry can not be called in question,"[25] "follow the lead of the . . . object,"[26] "let themselves be controlled by the subject-matter,"[27] and "follow the ordinary experimental methods of observation and tested generalization"[28] to refer to the shared qualities constituting the common method. Woodbridge also claims, "our procedure is defined at once as analytic."[29] The expression 'contextual analysis' appropriately refers to the method Woodbridge considers common to all realistic-scientific inquiry.[30]

The contextual analyst follows *the lead* of the subject matter of an observable activity—the way the subject matter behaves within its conditioning environment—in his drawing of the distinctions denoting *what that lead indicates* to be the factors conditioning the subject matter. In contextual analysis, therefore, the distinctions composing the hypothesis refer to factors that are believed to function in designated ways in the context of the subject matter. Accordingly, Woodbridge holds that the distinctions made by contextual analysts receive their meaning from the role they play in the analysis of the subject matter.

The contextual analyst must avoid preconceptions in initiating his inquiry. Furthermore, he will stress throughout the inquiry that the subject matter is the standard of both the meaning and the adequacy of the distinctions composing an hypothesis, rather than allowing these distinctions, once made, to distort the evident character of the subject.[31] On the other hand, when failure to sustain a realistic attitude allows the hypothesis and its distinctions to displace the subject matter's control over inquiry, contextual analysis degenerates into "reductive analysis." For example, Woodbridge warns that an analysis of the activity of seeing into distinctions denoting the factors conditioning vision should not become reductive:

There is always a need for caution in analysis if intellectual deception is to be avoided. Although nothing whatever in Nature is ever "left to itself" in such a manner that we can determine what it would look like, where it is, and what it would do if there were nothing else, analysis proceeds as if this were possible. . . . We are often deceived into thinking that we have found original elements which were once put together to make, by simply combining, what Nature herself is. Atomic theories of that sort have always been disputed and for the best of reasons: namely, Nature is never so disrupted. Atoms are at least in space, and we are always at our wits' end to determine where a single atom by itself would be or what it would do. So left to itself, it has lost all determination. It ceases to be even an atom. This simple illustration indicates that visibility is not a composition of the factors which are found to control it, but the effective cooperation of those factors in determining what is visible.[32]

Woodbridge claims that realistic-scientific inquiry is experimental, incorporating, in addition to observation, *tested* generalization. Thus, the inquirer's distinctions are tested by determining whether factors function relative to the subject matter in the manner claimed. This test of adequacy can be accomplished if the inquirer does not allow his distinctions to bring into question the character of his only standard of adequacy: the subject matter. The contextual analyst must avoid reductive analysis by sustaining an attitude of realism.

Language and Contextual Analysis

For Woodbridge, experience in and of itself is not knowledge. Although the process leading to the acquisition of knowledge begins with empirical subject matters, a necessary part of scientific inquiry is the formulation and testing of hypotheses expressing interpretations with regard to the factors conditioning these subject matters. Thus, language performs a necessary function in inquiry: it is the instrument through which interpretations are formulated and communicated; that is, it functions "informatively."[33] And Woodbridge maintains that when language functions informatively within inquiry it expresses claims regarding subject matters that are extra-linguistic or exist independently of the linguistic expression: the making of any claim about any subject matter implies, according to Woodbridge, the truth-functional nature of the claim — otherwise, nothing has really been claimed.[34] And if nothing has been claimed, then no interpretation, no hypothesis, has been formulated; inquiry itself does not exist. But if the making of a claim implies the possibility of its being false, then the claim's truth value must be contingent upon a state of affairs transcending the claim itself.[35] Woodbridge believes that it must be contingent upon the extra-linguistic, "obvious and familiar" contents of the world man experiences.

> Knowledge involves objects of discourse, things, entities, or events about which something is said. The status of objects of discourse is not a linguistic status, nor is it determined by linguistic considerations.[36]

In other words, a necessary condition for the undertaking of the contextual analysis of scientific inquiry is that the propositions of hypotheses involved in the inquiry express claims regarding extra-linguistic subject matters. Unless this condition is satisfied, Woodbridge holds that realistic inquiry does not occur.[37]

Realism, Naturalism, and Humanism

According to Woodbridge, the subject matter of realistic and, therefore, scientific inquiry is extra-linguistic, empirically accessible activities. Assessing the activities of subjects, scientific inquirers discover that the exercise of a subject's nature is conditioned by the natures of the objects in its environment. More specifically, a subject's activity is conditioned by the way its body cooperates with other bodies; its activity is a *cooperation* of these bodies, the subject's and those of its environment. Woodbridge believes, therefore, that the practice of realistic inquiry provides evidence for the metaphysical tenet: every activity is contingent upon the bodies or things composing its context.

The doctrine that all activities are contingent upon spatio-temporally located bodies is a basic tenet of contemporary naturalism. And this tenet implies another—the rejection, at least as regards the possibility of acquiring knowledge, of supernaturalisms.[38] Furthermore, as indicated in the tenet, mental activities, for example, perception and thought, require the cooperation of bodies as much as any other kind of activity.[39] Woodbridge holds, therefore, that neither these activities nor any other natural activity implies for the special sciences the presence of radical dualisms: traditional metaphysical distinctions—such as mind-body, appearance-reality, freedom-necessity, and teleology-mechanism—should not be allowed to degenerate into radical dichotomies, as they frequently did because of an unwarranted theoretical divorce of man as mental subject from his body and the rest of the physical world;[40] man is a natural being. The rejection of radical dualisms is yet another fundamental doctrine of contemporary naturalism. In summary, realism in the use of the scientific method of contextual analysis led to these basic tenets of naturalism: the acceptance of the naturalness of man, the repudiation of supernaturalisms, the rejection of radical dualisms, and the increased respect for scientific procedure as the method of acquiring knowledge.[41] Consequently, Woodbridge's realism led him to accept naturalism.

In addition to man's more complex activities, his simpler functions such as movement and digestion are also activities of cooperation between the human organism and its environment and, as such, are entirely natural. If human nature is to be understood, therefore, human activities must be examined in light of the fact that, when exercised, they are the mutual cooperation of human organisms and the environment. That is, according to Woodbridge, they must be examined within the context of Nature.

Man, from his lowest physiological functions to the highest aspirations of his thought, illustrates the propriety of nature. The world in which he lives is controlled not only by physical and chemical laws, it is controlled also by logical, moral and spiritual laws. Otherwise how could man doubt or know or believe? When a man walks, we readily admit that nature is appropriate to his walking. When he sees or thinks, should we say something different? Should we say something different when he prays? He is doing what is natural. A thorough going naturalism can not avoid the conclusion that nature is as adapted to the life of man as it is to animals, plants, and atoms. To be so adapted, nature must be so arranged and ordered that the spiritual life of man is not alien to her. The nature of man and the nature of nature coincide.[42]

By placing man within the context of Nature something happens to him; he becomes naturalized. But what exactly does this naturalization entail? Woodbridge raises this question, and his answer offers the key to an understanding of his naturalism:

What has naturalism really done to man? It has most certainly changed him. But how? It has changed him from an illustration of what nature is not, to a profound illustration of what nature is.[43]

Accordingly:

The incorporation of man into nature may well do something to man, but it must also do something to nature. It is impossible that the word "nature" can mean the same after this incorporation that it meant before.[44]

Man, placed within the context of Nature, will have to accept that as an organism his physiological processes are like any other within Nature. But Nature inclusive of man must be accepted as possessing many qualities not generally attributed to her: inclusive of man, she is self-aware, thoughtful, articulate, and even awesome. Woodbridge asks rhetorically, "How could naturalism be looked upon as a debasement of man and not an elevation of nature?"[45] Man's naturalization does not entail his debasement; that man finds his body need not imply that he loses either his mind or his soul. Rather, naturalized man is one being whose bodily movement can be rationalized for the sake of realizing his spiritual aspirations. The naturalization of man is, on the other hand, the elevation of Nature. For Nature is now recognized to be not only the space wherein bodily movement illustrates mechanical laws but also the abode of rational and purposeful behavior. In man, Nature reveals herself to be much more than atoms and the void. For a complete view of Nature, therefore, we must turn to man's activities, to human living.

Nature reveals herself in man more adequately than in anything else, that in him her laws come to expression and meaning, that human life is not set over against nature, but is nature illuminated and inspirited.[46]

Nature may incorporate possibilities not revealed in man, but a more complete view of her actualities is unavailable. So important was man to a metaphysical understanding of Nature that Woodbridge says, "the distinction between nature and human nature, if taken to be an absolute and unique dichotomy, can yield no theory of nature at all."[47] For Woodbridge, naturalism is correlated with humanism.[48] More generally, realistic metaphysical inquiry led Woodbridge to both naturalism and humanism.

Since human activities are the key to an understanding of Nature, Woodbridge holds that, in referring to the subject matter of realistic metaphysics, "Nature" must be taken to mean "the world and ourselves."[49] While the special sciences, in dealing with limited subject areas, cannot offer analyses of Nature as world *and* humanity, Woodbridge's view is that the realistic metaphysician's task is to clarify this most general of contexts and primary of subject matters. In summary, Dean Woodbridge's faculty at Columbia University wrote of him at his death,

His interests in philosophy were many. We of this faculty were chiefly struck by his recurring concern with nature; *but what he called nature was a greater thing than we who cultivate particular parts of nature usually recognize.* Nature to Woodbridge was "heaven and earth, the sea and all that in them is" or, as one of his favorite authors had it, "that universal and public Manuscript that lies expansed unto the eyes of all." Although he thought much of such special problems as light and optics, the Nature to which he ever returned was not in the external world — *it was Man*; and surely human nature could be the true domain of the humanist. [Italics mine][50]

Summary

According to Woodbridge, a realist (in principle) approaches his subject matter with a kind of naïveté: throughout the process of inquiry, the realist will attempt to avoid prejudice through the acknowledgment that the subject matter determines both the adequacy and the meaning of his interpretations, and not vice versa. Furthermore, Woodbridge holds that this realistic attitude of naïveté is also the attitude definitive of science; science as science, whether special or metaphysical, is realistic. Moreover, although the methods of the sciences differ according to variations in their subject matters, scientific methods, being realistic, share methodological qualities: all are forms of contextual analysis.

In general, scientific inquiry discovers that the activities it investigates are cooperations of bodies. Realistic-scientific inquiry, therefore, provides evidence for the basic tenets of naturalism. According to Woodbridge, the realistic metaphysician is led to accept naturalism. But, since human activities are natural, the realist's naturalism must be rich enough to account for the total range of human behavior, from physical to intellectual and purposeful, however complex. For Woodbridge, therefore, realistic metaphysics leads not only to naturalism but also to humanism.

Sterling Lamprecht relates a story told to him by his former teacher, Woodbridge, that illustrates the latter's realism: when Woodbridge was Dean, a young woman, interested in taking a Ph.D. degree, asked him to assign her a field of study. Being busy and annoyed with her desire to get a degree rather than acquire knowledge of a subject matter, he sent her away, suggesting, nonetheless, that she read Locke's *Essay* and Darwin's *Origin of Species* and return when she had something of importance to say about her reading. Two years later, the young woman returned.

> "Well," he inquired, "and what did you discover about Locke and Darwin?" "I discovered," she replied, "a difference in the relation between the beginning and the outcome in the two books. For when Darwin began, he had pigeons; and when he finished, he still had pigeons. But when Locke began, he had the world of many objects about him; and when he finished, he found that that world had disappeared from view and had become a problem of knowledge." Then Professor Woodbridge, telling the story, added that he felt like conferring a doctor's degree on the young woman on the spot.[51]

For Woodbridge, the point of the above story is: although Locke had begun his study with the objects of Nature, being prejudiced by the Newtonian mechanical theory of Nature, he concluded by calling into question the possibility of a genuine knowledge of the objects of Nature; for lack of realism, Locke had lost his original subject matter, and subsequent generations of philosophers have been perplexed by that loss, as is evident in the development of skeptical epistemologies. On the other hand, because Darwin's inquiry into the origins of species was realistic, he had followed the lead of his subject (rather than losing it) until he had clarified it; thereby, he presented evidence that encouraged later realistic philosophers, like Woodbridge and John Dewey, to develop naturalistic-humanistic metaphysics.

NOTES

1. Frederick J. E. Woodbridge, *Nature and Mind: Selected Essays of Frederick J. E. Woodbridge* (New York: Columbia University Press, 1937; reprint ed., New York: Russell and Russell, 1965), p. 7.

2. Ibid., p. 254.

3. John Herman Randall, Jr., "Epilogue: The Nature of Naturalism," in *Naturalism and the Human Spirit* edited by Yervant H. Krikorian (New York: Columbia University Press, 1944), p. 366.

4. Sterling P. Lamprecht, *Nature and History* (New York: Columbia University Press, 1950; reprint ed., Hamden, Connecticut: Anchor Books, 1966), pp. v–vi.

5. Woodbridge, *Nature and Mind,* p. 7.

6. Ibid., p. 10.

7. Ibid., p. 102.

8. Ibid., p. 6.

9. Henceforth, unless I state otherwise, I will use the term 'realism' (or 'realist') to refer to what Woodbridge holds is a "realism in principle."

10. Frederick J. E. Woodbridge, *The Realm of Mind* (New York: Columbia University Press, 1926), p. 115; see also, *Nature and Mind,* pp. 7, 290.

11. Woodbridge, "Papers, 1884–1940" (Woodbridge's unpublished correspondences, diaries, essays, and lecture and reading notes, Columbia University, Special Collections), essay entitled: "The Claims of Science," undated, p. 3.

12. Woodbridge, *Nature and Mind,* p. 8. The "realistic distinction," the distinction between subject-matter and discourse or interpretation, will be discussed more fully in Chapter 3.

13. Woodbridge, "Papers, 1884–1940," paper entitled: "Ideology," undated, p. 9.

14. Ibid., "Claims of Science," p. 12.

15. See, for example, Woodbridge, *Nature and Mind,* p. 240.

16. Frederick J. E. Woodbridge, *An Essay on Nature* (New York: Columbia University Press, 1940), pp. 209–10.

17. Woodbridge, *Nature and Mind,* p. 192.

18. Woodbridge, "Papers, 1884–1940," Essay entitled: "Interest and Will," undated, p. 59b.

19. I believe that John Herman Randall, Jr.'s, linguistically evidenced metaphysical categories reflect Woodbridge's influence. See *Nature and Historical Experience,* p. 176. On the other hand, Randall emphasizes the active involvement (i.e., the "universe" of action) of man in the "situation" giving rise to the metaphysical distinctions more than did Woodbridge (idem., p. 184).

20. Woodbridge, *Nature and Mind,* p. 257.

21. Ibid., pp. 290–91. A thorough description of Woodbridge's conception of the nature and uses of realistic metaphysical inquiry and his critique of unrealistic metaphysical theory will be presented in the next two chapters.

22. Woodbridge, "Papers, 1884–1940," "Claims of Science," p. 12.

23. Woodbridge, *Nature and Mind,* pp. 73–74, and 76.

24. Woodbridge, *Essay on Nature,* p. 24.

25. Woodbridge, *Nature and Mind,* p. 8.

26. Woodbridge, *Essay on Nature,* p. 24.

27. Woodbridge, "Papers, 1884–1940," "Claims of Science," p. 12.

28. Woodbridge, *Nature and Mind,* p. 108.

29. Woodbridge, "Papers, 1884–1940," untitled essay on knowledge, undated, p. 6. While Woodbridge used the terms 'analysis' and 'analytic' in characterizing this method, it is important to make clear at the outset that Woodbridge should in no way be associated with what has become known as "analysis." Woodbridge had little

to say about logical positivism even in his late writings and, as far as I can determine, he was not familiar with the pioneering work (e.g., Wittgenstein and Ryle) in linguistic analysis.

30. Woodbridge continually used the terms 'analysis', 'context', and 'factor' in characterizing this method. Furthermore, he contrasted this method with reductive analysis. Given the cumbersomeness of the above phrases and the contextualism to which Woodbridge believes realistic inquiry leads, I use 'contextual analysis' to refer to the procedure that Woodbridge believes is shared by all realistic-scientific inquiry. Although Woodbridge never used the expression 'contextual analysis' to refer to his method and this expression is associated with the method of John Herman Randall, Jr., I believe that it is an appropriate name for Woodbridge's realistic method.

31. See, for example, Woodbridge, *Nature and Mind,* p. 338; also see, Woodbridge, *Essay on Nature,* p. 114.

32. Woodbridge, *Essay on Nature,* pp. 77–78.

33. Ibid., p. 228. Woodbridge also calls this function of language, "communication." He recognizes that language can be used to perform other linguistic functions, e.g., the expressive and directive. See, for example, ibid., p. 229.

34. Woodbridge, "Papers, 1884–1940," "Lectures on Metaphysics: Spring, 1928–29," p. 22.

35. Woodbridge, *Nature and Mind,* p. 71.

36. Woodbridge, "Papers, 1884–1940," lecture entitled: "Greek Philosophy 1927–8)," p. 4.

37. Language use is empirically observable; therefore, it can be examined scientifically. When language becomes the subject matter of scientific inquiry, language as subject matter is extra-linguistic relative to the language functioning informatively within inquiry.

38. Nature is sufficient as a context for analyzing both man's physical and mental activities. Therefore, interpreting these activities in terms of some notion of the supernatural inevitably leads to a distortion of human nature. Thus far, Woodbridge's position reflects mainstream contemporary naturalism. As a realist, however, Woodbridge does not feel that the persistency of belief in the supernatural can be ignored. Following the lead of the subject matter, Woodbridge accepts what he believes this belief implies concerning man: man, in addition to being a physical and mental being, has a spiritual dimension. And man as spirit transcends Nature; he is a "supernatural" being. Here is support for my belief that Woodbridge's view of man is the key to his whole philosophy. Woodbridge's "supernatural" will be discussed in Chapter 7.

39. Woodbridge, *Realm of Mind,* pp. 91–92.

40. See, for example, Woodbridge, *Essays on Nature,* pp. 252–53.

41. This list of basic tenets reflects in general the more comprehensive description of characteristics of contemporary naturalism contained in Ernest Nagel's article, "Naturalism Reconsidered," found in his collection of articles entitled *Logic Without Metaphysics* (Glen-Coe, Illinois: Free Press, 1957), pp. 3–18.

42. Woodbridge, *Nature and Mind,* pp. 257–58.

43. Ibid., p. 254.

44. Ibid.

45. Ibid.

46. Ibid., p. 256.

47. Ibid., p. 290.
48. The application of terms like 'realism', 'naturalism', and 'humanism' to Woodbridge's thought can be misleading. To some extent, Woodbridge resisted the philosophical labeling of his positions.

> If the conclusions which I have now drawn are taken to suggest a philosophy, I suspect that that philosophy will be called materialism. Some people are glad to find a materialist among philosophers and others are sorry. The latter might be comforted if I claimed that I was not one. My own conviction is that gladness or sorrow in this connection are dependent on initial and not on eventual definitions. [Woodbridge, "Paper, 1884–1940," "The Claims of Science," p. 10.]

If in following the lead of a subject matter an inquirer discovers that the subject-matter necessitates the use of a label for its understanding, then, according to Woodbridge, its use is warranted. Inquirers, however, should not initiate inquiry with labels that, as initial definitions of the subject matter, prejudice inquiry. Woodbridge resisted labels because he did not want his philosophical examination of Nature to be prejudiced. Perhaps this is the reason that, although he claimed to be a realist, he did not join the realistic movement [See n. 18, Hae Soo Pyun, "Nature, Intelligibility, and Metaphysics" (Amsterdam: B. R. Grüner, 1971) p. 22]. Woodbridge accepted the label "realism in principle" but, as we have seen, this is an expression of his commitment to "follow the lead of the subject-matter." He did not initiate inquiry as a "naturalist" or "humanist"; rather, these were positions to which his realistic analysis of the subject matter of Nature led. Accordingly, we should understand the meaning of "realism," "naturalism," and "humanism" from the point of view of Woodbridge's use of them in his inquiries rather than on the basis of some other authority.

49. Woodbridge, "Papers, 1884–1940," "Lectures on Metaphysics: Spring, 1932–33," p. 4.
50. Woodbridge, "Papers, 1884–1940," memorial statement on the occasion of F. J. E. Woodbridge's death: "Minutes of the Faculty of Philosophy," 1940, pp. 6–7.
51. Lamprecht, *Nature and History,* pp. vi–vii.

2

Metaphysics: Stages in Woodbridge's Development of this Science

The distinction between nature and human nature, if taken to be an absolute and unique dichotomy, can yield no theory of nature at all.[1]

The acceptance of the evolutionary point of view is . . . no guarantee that mythology has been abandoned. . . . they too frequently display a tendency to turn the characteristic operations of things into causes why things so operate; to assign a superior efficiency to the past than to the present; to make evolution a substitute for a creator; and, in general, to suppose that the causes rather than the history of the world have been discovered.[2]

Introduction

In "The Influence of Darwin on Philosophy" (1910), John Dewey shows that Darwinian evolutionary thought has had a profound influence on philosophy, especially on that of the American pragmatists and naturalists. During this general period when evolutionary thinking was an influential part of the intellectual environment, Woodbridge was in the process of developing his metaphysical theory of Nature. Early on, his metaphysical thinking was shaped by evolutionism. But, through his criticism of evolutionism he came to believe that if allowed to become a presupposition, it prejudices metaphysical inquiry; therefore, he developed what he believed to be a more realistic theory of Nature. Given the influence of evolutionism on philosophy, Woodbridge's evolutionism, his critiques of it, and his eventual intellectual move beyond it have historical importance.

Woodbridge believes that the most general of the sciences, the analysis of what Nature is in general, is a philosophical task. This unique philosophical science is known by the curious, more or less accidental name of 'meta-physics.'[3] His conceptions of this science gives his philosophy an originality and a development that can be analyzed into four stages, in view of impor-tant addresses and papers he submitted to his philosophical colleagues: "The Problem of Metaphysics" in 1903; "Metaphysics" in 1908; "Natural Teleology" in 1911; "Evolution" in 1912; and three lectures under the title *The Purpose of History* in 1916.

This chapter and the one to follow discuss metaphysical subject matter; they constitute the most technical elements of our study.

Stage I: The Uniqueness of Metaphysics

Woodbridge's 1903 address "The Problem of Metaphysics"[4] presented his earliest conception of metaphysics. Although he would eventually empha-size that metaphysics and the special sciences possess a common realistic atti-tude and, therefore, a realistic method, within this address, Woodbridge claims that one of the lessons learned in the study of the history of metaphys-ical thought is the need for distinguishing metaphysics from other disciplines, especially science and religion. Here he offers his earliest description of the uniqueness of metaphysics and the metaphysical method.

I modestly shrink from a calling that imposes upon me the necessity of complet-ing the fragmentary work of the physicist, the chemist, and the biologist, or of instructing these men in the basal principles of their respective sciences. My work lies in a totally different sphere, deals with totally different problems, and can be pursued in independence of them as much as they pursue their work in independence of me. There is a scientific knowledge and there is metaphysical knowledge, and these two are widely different problems. Science asks for the laws of existence and discovers them by experiment. Metaphysics asks for the nature of reality and discovers it by definition.[5]

According to Woodbridge, the method of definition, by means of which the metaphysician discovers the nature of reality, is the method of discover-ing and defining both the presuppositions that determine the natures of intellectual methods and the basic concepts necessary "to preserve sanity in our thinking."[6] For example, he notes,

The concept of purpose occurs repeatedly in much of our thinking, but it does not explain how the spider spins its web. The history of science has been in one of its aspects, the history of the rejection of concepts that do not explain by leading to the formulation of laws. But these concepts may turn out to be the ones most important for a definition of reality. . . . They may also reveal their own use as concepts which we still must retain in order to preserve sanity in our thinking, to keep it from being absolutely detached and meaningless. One of the most significant illustrations of this is the concept of purpose. We may deny design in nature, we may reject final causes as explanations of existence; but we can not define a single problem, isolate a single field of inquiry, determine the requisites of the solution of a single question, without this concept as the determining factor. So deep seated in all our thinking does it disclose itself, that we are tempted to say it defines the nature of reality in at least one of its essential characters.[7]

As a practitioner of the method of definition, Woodbridge claims that, although the presuppositions of the special sciences exclude "purpose" as an explanatory concept, the metaphysician discovers that "purpose" is a quality of Nature's processes and, as such, it is a condition of Nature, being the subject of any type of inquiry, including scientific. That is, unless "purpose" is descriptive of an essential quality of Nature, thought cannot make contact with Nature; sanity has been lost, for Nature is unintelligible. Accordingly, while the concept of purpose does not explain, the metaphysician must admit that it defines an essential character of reality.

Within this address, Woodbridge expresses a desire to limit his inquiry to "the formal side of metaphysics, avoiding as far as possible its material content";[8] "we must know beforehand the conditions which our solution is to fulfill, in order to determine its correctness when attained."[9] In order to discover the formal conditions of a solution to the problem of metaphysics, an adequate description of the character of reality, he examines within this address the history of metaphysical thought:[10] by discovering the underlying concepts of previous thought and submitting these presuppositions to a logical examination, he seeks to discover in past conceptual failures some indication of the conditions an adequate metaphysical description must fulfill—conditions that, when fulfilled, would insure conceptual sanity and, therefore, the avoidance of conceptual failures.[11]

While Woodbridge's study of history provides several lessons, he believes that one promises to be most significant:

. . . we have to ask in most general terms. What does the solution demand in principle, under the conditions which we may discover as determining it logically? Here we come at once upon one of the most significant positive results of our previous discussion. It is this: reality can not be defined intelligibly as a system absolutely external to the one who formulates it, nor a system in which the one who formulates it is a mere incident, or of which he is a mere product. That is the positive contribution made by the weakness discovered in the traditional types of metaphysics, in the breach between reality and appearance in all thorough going evolutionary conceptions, and especially the weakness in the distinction between epistemology and metaphysics.[12]

According to Woodbridge, a logical examination of the conceptions that radically dichotomize appearance from reality or the subjective from the objective reveals their conceptual failures.

For the reduction of everything to one character either the phenomenal or the subjective whose opposite has been so shut out from us that we can neither know nor formulate it, makes of that opposite something which we do not need and can not value; and it gives to what we do have its old primary interest and its old need of metaphysical handling. . . . Absolute phenomenalism, subjectivism, and solipsism are to be rejected, not because they are false, but because they are meaningless and barren of all enlightenment.[13]

Woodbridge also criticizes the distinction between epistemology and metaphysics, especially where, for example, in Kant's transcendental philosophy, knowledge is defined from an analysis of its nature apart from any concrete content.[14] The result of an absolute separation of knowledge from its objects does not yield any knowledge of existing objects; epistemology is divorced radically from metaphysics.

The absolute separation of knowledge from its object can have, therefore, no metaphysical significance.

That is the lesson we have learned from the futility of such a separation. We can in no sense define reality in a way which makes it unrelated to knowledge, but this does not make a definition of reality impossible. It shows us rather that the conception of reality thus unrelated is quite meaningless. Knowledge is thus disclosed to be a real relation between things, a form of connection which has ontological significance in the general determination of reality's definition.[15]

These past conceptual failures indicate, according to Woodbridge, that a condition of an adequate metaphysical description of reality would be the acknowledgment of man as an inquirer present within reality.

The moment the definition of reality makes of reality an explicitly or implicitly complete system over against the metaphysician, or makes of him a merely incidental occurrence in its otherwise independent operations, reality has been put beyond any intelligible grasp of it. Reality absolutely external to the metaphysician will give him nothing besides himself. And reality, become momentarily conscious in the metaphysician, will give him no more than his moment of consciousness.[16]

More specifically, Woodbridge holds that if we acknowledge man as an inquirer included within reality, then a formal condition of offering an adequate metaphysical description is the acceptance of "individuality" as being definitive of an essential quality of reality: the inclusion of the inquirer within reality requires the recognition that man's definition of any subject matter implies a point of departure, man's own point of view, and that this point of departure displays the quality of "individuality."

We should give to this epistemological principle its metaphysical significance, and recognize that the definition of reality involves numberless points of departure from which reality may be grasped, and that each of these points, in its relation to what is thereby defined, is an absolute and undivided individual.[17]

By means of inquiry and man's individuality, which inquiry implies, knowledge occurs. And if man is included within reality, "whatever may be the nature of reality, it is, in a measure at least, held together in a degree of continuity by the knowing process, and to that extent definitely characterized."[18] Accordingly, another essential quality of reality is "continuity," or relation. Moreover, since human knowledge yields action and since reality changes as a result, Woodbridge claims that man's inclusion within reality requires the acknowledgment of other metaphysical traits: purpose, potentiality, and chance.[19] In summary, Woodbridge believes that an examination of past conceptual failures, failures to include man in reality, shows that the conditions for an adequate definition of reality—and, therefore, the maintaining of intellectual sanity—is the acceptance of the concepts of individuality, continuity, purpose, potentiality, and chance as being descriptive of essential characteristics of reality.

During this earliest period in the development of his metaphysics, like so many of his contemporaries, Woodbridge was concerned about the metaphysical implications of evolution; however, he was critical of evolutionists, especially Thomas Huxley. While he criticized in both the 1903 address and other articles of this period what he believed to be misconceptions associated with evolution, in these same articles he is critical not only of Huxley's evolutionism but also of his epistemological subjectivism[20] and epiphenomenalism.[21] When writing the 1903 address, Woodbridge had Huxley partly in mind, for the address offers a metaphysical rebuttal to each of these areas of Huxley's thought: if man's inclusion within reality is acknowledged, man can possess knowledge *of reality* and his knowledge can result in action that effectively modifies reality; therefore, epistemological subjectivism and epiphenomenalism are indefensible theories. In the 1903 address, however, Woodbridge's chief interest seemed to be to counteract the dualism that Huxley had created when he contrasted natural evolution, natural but immoral selection through selfish competition, with the moral adaptation required by human society. This irritated Woodbridge, because Huxley formulated an absolute dualism, something Woodbridge detested.[22] The 1903 address presented a metaphysical rebuttal to this radical dichotomy: if man as inquirer is within reality and Nature's processes displaying "purpose" is a condition of her being the subject of man's inquiries, then "purpose" is descriptive of an essential quality of reality. According to Woodbridge, the discovery of purpose in reality has

> the greatest practical importance. It validated the purposeful life of man. It fills nature with a content of surpassing value. It makes human history worth the reading.[23]

Man's moral activities do not divorce him from the cosmos. Rather, reality, or Nature, as knowable and purposeful supports man's quest for moral progress.

Stage II: A Realistic Metaphysical Conception of Evolution

A second address, "Metaphysics" (1908), reflects the growing influence of Aristotle on Woodbridge's conception of the nature of metaphysics.[24] Quoting Aristotle, Woodbridge writes of metaphysics:

> There is . . . a science which investigates existence as existence and whatever belongs to existence as such. It is identical with none of the sciences which are defined less generally. For none of these professedly considers existence as existence, but each, restricting itself to some aspect of it, investigates the general aspect only incidentally, as do the mathematical sciences.[25]

Under the influence of Aristotle, his conception of metaphysics became more explicitly realistic: although in the earlier address of 1903 he distinguished metaphysics from the special sciences primarily on the basis of their different methods, here he distinguished them on a more realistic basis, their difference in subject matters. Metaphysics is acknowledged to be a science among sciences; as such, it is the practice of essentially the same procedure as the other sciences, "the ordinary experimental methods of observation and tested generalization."[26] Because of his realism, by 1908 Woodbridge stopped using the term 'reality' in reference to the goal of metaphysics as the discovery of the nature of reality. For he says,

> the term "reality" . . . is intellectually agile. It tends to play tricks with one's prejudices and to lead desire on a merry chase. For to denominate anything real is usually to import a distinction, and to consign, thereby, something else to the region of appearance. . . . The term "reality," therefore, should inspire caution instead of confidence in metaphysics. . . . No; everything is somehow real; and to make distinctions within that realm demands caution and hesitation.[27]

In the 1908 address, Woodbridge continued to show interest in the metaphysical implications of evolution. He says of realistic metaphysics, "it finds a new interest in the interpretation of the process of evolution."[28] He presents a view of evolution, therefore, that he believes avoids misconceptions by evolutionists, especially Huxley's dualism.[29] In addition to his reflections on Aristotle's thought, the development of Woodbridge's view of evolution was influenced somewhat by Bergson's "creative evolution."[30] In his attempt to discover the general traits that are descriptive of existence as existence, Woodbridge reaffirms that man must be incorporated into the subject matter of metaphysics. Let us now develop these points expressed in the 1908 address.

Since the realistic metaphysician acknowledges man's presence within existence and accepts the realistic principle that "all things are somehow real," he must also accept that even the interpretations of unrealistic metaphysicians somehow disclose a real trait of existence: their preferential theories, according to Woodbridge, show that existence itself incorporates differing points of view. Replacing the earlier term "individuality" with the term "variety," he concludes, therefore, that a general quality of existence (or Nature) is "variety."

> For reality means either everything whatsoever or that a distinction has been made, a distinction which indicates not a difference in the fact of existence, but a difference in point of view. . . . Yet it is doubtless the business of metaphysics to undertake an examination and definition of the different points of view from which those questions can be asked and those statements made. Indeed, that undertaking may well be regarded as one of the most important in metaphysics. . . . [The outcome of it] is that existence, taken comprehensively, is an affair of distinctions; that existence is shot through and through with variety. . . .
> . . . and in this fact that differences are fundamental in the constitution of our world, we discover the reason why all those systems of metaphysics eventually

fail which attempt to reduce all existence to a single type of reality devoid of variety in its internal make-up.[31]

That man possesses preferences, according to Woodbridge, reflects the evolutionary nature of existence and that, in addition, the processes of existence display two other general characteristics: "teleology" and "mechanism."

> While all varieties as such are equally real, they are not all equally effective. They make different sorts of differences, and introduce, thereby, intensive and qualitative distinctions. The onward movement of the world is thus, not simply successive change, but a genuine development or evolution. It creates a past, the contents of which must forever remain what they were, but it proposes a future where variety may still exercise its difference-making function. And that is why we human beings . . . may not be indifferent to our performance or to the preferences we exalt. The future makes us all reformers, inviting us to meddle with the world, to use it and change it for our ends.[32]

Existence is a variety of different ends realized by means of efficient causes; existence is both teleological and mechanical.[33] Moreover, if man acquires a knowledge of Nature's efficient causes, then he can bring about desired ends. Because Nature presents man with opportunities for choosing ends, existence puts him in a position of moral responsibility; for in his making of choices, man begins to differentiate better from worse. Nature does, however, incorporate "natural goods"[34] — for example, man's biological need for food and water. Furthermore, since man cannot bring about chosen goods without a knowledge of Nature's efficient factors, existence puts man under the "natural obligation" to submit himself to the disciplines of inquiry necessary to acquire knowledge. As Woodbridge says,

> [S]ince all things are equally real, but all not equally important, the world's evolution presents itself as a drift towards results, as something purposeful and intended. While we may not invoke design to explain this relative importance of things, the world's trend puts us under the natural obligation of discovering how it may be controlled, and enforces the obligation with obvious penalties.[35]

Woodbridge concludes regarding existence as existence, especially when man's presence within Nature is acknowledged, "it seems difficult, therefore, not to describe evolution as a moral process. . . . evolution is movement controlled by the relative importance of things."[36]

The contrast between Woodbridge's concept of evolution and Huxley's dualism of natural evolution and moral adaptation should be apparent.

In summary, within the context of Woodbridge's critique of subjective ideal-ists, having divorced knowledge from its objective subject matter, he restates his conception of evolution in a manner that highlights the conflict between his views and those of Huxley, especially the latter's epistemological subjec-tivism and epiphenomenalism: when human intelligence is acknowledged to be included within the subject matter of Nature, then according to Wood-bridge, the metaphysician will discover that

> the dawn of intelligence in the world is an event of too great interest to be ac-cepted merely as a matter of record. If we are warranted in regarding it as a nat-ural good whose use is to acquaint us with the world, we are, doubtless, also warranted in regarding it as the situation in which the world's evolution is most clearly and effectively revealed. . . . From it we find little warrant to conclude that the present is simply the unfolding of a past, possibly of a very remote past, or that the future is simply the present unfolded. Evolution appears to be a process of a totally different sort. It appears to be always and eternally the unfolding of an effective present. . . . Behind it, it leaves the past as the record of what it has done, the totality of things accomplished. . . . It is a dead past. As such it may be conditioning; but it is not effective. . . .
>
> If such an interpretation of evolution is warranted, that process may indeed be described as having purpose. Only we may not understand by purpose some anciently conceived plan which the world was intended to follow.[37]

While Woodbridge does not wish to use the word "progress," according to his description of evolution, his theory is clearly a version of what had been conceived in evolutionary thought as a theory of progress. And he admits that it is a moral process.[38]

Stage III: From Evolution to Natural History

By 1911, Woodbridge apparently had had enough of evolution, for in an essay entitled "Natural Teleology,"[39] and a year later in an address entitled "Evolution,"[40] he discussed evolution as nothing but natural history. In the earlier paper, he argues both that an adequate metaphysical description of Nature's processes requires the use of the concepts of "teleology," "chance," "necessity," and "pluralism" and that these concepts refer to "ultimate" qualities of Nature; that is, these concepts can neither be reduced into one another nor into any other concept. Moreover, if these reductions are avoided, Nature's processes are recognized to be historical. Conceptions of evolution, however, have led too often to such reductions. Since the only metaphysically accurate theory of evolution is a conception identical with that of "natural history" and since misconceptions surrounded already existing theories of evolution, Woodbridge now preferred to use the term "historical" rather than "evolution" in his metaphysical description of Nature. A development of these points follows.

Woodbridge begins his 1911 paper by pointing out that, in human experience, "teleology" is a common quality of Nature.

> There . . . [things] are, constituting the great whole we call nature, each of them with its individual history culminating through many helps and hindrances in the present product. Illustrations are so abundant that choice is baffled in selecting the most appropriate. For while living things may at first appear to be more evidently the products of directive and selective forces, inanimate nature itself — the plain with mountains about it, the river with its course motived by the character of the land through which it flows — exhibits likewise the adaptation of means to ends.[41]

Furthermore, inquirers assume teleology.

> Thus we come to think that we have explained the origin of anything when we are able to view it as the kind of result we should expect from the operation of the factors which have produced it. But this means, of course, that these factors serve. They aid and abet the outcome in definite ways and will produce it if no obstacles of sufficient contrary influence thwart their natural productivity. . . . Nature is a domain, not of chaotic changes, but of definite, teleological changes pointing to particular results.[42]

"Natural teleology" is the way in which efficient factors help or hinder the outcome of Nature's processes; it is the adaptation of means to ends; it is the specific "uses" of factors relative to the realization of an end and, in turn, the end's own "uses."[43] Because Nature's processes are teleological, inquirers follow the lead of the products of processes in order to determine the contributions, or uses, of the efficient factors that condition these processes; and teleology is also evident in the uses to which products are put, enabling inquirers to determine the nature of various products. Overall, therefore, the uses of the products of various processes enable inquirers to understand how factors contributed to the development of products; Nature's processes display teleology.

According to Woodbridge, however, philosophers have not been content merely to accept teleology as a fact descriptive of a general characteristic of Nature; they have sought for an explanation of natural teleology by raising questions: Why do means adapt to ends? and Why do things have their specific uses? Woodbridge holds that the search for an explanation of teleology is stimulated by a misapplication of the analogy between nature and art.

> We find a ready explanation of the usefulness of the things man makes in the intention or design with which he makes them. . . . Furthermore our admiration of the product passes over into even greater admiration of the skill which could contrive a machine so useful. Thus in the products of art we seem to have instances where the explanation of use is obvious. The ease of the explanation readily begets a habit of thinking about use generally, leading us to regard all uses as designed for the ends they serve. . . . [S]o profoundly may this analogy between nature and art affect the mind, that it becomes incredible that the uses of nature have any other explanation than in a power great enough and intelligent enough to contrive their manifold adaptations. Thus philosophy is led to explain natural use by design and to see in the varied adaptations of means to ends in nature proof of intelligent direction. Nature becomes a work of art.[44]

The explanation of natural teleology as the work of an intelligent cosmic designer is in effect the reduction of the concept of "natural teleology" to the concept of "design": as a concept distinguishable from intentional "design," "natural teleology" is eliminated from the metaphysical description of Nature. The thesis that Nature is the creation of an intelligent designer is discredited, however, when it is discovered that Nature's processes produce tragic, as well as fortunate, results.

> Expected harvests blighted in a night, lives of promise lost through no discoverable fault . . . —these and a multitude of similar instances make nature as a work of art irrational and perverse. . . . Count only the gains, the seed breaking upward towards the life-engendering sun, and the inference to design looks easy; but count the losses also, the frost that kills before the blossom, and the inference is hard.[45]

Apart from the artistic activities of man, not only are the uses of the products of Nature's processes unintentional but also they are often unsuspected. Woodbridge claims, therefore, that the concept of "chance" seems to be descriptive of a general characteristic of Nature. And since "chance" is consistent with "necessity" and since the latter might account for the natural quality referred to as "teleology," the concepts of chance and necessity may adequately describe both Nature's perversity and her adaptation of means to ends; they may account for Nature's "accidental advantages."

> For contradictory as it may seem, the appeal to chance tends to become, when attention is focused on the thing that happens, an appeal to necessity. . . .

While the arrangement of plants in a garden may show the gardener's taste and skill, the distribution of vegetation about the shores of a lake, although no less remarkable in its arrangement, needs no gardener for its explanation; for, again, the fact that water and soil have happened to meet there under certain natural conditions excludes any other explanation of the resulting order. . . . It becomes no longer easy . . . to think of nature as a work of art. Its uses and adaptations appear rather *to be accidental,* because they simply befall under the conditions which happen to exist in any given case. They appear also *to be necessary,* because, given these conditions, no other results than the actual appear to have been possible. [Italics mine][46]

Although the concepts of chance and necessity are necessary to an adequate metaphysical description of Nature, they cannot replace "natural teleology" as another ultimate metaphysical concept. While "chance" is descriptive of the manner in which efficient factors enter into relationships and "necessity" is descriptive of the necessary adaption of means to ends that result, these adaptations could not occur except that the means, or efficient factors, were already potentially capable of these specific adaptations. Nature must already be essentially teleological.

Chance . . . can operate to produce adaptations only under conditions where that adaptation is already possible. A variation can turn out to be useful only in an environment where it has a possible use. It would be quite profitless, for example, for an organism to develop eyes in a world where there was nothing to see. Thus chance and necessity can operate to secure adaptation only in a world where things have their specific uses, only in a world already essentially teleological.[47]

Regarding the ultimateness of natural teleology, Woodbridge concludes,

If a thing is useful, it is useful irrespective of the causes which produced it, and no connection is discoverable between its use and its causes which warrants an inference from the one to the other. . . . A thing may originate by art or it may originate by chance, but whether it is useful or not is not thereby determined. . . . Use is, accordingly, to be set down, not as a product of nature or of art, but as a factor in their productivity. . . .
. . . Teleology is natural, something to build upon, not something to be explained.[48]

Having shown that natural teleology, the Aristotelian "final factor,"[49] is necessary to a metaphysical understanding of Nature's processes, Woodbridge asks whether or not a final factor is also an efficient factor in

Nature's processes. Within biology, vitalistic theories raise this question. He rejects the notion that final factors are also efficient factors, for if Nature's uses were sufficient to bring themselves into existence, then everything would have already been accomplished and Nature would be static.

> To put the end of a process into the beginning of it in order to explain why that end is reached, is either meaningless or absurd. For, assuredly, if the end existed at the beginning we should need more than all our wit to distinguish the one from the other. A world so constructed would be a world where nothing could happen, a perfectly static world.[50]

The denial that Nature's final factors are also efficient factors reaffirms the importance of the metaphysical concept of "chance": Nature is not static; everything has not been accomplished, for the accomplishment of Nature's uses must wait upon the co-incidence of appropriate efficient factors. And the accomplishment of ends being dependent upon the cooperation of *appropriate efficient factors* shows that Nature includes a plurality of factors, many of which differ in nature. Therefore, "pluralism" is also descriptive of a general characteristic of Nature. The failure to reduce causation to teleology

> points . . . to the fact that any definition of teleology must recognize an essential diversity of character in the processes involved in any change. Things and the elements of things are specifically different in their character and their operations.[51]

According to Woodbridge's analysis in the 1911 essay, an adequate metaphysical description of Nature requires the use of the ultimate concepts of natural teleology, chance, necessity, and pluralism.[52]

Having summarized his arguments in the essay of 1911 against the reduction of natural teleology to design or chance-necessity, we now turn to "Evolution," his address of the following year, in order to discover his reasons for preferring the use of "natural history" to "evolution" in his metaphysical description of nature's processes.

> My purpose is to express the opinion that evolution is history; that antecedents and causes should consequently be historically construed. . . .
> . . . It . . . is easier and often more congenial to make mythologies than to write history.
> The acceptance of the evolutionary point of view is . . . no guarantee that mythology has been abandoned. Speculations about energy and force, about

the origins of variation, about heredity, about nature and nurture, as well as such controversies as often mark the engagements between vitalists and the supporters of mechanism . . . seem frequently to indicate that mythology still finds a place among the general doctrines of evolution. I do not mean to imply that these speculations and controversies point to no problems in need of solution. I mean only that they too frequently display a tendency to turn the characteristic operations of things into causes why things so operate; to assign a superior efficiency to the past than to the present; to make evolution a substitute for a creator; and, in general, to suppose that the causes rather than the history of the world have been discovered.

When, for instance, we ask, Why does a hen sit on eggs? we are often forbidden to give the natural and obvious answers, Because she wants to, or, in order that chicks may be hatched; and are urged rather to give the mythological answers, Because she has an instinct to sit, or, Because her ancestors sat. Now the first of these latter answers is the attempt to turn the characteristic behavior of the hen into a cause why she so behaves, and the second is the attempt to regard her past as more efficient than her present.[53]

These are Woodbridge's reasons for replacing the concept of evolution with that of history, and these reasons are reflected in his arguments in the earlier essay of 1911 against the reduction of ultimate metaphysical concepts. For evolutionists, making evolution a creator is an instance of the attempt to explain natural teleology as the work of a cosmic designer; it involves a misapplication of the analogy between nature and art and a reduction of the concept of natural teleology to the concept of design. The attribution of a superior efficiency to the past rather than to the present is illustrative of the attempt to reduce natural teleology to chance-necessity or, more specifically, causation. The evolutionist's tendency to transform the characteristic operations of things into causes of their operation is an example of the attempt to reduce Nature's efficient factors to final factors. Accordingly, Woodbridge's arguments against reductionism in the essay "Natural Teleology" are also arguments for the abandonment of "evolution" in favor of "history." "Natural teleology," "chance-necessity," and "pluralism" must be maintained as ultimate metaphysical concepts against every attempt at reductionism.

It seems, however, that when we ask such a question as has been proposed about the hen [i.e., Why does a hen sit on eggs?], we desire an answer which will make clear to us the result to be attained by her behavior, . . . or we desire one which will disclose what it is that induces the hen so to behave. We do not desire, or rationally ought not to desire, an answer which will disclose why the hen sits irrespective of the end to be attained by her behavior or of the stimulus which excites her. In other words, unless we are mythologists, we do not expect to be told why in a world like ours it is characteristic of hens to sit. . . . There are hens, they do sit, they thus perpetuate their kind, and they have had a history which is measurably ascertainable; but hens must be given first, if there is to be any investigation of them or any discovery of their evolution. . . . Evolution . . . discloses and is the history of what exists or what has existed, but it is always with the existent that it begins.[54]

Even though by 1911, Woodbridge had replaced his metaphysical concern for evolution with a concern for history, he continued to think of Nature's processes as movements of progress; and especially human history, he regarded as the progress that mankind had made.[55] While the same metaphysical concepts of natural teleology, chance, necessity, and pluralism, are descriptive of Nature's processes, whether natural or human history, when inclusion of the intelligence within Nature is acknowledged, Nature's progressive movements are also moral processes. Apparently, Woodbridge was becoming more and more interested in the theory of human history.

With consciousness today's changes occur in view of yesterday and of the possible tomorrow. With consciousness the processes of the world become at once retrospective and prospective in their operation.

There is, therefore, design in the world. Only, as we have seen, that design may not be invoked to explain the world's teleology, because it is one instance of that teleology. But the fact that it is such makes it unnecessary to seek further for the ground of moral distinctions or for a rational confidence that nature is sufficient for the demands design may make upon it. Responsibility is not imposed from without. It arises from no authoritative command. It is, rather, the inevitable consequence of design. For to plan and put the plan in operation is to become the cause of the issuing result, the point where responsibility is definitely lodged. So we do not hold rocks responsible because they fall, but we do hold men responsible because they think. Because they think today is changed in view of yesterday and tomorrow, and consciousness being the possibility of such a change takes upon itself the thoughtful construction of the issue in the light of the world's natural teleology. That is the essence of morality. . . . Thus, with consciousness, the world's teleology is a moral teleology.[56]

Stage IV: From History to Science of Existence

Three lectures Woodbridge delivered in 1916 on the subject of history, published later the same year under the title *The Purpose of History,* expressed in general his final conception of the nature of metaphysics.[57] Whereas earlier he had claimed the identity of history and evolution, here he offers a more precise description of evolution as it relates to history: evolution refers to the *integrations* characteristic of Nature's historical processes rather than the differences integrated.

Evolution is . . . only a name for historical continuity, and this continuity itself is a fact to be investigated and not a theory which explains anything, or affords a standard of value.[58]

Accordingly, in the lectures of 1916, he continues to express greater metaphysical concern toward history than evolution. Most distinctive of this new conception of the nature of metaphysics, however, is Woodbridge's rejection of his earlier belief that the primary metaphysical concern is history.[59]

In *The Purpose of History,* Woodbridge defines 'history' as follows:

History is itself essentially the utilization of the past for ends, ends not necessarily foreseen, but ends to come, so that every historical thing, when we view it retrospectively, has the appearance of a result which has been selected, and to which its antecedents are exclusively appropriate.[60]

Given his definition of history, the history of any natural thing would be a description of how means cooperated in bringing about its occurrence. From Woodbridge's point of view, therefore, the sciences which attempt to discover experimentally Nature's efficient factors are, in effect, trying to describe *the history* of specific kinds of occurrences. Metaphysics, however, is not like *these* sciences, for it cannot offer a history of its subject matter: the subject matter of metaphysics is the most general subject matter; accordingly, if the metaphysician could offer the history of his subject matter, he would have to offer the history of the cosmos as a whole, the history of history. This history, however, can neither be discovered nor expressed; it does not exist. In order to present the history of the cosmos as a whole, the metaphysician would have to discover the means, or factors, which brought about its existence. But this is impossible, for since the end which would be the metaphysician's subject matter is the cosmos *as a whole,* an *all inclusive* subject matter, there is nothing beyond it that could function as the means which effected its existence. Indeed, since there is nothing beyond it, over against which the Whole can be determined, the cosmos as a whole is indeterminable; the history of history cannot be disclosed. As early as 1912, Woodbridge anticipated somewhat his 1916 critique of metaphysical history:

[N]o history of evolution [or history of history] can be written. Every attempt to write one always gives us something other than a history and something other than an evolution. It converts the world into a product or into an effect of causes, and must at last confess its inability to find the producer of that product or the causes of that effect. Its failure does not indicate a lack of intellectual power, but a misdirection of intellectual effort. It proves that evolution is pluralistic, not that monism is necessary.[61]

In 1916, therefore, Woodbridge concludes,

> The only universal history is the exposition of what history itself is, the time process stripped of all its variety and specific interests. Consequently, a single purpose is not discoverable; there are many purposes. When we try to reduce them all to some show of singleness we again do no more than try to tell what a temporal order is like. *It is metaphysics and not history we are writing.*[Italics mine][62]

Accordingly, metaphysics is the science that seeks to discover the "ontological categories" descriptive of the common qualities displayed by any and every natural, historical process: metaphysics presents a description of what Nature's processes, when taken separately rather than as a whole, display most generally.[63]

Summary

In the first stage of Woodbridge's development of his conception of metaphysics (1903), he emphasized the uniqueness of metaphysics: whereas the sciences seek to explain how events occur and, therefore, reject nonexplanatory concepts such as "purpose," metaphysics, which defines concepts necessary to avoid intellectual confusion, discovers that, although "purpose" does not explain, "purpose" must be a quality of the natural processes studied by science for scientific explanation presupposes its presence. (Even as early as 1903, Woodbridge's influential conception of natural teleology was taking shape.) More generally, Woodbridge believes that metaphysics shows that man's presence within reality, the reality man also seeks to know, must be acknowledged and, therefore, not only "purpose" but also "individuality," "continuity," "potentiality," and "chance" are qualities descriptive of reality. Moreover, since man as inquirer is included within reality, a purposeful reality provides knowledge of itself enabling man to effect his situation; therefore, Thomas Huxley's evolutionary theories, that is, his epistemological subjectivism, implying man's lack of knowledge of reality, and his epiphenomenalism, implying man's inability to effect reality, are indefensible theories.

By 1908, under the growing influence of Aristotle, Woodbridge entered a second stage where he held a more explicitly realistic conception of metaphysics and of evolution. He now conceives of metaphysics as one of the sciences distinguishable from the other sciences on the basis of its different subject matter. He believes that "variety," "mechanism," and "teleology" (re-affirming his earlier acknowledgment of "purpose") are descriptive of general characteristics of Nature; for the world's occurrences are not simply succes-sive changes but processes to which factors have made different contributions in bringing them about. According to Woodbridge, therefore, a realistic con-ception of evolution based upon an examination of Nature's processes shows that "evolution" refers to the fact that factors contribute differently to and, therefore, vary in importance in bringing about Nature's changes.

During 1911–12, Woodbridge reached a third stage where he concludes that, since the only metaphysically accurate theory of both Nature's processes and evolution is a conception identical with that of "natural history" and since misconceptions surround already existing theories of evolution, the term 'historical' is preferable to 'evolution' in developing a metaphysical descrip-tion of Nature. In effect, the primary metaphysical concern becomes history.

In 1916, Woodbridge reached his fourth and final conception of meta-physics: although the special sciences are attempting to describe the history of specific kinds of occurrences, metaphysics cannot describe *a* history since Nature as a whole does not have a history. Rather, metaphysics is the science that seeks to discover the ontological categories descriptive of the common qualities displayed by any and every natural, historical process. In part, Woodbridge's rejection of evolution and history as the primary con-cerns of metaphysics shows his desire to disassociate himself completely from speculative metaphysical beliefs: for example, that Nature's processes reveal an overall meaning or purpose because they participate in a cosmic evolution or history.

Before proceeding, an important influence Woodbridge's criticism of evolutionary thought has produced should be noted: Woodbridge insisted that "natural teleology" is descriptive of a general quality of Nature even though scientists questioned its explanatory value and philosophers under the influence of the sciences, especially evolutionists, severely criticized the concept of teleology. According to Randall, Woodbridge impressed upon contem-porary naturalists the importance of "natural teleology," and thereby con-tributed substantially to the tempering of the "excesses of the genetic method of the evolutionary enthusiasts" with a functional or operational analysis.[64] Contemporary naturalists believe that scientific control requires the discovery of natural mechanisms. Largely because of Woodbridge's intellectual influ-ence, however, naturalists generally hold that it is in light of natural ends that the discovery of natural means is made. As Randall says,

a second issue between naturalists . . . can be said to arise between a naturalism whose inspiration is fundamentally Greek [such as Woodbridge's], and one strongly influenced by evolutionary thought. The latter tends to construe the relation between the different types of activity encountered in the world in terms of their temporal genesis in the evolutionary process. In general it sets high store by genetic analyses. The former, true to its Aristotelian inspiration, prefers to read those relations as obtaining between factors discriminated in an experimentally observable subject-matter. It employs rather a functional or operational analysis. . . .

Both [Morris] Cohen and Woodbridge were keen critics of the excesses of the genetic method of the evolutionary enthusiasts; they have transmitted their suspicion to their students. Mr. Dewey's evolutionism, especially when under the influence of G. H. Mead, has put much more emphasis on various types of genetic analysis—though he would in fact pretty much agree with the specific criticisms advanced by Woodbridge. . . .

. . . it is well to observe that the concern with a functional analysis and with the means-end relationship has led nearly all present-day naturalists to recognize the importance of what Woodbridge called "natural teleology." . . . From the time of Spinoza and Hobbes through the Darwinian period, the older naturalism overlooked natural teleology in its hostility to explanations in terms of "purpose," conscious or unconscious. But present-day naturalists, though finding no evidence that ends operate apart from human action, recognize that ends are nonetheless achieved through natural means, and that a concern with means and ends is fundamental for human understanding.[65]

In addition to a description of Woodbridge's mature metaphysical theory of Nature in the next chapter, more of his criticisms of the evolutionists, especially pragmatic evolutionists such as Dewey, are presented later in Chapter 5.

NOTES

1. Frederick J. E. Woodbridge, *Nature and Mind: Selected Essays of Frederick J. E. Woodbridge* (New York: Columbia University Press, 1937; reprint ed., New York: Russell and Russell, 1965), p. 290.

2. Ibid., p. 135.

3. Woodbridge notes that it was an accident in the editing of the writings of Aristotle which established 'metaphysics' as the name of the science of philosophers. According to tradition, Andronicus of Rhodes, in the first century B.C., discovered some loosely connected but unnamed writings of Aristotle, placed them after Aristotle's books on physics, naming them accordingly, Meta-physics, the books after the books on physics (ibid., pp. 95–96). "Metaphysics" is a curious, even unfortunate, title for the inquiry developed in these writings of Aristotle, a science of Nature which investigates existence as existence.

[For the title] appears to indicate that when you have finished your physics, the science which was originally thought to embrace nature, you must then pass beyond physics and somehow cut loose from nature herself. After physics, metaphysics; after nature, the supernatural—that is an invitation at once to titanic effort and to Icarian folly. [Ibid., p. 95]

4. Ibid., pp. 37–55. This was presented as the Presidential Address at the third annual meeting of the Western Philosophical Association, April 10, 1903. It was originally published in the *Philosophical Review*, Vol. 12 (1903):367–85.

5. Ibid., pp. 40–41.

6. Ibid., p. 42.

7. Ibid., pp. 42–43.

8. Ibid., p. 53.

9. Ibid.

10. Ibid., p. 38.

11. Ibid., pp. 44–45.

12. Ibid., p. 45.

13. Ibid., p. 39.

14. See Ibid., pp. 43–44.

15. Ibid., p. 44. Woodbridge's realism is already evident.

16. Ibid., p. 45.

17. Ibid., p. 46.

18. Ibid., p. 44.

19. See Ibid., pp. 49–53.

20. Ibid., "The Nature of Consciousness (1904)," p. 307; and, "The Problem of Consciousness (1906)," pp. 328–29.

21. Ibid., "The Field of Logic (1905)," p. 65.

22. Professor Herbert W. Schneider, a former student and colleague of Woodbridge's at Columbia University, gave this information to me during our conversations, June 5–10, 1977 and January–June, 1979. Cited hereafter as "Herbert Schneider, conversations."

23. Woodbridge, *Nature and Mind*, p. 43.

24. Ibid., pp. 95–112. This was a lecture delivered at Columbia University in the series on Science, Philosophy, and Art (March 18, 1908) and was published originally by the Columbia University Press.

25. Ibid., p. 96.

26. Ibid., p. 108.

27. Ibid., pp. 99–100.

28. Ibid., p. 99.

29. Herbert Schneider, conversations.

30. Ibid.

31. Woodbridge, *Nature and Mind*, pp. 102–03.

32. Ibid., p. 103.

33. Ibid., pp. 104–05.

34. Ibid., p. 104.

35. Ibid., p. 103.

36. Ibid.

37. Ibid., pp. 111–12.

38. Herbert Schneider, conversations.

39. Woodbridge, *Nature and Mind*, pp. 113–133. This essay was published

originally in *Essays in Modern Theology and Related Subjects* (New York: Scribners, 1911), pp. 307-326.

40. Ibid., pp. 134-48. This was delivered as the presidential address before the Eleventh Annual Meeting of the American Philosophical Association at Harvard University (December 28, 1911) and was published originally in the *Philosophical Review,* 21 (1912):137-151.

41. Ibid., p. 113.

42. Ibid., pp. 113-14.

43. While Woodbridge refers to both forms of the manifestation of "uses," or natural teleology, he did not clearly distinguish them. He spoke of the specific "uses" of factors relative to a realized end as follows: "That ends are reached in nature through the utilization of *serviceable means* is as simple and unsullied a fact of observation as any other" [ibid., p. 121 (italics mine)]. On the other hand, Woodbridge noted the "use" of products, or ends of processes: "Art, when consciously productive, evidently intends its products to be useful. A house is made for shelter, clothing for protection or adornment, pictures to delight the sense" (ibid., p. 115). John Herman Randall, Jr., who in his exposition of Aristotle's thought generally reflects the positive influence of his teacher Woodbridge, clearly distinguishes in Aristotle's thought these two forms of "uses," or natural teleology, in a manner that I believe clarifies Woodbridge's own view. In regard to Aristotle, Randall illustrates one manifestation of natural teleology, the discovery of the natures, or powers, of factors in terms of their operations or, as Woodbridge would have it, the specific "uses" of factors relative to a process's realized end.

> We understand the powers in terms of their operations. We understand the power of sight or vision in terms of the activity of seeing; and likewise the instrument by means of which vision operates, the eye. We understand the power of thinking, nous, in terms of the activity of thinking and likewise the instrument by means of which thinking operates. [*Aristotle* (New York: Columbia University Press, 1960) p. 65.]

Randall also illustrates a second form of natural teleology in Aristotle, what I believe would be for Woodbridge the "use," of the products, or ends, of processes.

> Moreover, activities and functions are themselves understood in terms of that toward which they are directed, of that to which they are a response, their "correlative objects." . . . Seeing is understood in terms of what is seen, the visible; . . . thinking is understood in terms of what is thought. There is some object or objective in the environment, in the situation or context, to which the activity is a response, and toward which it is directed. The activity cannot be understood without reference to such an environment or context and to the objective to be found in it. [Ibid., pp. 65-66]

Accordingly, Randall summarizes Aristotle's and, I believe, Woodbridge's position as follows: "It is in terms of this objective or end in the context that we understand the activity; and it is in terms of the activity that we understand the power" (Ibid., p. 66).

44. Woodbridge, *Nature and Mind,* p. 115.

45. Ibid., p. 116.

46. Ibid., p. 117.

47. Ibid., p. 118.

48. Ibid., 119–20.

49. Ibid., p. 120.

50. Ibid., p. 125.

51. Ibid.

52. During this period in the development of his metaphysical thinking, Wood-bridge also acknowledges both the "continuities" and "discontinuities" in the historical processes of Nature (Herbert Schneider, conversations). When attention is drawn to "necessity" and "teleology" as characteristic of Nature's processes, both of which refer to the manner in which things *are integrated,* then Nature's continuities become prominent. On the other hand, when attention is placed upon the "chance" and "pluralism" in Nature, her discontinuities are more evident. Nature's processes, however, are never *absolutely* discontinuous.

53. Woodbridge, *Nature and Mind,* pp. 134–35.

54. Ibid., pp. 135–36.

55. See, Frederick J. E. Woodbridge, *The Purpose of History* (New York: Columbia University Press, 1916; reissued, Port Washington, New York: Kennikat Press, 1965).

56. Woodbridge, *Nature and Mind,* pp. 130–31.

57. The lectures which compose *The Purpose of History* are: "From History to Philosophy," "The Pluralism of History," and "The Continuity of History."

58. Woodbridge, *Purpose of History,* pp. 4–5.

59. As early as 1912, however, Woodbridge was beginning to see that the science of metaphysics is not theory of history even though a metaphysical analysis of "history" was necessary for him to come to his mature understanding of the nature of metaphysics.

60. Woodbridge, *Purpose of History,* p. 4.

61. Woodbridge, *Nature and Mind,* p. 142.

62. Woodbridge, *Purpose of History,* p. 49.

63. Even as early as 1912, Woodbridge's mature conception of the nature of metaphysics was beginning to take form. See, for example, Woodbridge, *Nature and Mind,* pp. 142–43.

64. John Herman Randall, Jr., "Epilogue: The Nature of Naturalism," in *Naturalism and the Human Spirit,* edited by Yervant H. Krikorian (New York: Columbia University Press, 1944), p. 378.

65. Ibid., pp. 378–79.

3

Metaphysics: Woodbridge's Philosophical Science of Existence

> Metaphysics . . . should come before and not after as a discipline to keep us sane in what we do after — an examination one might say of the grounds and method of intelligibility, or a general theory of nature prior to theories of specific traits.[1]

> The distinction between nature and human nature, if taken to be an absolute and unique dichotomy, can yield no theory of nature at all.[2]

Introduction

The influence Woodbridge's realism has had on American thought was acknowledged in the Preface. Although a discussion of his influence is beyond the purpose of this book, it should be noted that metaphysical reflection has been significantly effected by the realism of Woodbridge. Sterling P. Lamprecht has this to say about his former teacher:

> [He] did much to revive metaphysics, rescuing it from the inferior status to which modern epistemologists had relegated it and re-establishing it as a *first science* in Aristotle's sense of that term.[3]

That Woodbridge opened others to similar metaphysical visions of Nature is evident, for example, in the writings of John Herman Randall, Jr., and Sterling P. Lamprecht. In addition to the influence of Aristotle and Dewey, Randall notes in *Nature and Historical Experience* his special indebtedness

51

to his teacher, saying of Woodbridge that he "taught me all the metaphysics I know. . . ."[4] Moreover, Lamprecht says,

> I can hardly distinguish what in my own views I owe to [Woodbridge] and what I may have somewhat independently added or modified. For what I may have independently added or modified surely stems from what he enabled me to discover from the vantage point of his frank and disinterested concern with man's place in nature.[5]

This chapter presents the conception of metaphysics and the metaphysical theory of Nature to which Woodbridge's reflection eventually led.

Realistic metaphysics, according to Woodbridge, acknowledges the fact of human activities in nature; as was shown in Chapter 1, realism led Woodbridge not only to naturalism but also to humanism. He believes that a realistic and, therefore, scientific metaphysical description of the common qualities displayed by Nature's activities, inclusive of human activities, requires acceptance of the following metaphysical distinctions: the realistic distinction, individuality, structure, natural teleology, dynamism, activity, potentiality, and contingency. In addition, Woodbridge claims that an adequate metaphysical theory of Nature would recognize three "realms of being," the realms of vision, matter, and mind, which are descriptive of three kinds of natural cooperation, spatial, temporal, and logical.

Even during the period of his mature metaphysical reflection, after 1916, Woodbridge discovered that earlier distinctions, which had been made when he was primarily concerned with evolution and history, were still appropriate to a set of ontological categories descriptive of Nature. In unpacking Woodbridge's mature metaphysics, therefore, I will have to make some use of the language from the addresses and papers already discussed.

The Subject-matter of Metaphysics

Of his mature conception of metaphysics, Woodbridge says, "metaphysics is here conceived in the spirit of Aristotle's enterprise."[6] He continued to hold that metaphysics is the science of existence *as* existence or of being *as* being. In addition, given his realism, he continued to distinguish metaphysics from the special sciences on the basis of the difference in generality of subject matter rather than any difference in method: while the special sciences seek knowledge of the natures of specific kinds of subject matter, metaphysics is the science of the general nature of Nature. It is not, however, a science of Nature or existence *as a whole*. Woodbridge claims that things are determined contextually; they are determined relative to the content of their environment.[7] Nature as *the whole,* therefore, could not *as a whole* be the subject matter for scientific inquiry, for she is not as such definable: nothing lies beyond her relative to which she might be identified. In other words, Nature as a whole serves as the general context for all other things without having a determinate context of its own.

> It [i.e., the Aristotelian enterprise] was based on the recognition of the facts that knowledge invariably consists of affirmations and denials about some object or other of inquiry: of propositions about some subject-matter. As the subject-matter varies, the propositions will vary. Recognizing this Aristotle raised the question, in effect, whether there were propositions which do not vary in spite of the variations in subject-matter? He answered that there were such propositions and concluded that these propositions constituted knowledge of existence as existence or being as being. By *as* existence or *as* being he did not mean something more fundamental or other than existence or being as specific subject-matter. He meant rather what could be said about *any* specific subject-matter. . . .
> . . . At any rate it should be a means of clarifying what existence is or what it is to be. It should indicate at least what existence seems to imply.[8]

Metaphysics will attempt to discover categories descriptive of the common qualities displayed by any or every subject matter, that is, activities in context.

The Method of Metaphysics and the Realistic Distinction

The method of metaphysics is the realistic method of contextual analysis:

> The analytic character of the method as opposed to a synthetic character may be illustrated as follows: Let us suppose that we are led by our study to the recognition of certain ultimates which we may call factors or elements or categories of existence or types of being. These are discovered by analyzing situations with which we are confronted. But we are not now to suppose that a synthesis of these factors gives us the situation we have analyzed. The factors of existence are not first independent of each other and later in combination. They are together in existence but do not go together to make existence.[9]

Elsewhere, in his "Confessions," Woodbridge says the following:

> I would make this the first step in metaphysics — the recognition that existence is primarily what it is and can neither be explained nor explained away. The most

that can be done is to find out what it implies. And the great error of meta-physicians is the supposition that the implications of existence are its causes and lead us to something more fundamental than existence, or prior to it, or in itself irrelevant to it.

I have, consequently, often called myself a realist, and one of a very naïve sort.[10]

The realistic-scientific inquirer practicing contextual analysis will respect the subject matter as the standard of both the meaning and the adequacy of the distinctions composing his hypotheses, rather than allowing these distinctions once made to cast doubt on the evident character of his subject. In those cases of reductionism where either preconceptions or distinctions made during inquiry displace the authority of the subject matter, the subject ceases to be a genuine subject matter, for it no longer functions as a subject matter; therefore, realistic-scientific inquiry ceases to exist. Accordingly, if metaphysics attempts to discover distinctions descriptive of *any* subject matter and the preservation of subject matters over against their reduction is implied by *the existence* of subject matters, then the distinction between subject matters and their linguistically expressed interpretations is a meta-physical distinction descriptive of a general trait of existence, the existence of any subject matter as a subject matter. Woodbridge referred to this distinction, between subject matter and its linguistically expressed interpretations as the subject matter and discourse distinction, but he also called it the "realistic distinction," for it is a metaphysical expression of his realism.[11]

Whatever we explain and however we explain, explanations are all ultimately made in terms of language. In general, it is in language that anything whatever is understood or becomes intelligible. As we consider this fact we seem forced to conclude that what existence is or what things are, is ultimately a matter of what they are said to be. . . .

. . . Language is . . . the embodiment of the distinction between X and what is said about X, or between subject-matter and discourse. This distinction is present and unavoidable in all inquiries whatsoever. It is metaphysical. Without it, no discourse is intelligible.

. . . The distinction between subject-matter and discourse is one of the most ultimate distinctions we make and one without which subject-matter and discourse are meaningless.[12]

Metaphysically speaking, Nature as the subject matter, either actual or potential, of all inquiry,[13] according to Woodbridge, is a "universe of discourse."

Woodbridge's solution to the problem of theorists, such as evolutionists, reducing one ultimate category to another is realistic; respect for the metaphysical distinction of subject matter and discourse. For in a realistic metaphysical inquiry, the ultimacy of the categories is sanctioned by the subject matter. "They are ultimate distinctions *in analysis*" (italics mine).[14] Accordingly, ultimate categories can be reduced only by displacing the legitimate subject matter with some prejudicial conception, an instance of the failure to maintain the realistic distinction. Respect for the realistic distinction also prevents turning the distinction into a radical dichotomy:[15] in order for the subject matter to be divorced from discourse, that is, in order for the subject to be put beyond the reach of inquiry and knowledge as it was for Kant, the subject matter's authority over inquiry must be replaced by some prejudicial conception. Even as early as his 1903 address, "The Problem of Metaphysics," Woodbridge rejects this divorce:

> For when we say that there are certain [metaphysical] conditions which must be fulfilled in order that knowledge may be knowledge, we must recognize that it is the constitution of reality which determines those conditions. We may ascribe what *a priori* powers we like to knowledge; but these powers would never receive an atom of significance in experience, if reality did not call them out and fit into them.[16]

Later, in 1930, he says, "the realism I would urge is one of principle rather than one of selection. As a principle it does not dichotomize existence. . . . The subject-matter of inquiry can not be called in question."[17]

Of the failures to maintain the realistic distinction, Woodbridge was concerned primarily with a lack of respect for the distinctive differences in the subject matters of the sciences. For according to his realism, differences in the natures of subject matters determine differences in the procedures of the various sciences, not the converse. He was especially concerned where scientists of the special sciences, through a loss of realism and failure to maintain the realistic distinction, no longer limited their inquiries to their restricted subject matters; therefore, they attempted to apply procedures and concepts appropriate to the limited contexts of their own inquiries to Nature in general, the legitimate context for metaphysical inquiry alone. The theoretical confusion resulting from this lack of respect for differences in context and this reductionism of subject matter can best be corrected by a realistic metaphysical analysis that draws attention to the importance of a respect for contexts through an acknowledgment of the realistic distinction.

> In thus conceiving a science [i.e., first philosophy or metaphysics] whose distinguishing mark should be that it applies to all existence, Aristotle noted a fact which the history of intellectual progress has abundantly illustrated, the fact,

namely, that knowledge grows in extent and richness only through specialization. Nature herself is a specialized matter. She does things by producing differences, individuals, variations. To grasp this variety, a variety of sciences is necessary. Indeed, as Aristotle estimates the achievements of his predecessors, he finds the source of their confusion, inadequacy, and limitation to be in their habit of regarding each his own special science as a sufficient account of the cosmos. What they said may have been true under the restrictions which their limited field imposed upon their utterance; but it became false when it was transferred to other fields differently limited. Following his own illustrations we may say, for instance, that the Pythagoreans were quite right in trying to formulate the undoubted numerical relations which obtain in nature; but they were quite wrong if they conceived arithmetic to be an adequate astronomy. The soul may be a harmony of the body and thus capable of numerical expression, but to think one has exhausted its nature by defining it as a moving number is to forget the natural limitations of inquiry and to make a rhetorical phrase the substitute for scientific insight. We may properly speak of a sick soul as out of tune, but we should not thereby become either psychologists or physicians. No; knowledge is a matter of special sciences, each growing sanely as it clearly recognizes the particular and specialized aspect of nature with which it deals, but becoming confused when it forgets that it is one of many.[18]

Metaphysics . . . should come before and not after, as a discipline to keep us sane in what we do after—an examination one might say of the grounds and method of intelligibility, or a general theory of nature prior to theories of special traits.[19]

The Importance of Maintaining the Realistic Distinction

Woodbridge believes that a common result of the failure of special scientists to respect the realistic distinction in the misapplication of their special procedures and limited concepts to the most general of contexts and subject matters—Nature—is a loss of the richness of variety of Nature's activities, especially those most characteristic of human living. Since Newton, physical scientists and philosophers under the influence of the physical sciences have sometimes forgotten the limitation implied in the title of Newton's *Principia Mathematica Philosophiae Naturalis* and have applied to Nature in general the mathematical concepts underlying their special procedures, with the result that Nature's qualitative richness has been eliminated, leaving only what could be expressed in a manner consistent with their procedures, the quantitative.

I often think of the title of Newton's great book. . . . It made a discrimination between the natural and its mathematical principles; it refused to admit within its scope anything natural of which a mathematical expression could not be given or attempted. . . . It is clear enough to the historian that most of his followers and his opponents saw in that book a new system of the world, a new view of nature of revolutionary proportions. But the historian must recognize that the implications of that title and also the superb development of it in the book itself were a limitation of the study of nature and not a comprehensive extension of it. One has only to consider what that book left out to see how inadequate it is as a theory of nature, how preposterous even. In a nature of mathematical principles alone, or of the natural mathematically delineated, there is no going to school, no cities, no wars, no buying or selling, no life or death; there, however, space is squared without a blush and time exponented without shame. In the nature in which we live, however, no man ever walked a square mile or ate his dinner in fifteen minutes with the exponent -1. In a nature of mathematical principles alone, those fabulous twins of relativity, Peter and Paul, might part and meet again with each other's times a seeming miracle, but they could neither eat breakfasts nor grow old. Such things aren't done in a nature of mathematical principles. If the modern man has lost a conventional faith, it is far from likely that he has lost something of great value to him, but if he has lost nature in the complexity of its mathematical principles he has lost the one thing that can keep him sane.[20]

While drawing attention to the procedural importance of the realistic distinction, therefore, a realistic metaphysics should present a theory of Nature that would keep a vision of Nature's richness before the scientific community.

Woodbridge, however, goes even further in stressing the importance of metaphysics; for he says that the principles discovered by the realistic metaphysician are more fundamental than those of the special sciences:[21] while the nature of the subject matter for a special scientist may prevent him from considering much of the richness of the data, especially his own living presence, the metaphysician's context of inquiry is all-inclusive and, therefore, the latter cannot ignore any of Nature's richness, including his own presence and the presence of other inquiries within the situation of inquiry. Accordingly, a realistic metaphysics should present a theory of Nature that would remind the scientific community of the importance of man's presence within Nature. Without this reminder, special scientists are more liable to violate the realistic distinction by extending the fact that their limited subject matters exclude consideration of human life in a metaphysics that rejects the presence of human (e.g., mental and spiritual) activities in Nature. Intellectual confusion is the result of this confusion of contexts and subject matters: since the process of inquiry itself necessarily includes human vital functions such as perceiving and reflecting, the inquirer adopts a theory of Nature that excludes the very process required to generate his metaphysics. By theoretically eliminating human activities from Nature, unrealistic scientists have in effect divorced discourse from subject matter with the result that Nature is thought to be beyond the reach of experience and knowledge.

We are not in the habit of setting a moving body over against nature as if the two were so dichotomized that the body's motion defined a region discontinuous with nature's space instead of being a sample of what that space is. Why then should we set a perceiving and thinking man over against nature as if the two were so dichotomized that his perceiving and thinking defined a region discontinuous with nature instead of being a sample of what nature is? When we do the latter, philosophical scepticism becomes inevitable because we are then forced to admit that no samples whatever of what nature is, are accessible to us. Nature then becomes . . . a name for something wholly irrelevant and inaccessible to knowledge.

The recognition of this impresses me as a great intellectual liberation. It has become for me convincing evidence of two conclusions. One is that the distinction between nature and human nature, if taken to be an absolute and unique dichotomy can yield no theory of nature at all.[22]

Regarding the scientific community's need for a realistic metaphysics that would illustrate respect for the realistic distinction by presenting a theory that takes into account the rich variety of Nature's activities without divorcing human activities from Nature, Woodbridge concludes,

[M]etaphysics . . . should come before and not after, as a discipline to keep us sane in what we do after. . . . When I try to work this out with the emphasis primarily on [human] life, those problems to which I have referred seem largely if not wholly to disappear. They seem to have not natural but artificial support.[23]

Metaphysics is able to perform these important functions within the scientific community only so long as it is realistic and, therefore, is limited to the analysis of its own subject matter, existence *as* existence. Those metaphysicians who believe metaphysics to be a super-science that, for example, completes the fragmentary work of the other sciences or instructs other scientists in their basic principles follow the lead of the subject matter of the special sciences rather than their own; they have failed to maintain the realistic distinction.

The intent of laying metaphysics down as the foundation of science, of morality, and of religion . . . is obviously false and iniquitous. In our enthusiasm we may indeed speak of metaphysics as the queen of all the sciences, but she can wear the title only if her behavior is queenly; she forfeits it when, ceasing to reign, she stoops to rule.[24]

The Categories of Individuality and Structure

Nature as experienced is qualitatively punctuated.[25] And its punctuators as such are irreducibly unique self-identicals. Woodbridge uses the term 'individual' to refer to a punctuator's unique self-identity and the term 'individuality' to refer to a common trait: that any of Nature's punctuators displays unique self-identity. According to Woodbridge, the fact of individuality is an ultimate fact. The metaphysician, therefore, cannot explain why Nature is individuated, for any explanation requires the use of individuals; rather, he must simply acknowledge the fact of individuality.

Woodbridge claims that the quality of individuality can be acknowledged only denotatively.[26] Even so simple a form of acknowledgment, however, assumes that the individuals acknowledged are related to other individuals. The metaphysician discovers, therefore, that an individual as such is meaningless and unintelligible; "thought demands that individuality be transcended."[27] Woodbridge concludes that the fact of individuality can neither be acknowledged nor understood apart from an acknowledgement of the fact of relations. The category of "relations" Woodbridge called 'structure'.[28]

On the other hand, however, structures — relations — are not *actually* evident unless punctuated by individuals; they cannot be acknowledged without individuals.

> If one should claim that thought immediately demands that we should transcend individuality, we can answer that the attempt to transcend it is to reinstate it. Thus it is that individuality can not be defined or argued out of existence. It is here to stay.[29]

Accordingly, a pair of ultimate distinctions necessary for the metaphysical description of Nature's general character is individuality and structure. Since the acknowledgement of one requires the acknowledgement of the other, neither category can be divorced from the other; they must not be allowed to degenerate into a radical dualism.

> Individuality and continuity [i.e., structure] are bound together in all our thinking. Indeed the assertion that thought demands that individuality be transcended is really the demand for continuity as a supplementary conception. . . .
> If we are bound to recognize that individuality enters into the constitution of reality [i.e., Nature], we are equally bound to recognize that continuity enters also.[30]

So important is each category to a metaphysical understanding of Nature that Woodbridge says of individuality:

> Thus we may claim that the problem of metaphysics is fundamentally the problem of individuality, the definition of reality is primarily the definition [or

the understanding] of individuality. But individuality can not be defined away or argued out of existence. Its definition must give to it the fullest ontological recognition.[31]

Later, he says of the importance of structure, "we may then say not that the world has structure, but that structure is the world."[32] It is not surprising that Woodbridge holds that the ways in which this distinction is displayed by Nature are many. For example, each of the following pairs exhibits individuality and structure: the finite and the infinite, the discrete and the continuous, the particular and the general, the individual and the universal, subject matter and knowledge, subjects and predicates of propositions, members and classes, and terms and relations.[33]

Woodbridge believes that every existent, even if it is a composite of simpler existents, displays, as a whole, unique self-identity;[34] as such, it is an individual. However, apart from its *relation* with other individuals, a completely isolated individual, although unique, does not display difference or contrast: "nothing whatever in nature is ever 'left to itself' in such a manner that we can determine what it would look like, where it is, and what it would do if there were nothing else."[35] Empirical identification requires, therefore, not only individuality, but also structure. And since the subject matters of scientific inquiry are empirical, this distinction is necessary to a general understanding not only of Nature's perceptibility but also her suitability as the subject matter of empirical science.

Woodbridge holds that philosophers have developed skeptical epistemologies, denying the reliability of experience and the possibility of a posteriori knowledge, because they have either failed to include the inquirer or have misunderstood the manner in which he is included within the natural situation giving rise to knowledge.[36] Man, like any other existent, displays individuality. He is an especially important individual, however, because of the role he plays in determining empirical subject matters and in the inquiry that follows: human individuals do not occupy privileged positions within Nature (there are no absolute perspectives within Nature as a realm of experience—what Woodbridge called the "realm of vision"—for Nature as a realm of vision is essentially relativity of positions);[37] nonetheless, since human perception is from the perspective of the human body's location, the temporal duration of the human body's occupancy of a given location is a factor conditioning the spatial and temporal qualities of a subject matter. Man's bodily inclusion in the context that determines empirical subject matters does not present any problems beyond those associated with the inclusion of any other physical individuals. When man's physical presence is ignored in the situation determining the character of the perceived, however, problems develop in the attempt to account for human experience.[38]

Man's individuality continues to express itself in inquiry. As already shown, Woodbridge believes that the making of claims is required for scientific inquiry and that this activity implies that claims are made of an extra-linguistic subject matter. In addition, however, the making of claims implies a claim maker. In other words, a necessary condition for the assertion of propositions—and, therefore, the existence of inquiry—is the individuality of the point of view displayed by the inquirer in the judgments he makes regarding a subject matter.[39] According to Woodbridge, "reality can not be defined intelligibly as a system absolutely external to the one who formulates it, nor a system in which the one who formulates it is a mere incident, or of which he is a mere product."[40]

Natural Teleology and Mechanism

While mechanism and teleology are qualities displayed by all of Nature's processes, Woodbridge believes that both are especially evident in human living: during the process of inquiry, man assumes that both mechanism and natural teleology are general traits of Nature; and the basis for this assumption is natural rather than transcendental. Given the nature of their subject matters, for example, many special sciences limit their study to *how* Nature's activities occur. And, since the acknowledgment of qualities that display teleology, such as uses, purposes, or ends, are not necessary to an explanation of how events occur, these sciences intentionally ignore natural teleology.[41] Indeed, as Woodbridge notes, "to look for them with an eye on use is to rob science of its disinterestedness."[42] Taking these human activities of inquiry to be indicative of Nature's general character, the realistic metaphysician will acknowledge that a general quality of Nature is mechanisms, or means: Nature is the kind of realm wherein knowledge of many types of subject matter requires discovering how they work; discovering *how* something works is determining the mechanisms; or means, by which it operates.

On the other hand, given the more general context of metaphysical inquiry, the realistic metaphysician can acknowledge what these special scientists cannot: scientists would not be able to identify the mechanisms conditioning a subject matter except that Nature's means-end relation is also a common characteristic. Woodbridge, like Aristotle before him, claims that it is only in terms of Nature's ends, or products and the uses of products, that Nature's means are either identifiable or understandable;[43] for mechanisms are intelligible only as accomplishments. The discovery of mechanism implies, therefore, that teleology is another common quality of Nature. Mechanism and teleology constitute another metaphysical distinction.

It is always what happens that leads to the discovery of what has happened. Were no results attained in Nature, were there no composition of forces determining

one direction rather than another, it is difficult to see how we could have any
interest in causes or in the conservation of the past in some manner in the
effected and effecting present. The search for origins always runs back from
specific products which define the lines which the search must follow to be successful. The questions are always: What did produce this specific product?
What can produce it? What product may be expected or will eventuate when
specific factors are artificially combined? Teleology in this sense is both
unescapable and the source of intelligibility in historical processes.[44]

We may deny design in nature, we may reject final causes as explanations of
existence; but we can not define a single problem, isolate a single field of
inquiry, determine the requisites of the solution of a single question, without
this concept [i.e., teleology] as the determining factor.[45]

The realistic metaphysician will not allow the metaphysical distinction of
mechanism and teleology to become a radical dichotomy.

It should be clear . . . that teleology and mechanism are correlative rather than
opposed. They are contrasted in that without the teleology the mechanism
would not be discovered and that the mechanism alone does not reveal what the
teleology is. But we are under no obligation whatever to assign to either a rival's
privilege.[46]

Woodbridge believes that the main reason so many philosophers reject
teleology as a characteristic of Nature is their belief that it implies the productive capacity of ends rather than means. According to Woodbridge, however, ends *as* ends are never productive. Only mechanisms are productive.

[Natural teleology] is at least relatively harmless. It calls attention to such facts
as that origins cannot be discovered or histories portrayed unless there are specific and identifiable products or ends. . . . [The] end justifies the means,
. . . it clearly does not produce them.[47]

What he calls 'natural teleology' simply denotes the specific *uses* of factors
in the realization of an end and, in turn, the end's own uses; it is the ultimate
fact of the adaptation of means to ends within Nature. Although this is the
minimal meaning of "natural teleology," it is most evident in the human
activity of inquiry, the fact that within Nature means are identified and
understood in terms of ends.

Dynamism of Nature

For an empiricist like Woodbridge, perhaps the least debatable quality that can be attributed to existence is change. Indeed, since experience of Nature is both the source and standard of the adequacy of man's knowledge and, moreover, change is a common quality of experience, it must be accepted as a general characteristic and fact of Nature. Furthermore, Nature's changes are productive, or "dynamic," for they generally display mechanism and teleology. Since the realistic metaphysician is particularly interested in what human activities reveal regarding Nature's general character, Woodbridge examines nature's dynamism as it is displayed in man's involvement with the rest of Nature.

Scientific inquiry is itself a process, a movement from a subject matter as end to an identification of the means conditioning that end. Accordingly, it is change that nonetheless displays the qualities of mechanism and teleology. While scientific inquiry is a form of art and as such can be distinguished from other natural processes, it is also natural. Like Aristotle, Woodbridge believes that art is an extension or perfection of Nature; art is the intentional use of natural conditions. Woodbridge claims that it simply does not make sense to believe that a static world would incorporate a being whose use of natural conditions to acquire knowledge nonetheless requires a process; the process of inquiry could only be an extension of a Nature already essentially dynamic.

> He [i.e., man] belongs to his world as much as anything else and is a product of it as much as anything else. Since, as a product, he attempts to understand his world, the terms in which he understands it can not intelligibly be said to be irrelevant to it any more than the terms in which other beings react to it can be said to be irrelevant to it. . . . In other words, man is to be set down as that illustration of a world in the making which has thoughtful regard for the fact. . . . There can be no consideration of things where the conditions of consideration are not allowed. Man is not the only, but perhaps the best, illustration of essential dynamism.[48]

Activity and Possibility

The acknowledgment of Nature's dynamism makes possible a fuller appreciation and understanding of the other metaphysical distinctions. Dynamic existence incorporates change—a change that is a passage from what can be to what is, from potentiality to actuality. Like Aristotle, Woodbridge believes that change in anything implies that the change must have been already possible; "what philosophy and science both need to recognize is that not only are actualities real, but possibilities are real also."[49] Since Nature's mechanisms, or means, condition every change taking place, they in turn reveal Nature's possibilities. Given the fact of natural teleology, however, Nature's mechanisms are neither identifiable nor understandable until changes are accomplished as natural ends; Nature's possibilities are discovered only from the point of view of the actual.

After 1917, Woodbridge used the terms 'behavior' or 'activity' more often than the terms 'individual' or 'individuality' to refer to the particular actual.[50] Even so, he did not deny the ultimateness of individuality, for every activity and non-active entity displays it.[51] Since individuality can be non-active as well as active, the metaphysician is more liable to properly acknowledge Nature's dynamism if he describes active "individuality" from the point of view of Nature's activities rather than conversely.

> Pluralism does not start with a self-contained system of terms [i.e., individuals] and relations which is, in general, responsible for everything that happens, and then claim that there may be free and spontaneous infractions of the system. It starts rather with the conception of activity as empirically exhibited in any change, and tries to generalize this conception and draw out the implications that seem to be empirically involved.[52]

Again, for Woodbridge, "activity" is any sort of "doing"—"from the movement of an ion to the thinking of a man";[53] and it is equivalent in meaning to Aristotle's notion of "actuality." Moreover, Nature's mechanisms are defined and clarified (and, therefore, her possibilities are discovered) relative to the *activity* of her individuals as ends. For Woodbridge, therefore, the extralinguistic subject matters of scientific inquiry are actually existing individuals.[54] Although Nature's mechanisms reveal her possibilities, they obviously do not exhaust the possible. Otherwise, inquiry would not exist. For the fact that natural possibilities already revealed through mechanisms can be revealed again and again experimentally implies that the possibilities revealed in activity are not exhausted by that activity.[55] Accordingly, the concept of structure must be rich enough in meaning to cover not only the actual relations of the internal organizations of individuals and of their ways of cooperating with each other but also the possibilities displayed thereby.[56] Therefore, although both potentiality and structure are categories, potentiality is not an ultimate one, for "possibility" is an essential characteristic of "structure." Moreover, as already shown, possibilities and, therefore, the structures to which they inhere cannot be reduced to characteristics of individuality, or actual existence.[57] Along with natural teleology, therefore, individuality, activity, and structure, are ultimate metaphysical categories descriptive of general qualities of Nature.

Since the internal organization of an individual thing determines what it is capable of doing within suitable fields of other individuals, like Aristotle, Woodbridge holds that an individual's "frame," or internal organization, is, in a manner of speaking, its powers, capabilities, even its nature.[58]

The dependence of the way things behave on the way they are put together seems to be sufficiently proved. Every act, from the movement of a body in space to the movement of thought in an inference, seems to be done by an agent in which can be found a structure, constitution, or organization without which the act is not done. Specific activity and specific structure go together.[59]

On the other hand, a thing would not possess these powers apart from a field of other individual frames appropriate to its exercise. As Woodbridge says,

Undoubtedly a thing has the power to do what it does, but this power of doing is not a force resident in it independent of the things to which it reacts. Its power is exercised only in co-operation with other things, and when we examine the means and occasion of this co-operation we discover only structural determinations.[60]

So the powers attributed to an individual thing as subject are a function of both its internal organization, or its frame, and the "relational" structure of the way in which the individual frames of its field or content can cooperate with its frame.[61] As he says, "an explosion is not in the powder, but in the world where the powder explodes. . . ."[62] Relational structure, however, is not the structure *of* the field *apart from* (and, therefore, over against) the subject's frame. When actualized, relational structure *is* the structure of cooperation between the subject's frame and the other individual frames of its environment. And, as is true of any structure, the possibilities it displays when actualized are not exhausted in that actualization; structure retains as an essential characteristic, possibility, and these possibilities maintain their ontological status as possibilities.

According to Woodbridge, Hume's analysis of cause-effect and necessary connection is persuasive. For, no matter how thoroughly the frame of anything is examined, that examination will not reveal what it is capable of doing when actualized.[63] "The lack of what Hume called necessary connection between what a thing is and what it does is here admitted and taken for granted. . . ."[64] An a priori knowledge based on *necessary connection* must be denied. For the frame of any thing exercises its capacities only in cooperation with other frames. Accordingly, the possibilities of these frames are revealed only through the possibilities displayed in the relational structure when an activity occurs; the disclosure of a frame's possibilities, therefore, is always a posteriori, never a priori. After activities take place, however, the way the field and the subject's frame cooperate in bringing about the activities reveals that the subject's frame together with the frames of its field and the presence of appropriate agency are a sufficient condition necessitating the activities—thus making possible an a posteriori science based on sufficient conditions.

Necessity and Chance

Woodbridge holds that the acknowledgment of Nature's dynamism implies the acknowledgment of two other general traits: chance and necessity. For the fact of dynamism implies the genuineness of change and, therefore, the occurrence of novel qualities that nonetheless conform to the structural limitations imposed by already existing things.

> Each of them, if started on the road toward realization, has its path determined. . . . The determined path presents us with all the elements of a necessary connection, but we look in vain for such connection when we seek among the untold possibilities the one which is in effect to be. Something new must add itself, must emerge, as it were, out of nonexistence into being. [A] . . . point of departure must arise, and when once it has arisen, the movement proceeds with definiteness. It is thus, whether we like it or not, that the doctrine of chance originates.[65]

While "chance," or "contingency," is a metaphysical category descriptive of an ultimate trait of Nature,[66] according to Woodbridge, "necessity" is a characteristic of the category of structure:[67] "it is the structural concatenation of things which determines the limits of possible behavior. . . ."[68] Accordingly, "given such or such activity of agents under such and such structural conditions, such and such consequences are necessary. . . ."[69] Since every activity (and, therefore, every existing individual) conforms to the limits imposed by Nature's structures, Woodbridge holds that the discovery of structure *is* the possession of a knowledge of Nature.

> For whatever the end may be which any operation serves and whatever the cause may be which initiated the operation, our curiosity is largely satisfied and our efficiency is enhanced when we have discovered the structure to which the operation conforms.[70]

On the other hand, although structure is a necessary condition for the production of activity, it is not also a sufficient condition. For Woodbridge claims that "structure is the inert principle of all existence."[71] "We can not say that given such and such structural conditions such and such active consequences will follow."[72] In addition to structure, the agency of active individuals is a condition for the production of activity.

Nature's "necessity," therefore, does not exclude chance. If Nature's necessity were the "simple necessity" of necessary connection—that is, a thing as cause necessarily determines of itself an effect—then chance would not be a genuine characteristic of Nature. In such a world, a belief in chance could only reflect the believer's ignorance. According to Woodbridge, however, "events both in their character and occurrence are bound up with the interaction of agents and are not end products of series."[73] Every individual frame populating a given environment is necessarily what it is and where it is because each is the result of previous cooperations of individuals; nonetheless, since the existence of each individual frame is the result of a *different* cooperation from the other individual frames, their assembly at a given time, though individually *necessary,* is, as a group, coincidental, or a matter of chance.[74] And, unless a subject's frame is within a suitable environment of other frames with appropriate agency, neither its capacities nor theirs will be exercised.

Moreover, chance does not exclude necessity: for as Woodbridge says, "contradictory as it may seem the appeal to chance tends to become, when attention is focused on the thing that happens, an appeal to necessity."[75] Although the natural assembly of any group of frames is co-incidental, if and when through their assembling they interact, the resulting activity is *necessary*—that is, given the presence of these frames, no other result could have taken place.[76] Woodbridge's view of necessity is what Randall calls "hypothetical necessity."[77] It is most appropriately expressed in the "if-then" form of the implication: "If the sufficient conditions are satisfied (i.e., 'If suitable frames and agency are present . . .'), then a determinate activity will necessarily result." The "if" of the antecedent expresses the *contingent* characteristic of the intersection of Nature's processes; but what follows from their intersection *necessarily* follows.

In summary, in his "Lectures on Metaphysics," Woodbridge lists the categories to which his metaphysical analysis has led:

Considerations of structure, activity, dynamism, individuality, contingency, potentiality and teleology make up the fundamental considerations of metaphysics. We should not think that these . . . indicate anything like the elements of a compound, elements which have being independently and are somehow combined to produce existence as we are familiar with it. They are ultimate distinctions in analysis. They involve propositions not restricted to any subject-matter.[78]

Like all scientific propositions, the propositions expressing these metaphysical distinctions, though formulated in discourse, refer to an extra-linguistic subject matter; therefore, another ultimate metaphysical distinction that must be acknowledged is subject matter and discourse, the realistic distinction.

Realms of Being

In addition to the above categories, Woodbridge distinguishes three "realms of being" that he believes are necessary to an adequate metaphysical understanding of Nature. According to Woodbridge, the realistic metaphysician discovers when he examines his subject matter of any or every activity in context, especially when he considers human activities, that Nature's activities display fundamentally different kinds of cooperation; that is, he discovers that Nature's individuals participate in different kinds of cooperation and, therefore, different kinds of structures or contexts. Woodbridge claims that the different ways in which Nature's individuals cooperate structurally are spatial, temporal, and logical, and that, therefore, Nature displays three kinds of context or, as he calls them, "realms of being":[79] a spatial "realm of vision," a temporal "realm of matter," and a logical "realm of mind." Although these realms and their distinctive kinds of structure are distinguishable, according to Woodbridge, these realms cannot be divorced from each other; they are all realms of Nature. Woodbridge's realms of being are discussed throughout the remainder of this book but with more specific detail in the following chapters: the realms of vision and mind in the chapter on "Man in Nature" (Chapter 4); and the realm of matter in the chapter titled "History and Historical Comprehension" (Chapter 6).

Woodbridge believes that his categories and realms of being provide the distinctions needed for an adequate metaphysical description of Nature. In order to avoid intellectual confusion, however, Woodbridge claims that the realistic metaphysician must acknowledge yet another distinction; this distinction, unlike the others, does not refer to qualities of Nature but instead to a radical dichotomy between Nature and the "supernatural" where Nature is transcended in certain kinds of human activities. Woodbridge's acknowledgment of the supernatural (even though he is a naturalist) is thoroughly discussed in the final chapter on "The Pursuit of Happiness and the Supernatural."

Summary

Increasingly under the influence of Aristotle, Woodbridge reached his mature conception of metaphysics in 1916. He contends that realistic metaphysics is a science that is distinguishable realistically from the other sciences, that is, on the basis of difference in subject matter rather than difference in method: while the special sciences seek knowledge of the natures of specific kinds of activities, metaphysics is the science that seeks to discover the categories descriptive of the common qualities displayed by any or every subject matter.

Moreover, since the subject matter determines the adequacy of the method of inquiry, realistic-scientific method, both in metaphysics and in the special sciences, is contextual analysis, where the subject matter is the standard of the meaning and adequacy of the hypotheses of inquiry. According to Woodbridge, therefore, in cases of reductionism, that is, when interpretations either as preconceptions or those expressed in the hypotheses displace the authority of the subject matter within inquiry, the subject ceases to be a genuine subject matter and, therefore, realistic-scientific inquiry ceases to exist. Woodbridge claims, therefore, that the "realistic distinction" of discourse and subject matter, where the subject matter continues to be distinguished from rather than being reduced to its linguistically expressed interpretations, is a metaphysical distinction descriptive of a general trait of existence, the existence of any subject matter as a subject matter.

While Woodbridge believed that the realistic distinction should be used to combat every kind of reductionism, he was especially critical of the special scientist's misapplication of his procedures and concepts to the different subject matters of metaphysics with the result that the rich variety of Nature's activities is lost, especially those activities characteristic of human living. For example, through the theoretical elimination of human activities from Nature, unrealistic scientists have divorced discourse from subject matter with the result that Nature is thought to be beyond the reach of experience and knowledge. Accordingly, a realistic metaphysics that would illustrate respect for the realistic distinction is needed to correct these reductionist confusions.

According to Woodbridge, when the realistic distinction is respected and reductionism is avoided, the metaphysician discovers that, in addition to the realistic distinction of discourse and subject matter, other ultimate metaphysical distinctions descriptive of Nature's common qualities are "individuality," "structure," "natural theology," "dynamism," "activity," "potentiality," and "contingency." Furthermore, Nature's individuals structurally cooperate in three different ways, spatially, temporally, and logically; therefore, Nature displays three kinds of context or "realms of being": a spatial "realm of vision," a temporal "realm of matter," and a logical "realm of mind." Woodbridge's discussion of these metaphysical distinctions and realms is his mature metaphysical theory of Nature. Since his metaphysical theory influenced every area of his thought, this survey of his metaphysics is preparation for discussions in later chapters.

To indicate the important general influence of Woodbridge's metaphysics on contemporary naturalism, I close this chapter with John Herman Randall's assessment of Woodbridge's influence on the contributors to *Naturalism and the Human Spirit*:

> Much as they have learned from Dewey, it is clear to the discerning reader that most of them owe their fundamental naturalism to Woodbridge.[80]

NOTES

1. Frederick J. E. Woodbridge, *Nature and Mind: Selected Essays of Frederick J. E. Woodbridge* (New York: Columbia University Press, 1937; reprinted, New York: Russell and Russell, 1965), pp. 290–291.

2. Ibid., p. 290.

3. Sterling P. Lamprecht, *Our Philosophical Traditions* (New York: Appleton-Century-Crofts, Inc., 1955), p. 486.

4. John Herman Randall, Jr., *Nature and Historical Experience: Essays in Naturalism and in the Theory of History* (New York: Columbia University Press, 1958; Softcover edition, 1962), p. 136.

5. Sterling P. Lamprecht, *Nature and History* (New York: Columbia University Press, 1950; reprinted ed., Hamden, Connecticut: Anchor Books, 1966), p. v.

6. Frederick J. E. Woodbridge, "Papers, 1884–1940" (Woodbridge's unpublished correspondences, diaries, essays, and lecture and reading notes, Columbia University, Special Collections), lectures entitled "Lectures on Metaphysics: Spring, 1928–1929," p. 2.

7. Frederick J. E. Woodbridge, *An Essay on Nature* (New York: Columbia University Press, 1940), pp. 77–78.

8. Woodbridge, "Papers, 1884–1940," "Lectures on Metaphysics: Spring, 1928–29," pp. 1–2. See also, Woodbridge, *Nature and Mind*, pp. 97–98.

9. Ibid., p. 3.

10. Woodbridge, *Nature and Mind*, p. 7.

11. For the sake of conciseness, hereafter the expression "the realistic distinction" refers to the metaphysical distinction of subject matter and discourse.

12. Woodbridge, "Papers, 1884–1940," "Lectures on Metaphysics: Spring, 1928–29," pp. 10 and 13.

13. Woodbridge, *Essay on Nature*, pp. 3–4.

14. Woodbridge, "Papers, 1884–1940," "Lectures on Metaphysics: Spring, 1928–29," p. 46.

15. Woodbridge says of Kant's transcendentalism: "But to make nature nothing but a collection of appearances in the mind, united according to the supposed necessities of thought, is really to discourage experience and bid imagination riot" (*Nature and Mind*, p. 109). Also see, ibid., pp. 8 and 323.

16. Ibid., p. 54.

17. Ibid., pp. 7–8.

18. Ibid., pp. 96–97; cf., ibid., pp. 288–91.

19. Ibid., pp. 290–91.
20. Woodbridge, "Papers, 1884–1940," "Claims of Science," pp. 14–15.
21. Ibid., p. 15.
22. Woodbridge, *Nature and Mind*, pp. 289–90.
23. Ibid., pp. 290–91.
24. Ibid., p. 106.
25. I am using 'punctuated' to refer to any empirically observed, irreducible quality of the world. Woodbridge does not use this term.
26. Woodbridge, *Nature and Mind*, p. 46.
27. Ibid., p. 47.
28. Ibid., p. 154.
29. Ibid., p. 46.
30. Ibid., p. 47. In his early (1903) article "The Problem of Metaphysics," from which much of the above is taken, Woodbridge uses the term 'continuity' in referring to the category of "relations." After 1916, however, he generally uses the term 'structure' in referring to the same category. For the sake of consistency, I have chosen in most instances to follow his later usage.
31. Ibid., p. 46.
32. Ibid., p. 157.
33. Woodbridge, "Papers, 1884–1940," "Lectures on Metaphysics: Spring, 1928–29," p. 36.
34. Ibid.
35. Woodbridge, *Essay on Nature*, p. 77.
36. Woodbridge, *Nature and Mind*, p. 295.
37. Woodbridge, *Essay on Nature*, pp. 86–88.
38. See, for example, Woodbridge, *Nature and Mind*, pp. 281–82.
39. Ibid., pp. 45–56; also see above discussion of 1903 address, "The Problem of Metaphysics."
40. Ibid., p. 45.
41. Ibid., p. 42.
42. Ibid., p. 120.
43. Ibid., p. 43. Woodbridge still accepts the conception of natural teleology presented in the 1911 essay entitled "Natural Teleology." Accordingly, see the above discussion of that essay.
44. Woodbridge, *Essay on Nature*, pp. 195–96.
45. Woodbridge, *Nature and Mind*, pp. 42–43. Actually, in this essay Woodbridge uses the term 'purpose' rather than 'teleology.' They may be used interchangeably, however, for Woodbridge uses both words to refer to the same concept.
46. Woodbridge, *Essay on Nature*, p. 196.
47. Ibid., p. 198.
48. Woodbridge, "Papers, 1884–1940," "Lectures on Metaphysics: Spring, 1928–29," p. 38.
49. Woodbridge, *Nature and Mind*, p. 303.
50. See, for example, F. J. E. Woodbridge, "Pluralism," *Encyclopedia of Religion and Ethics*, 10 (1919):66–70. Because the term 'behavior' is too closely associated with theories like that of radical behaviorism, I will in most cases use the term 'activity' to denote this general trait.
51. In his unpublished lectures on metaphysics, Woodbridge lists among the

illustrations of activity the finite, the discrete, the particular, and the individual ("Lectures on Metaphysics," p. 36). On the other hand, at the end of the same lectures, he distinguishes individuality from activity as "fundamental considerations of metaphysics" (ibid., p. 46). All in all, he holds that both activity and individuality are ultimate metaphysical categories, although he emphasizes the former for the reason given above. Also he says, "behavior is always specific behavior, meaning the behavior of an individual, and this specific character is attached to the individual . . ." (ibid., p. 25).

52. Ibid., p. 68.

53. Woodbridge, *Nature and Mind,* p. 192.

54. Woodbridge says that "subject-matter" and "subjects of propositions" are illustrations of activity ("Papers, 1884–1940," "Lectures on Metaphysics," p. 38).

55. Evidently, Woodbridge does not consider "mechanism" to be an ultimate metaphysical trait, for he did not include it in the list of "fundamental considerations of metaphysics" in his "Lectures on Metaphysics" (p. 46). Mechanism can be accounted for by the categories of individuality, activity, and structure: nature's mechanisms are her already *actual individuals* that, because of the nature of their internal *structures,* either enter or are available to enter into ways of cooperating (which are also structures) that produce Nature's activities.

56. Although Woodbridge, in his published writings, never clearly distinguishes between "structure's" reference to "ways of cooperating" and "internal organization," in his unpublished "Lectures on Metaphysics: Spring 1928–29," he explicitly states the distinction.

> Now individuals apart from their operations are often said to have a structure which is defined in terms of the instrumentalities by which the operation is effected. In other words, the concrete and specific make-up of the individual is called its structure. The structure which is thus the individual in a sense, is not to be confused with the structure that controls the operations of the individual [i.e., the structures of the ways in which the subject and other individuals cooperate]. Yet the two are correlated [sic] in terms of the individual's operations. [p. 25]

57. Woodbridge says:

> Relations can not intelligibly be treated as terms to the undoing of the distinction between terms and relations. Terms are in relations but are not related to relations. Continuity forbids any final and complete atomizing of being. [ibid., p. 36]

58. Henceforth, for the sake of conciseness, I shall use the term 'frame' to refer to the internal organization or structure of a thing.

59. Woodbridge, *Nature and Mind,* p. 183.

60. Ibid., p. 188.

61. Henceforth, when I use the phrase 'relational structure,' it will refer to "the structure of the way in which the individual frames of a thing's field cooperate with its frame."

62. Frederick J. E. Woodbridge, *The Realm of Mind* (New York: Columbia University Press, 1926), p. 127.

63. Woodbridge, *Nature and Mind,* p. 183.

64. Ibid., p. 184.

65. Ibid., p. 52. Woodbridge's discussion of "chance" in his "Lectures on Metaphysics: Spring, 1928–29," indicates that he still accepts his conception of chance as presented in the 1911 essay, "Natural Teleology." Accordingly, see the above discussion of that essay.

66. Ibid., p. 53; "Papers, 1884–1940," "Lectures on Metaphysics: Spring, 1928–29," p. 46.

67. Ibid., p. 41. The nature of the relation between an occurrence and the conditions of its occurrence is a much debated issue in philosophy of science; and the nature of the "necessity" involved in this relation is highly controversial. Nonetheless, rather than getting involved in the controversy, my task here is simply to present what I believe is Woodbridge's position.

68. Woodbridge, *Nature and Mind,* p. 192.

69. Woodbridge, "Papers, 1884–1940," "Lectures on Metaphysics: Spring 1928–29," pp. 41–42.

70. Woodbridge, *Nature and Mind,* p. 149.

71. Ibid., p. 158.

72. Woodbridge, "Papers, 1884–1940," "Lectures on Metaphysics: Spring, 1928–29," p. 42.

73. Woodbridge, "Papers, 1884–1940," "Lectures on Metaphysics: Spring, 1928–29," p. 40.

74. Woodbridge, *Nature and Mind,* p. 117.

75. Ibid.

76. Ibid.

77. See, Randall, *Nature and Historical Experience,* p. 186. I suspect that Randall was influenced by Woodbridge in his development of this concept.

78. Woodbridge, "Papers, 1884–1940," "Lectures on Metaphysics: Spring, 1928–29," p. 46.

79. That Woodbridge calls these different kinds of cooperation or contexts "realms of being" can be misleading, for it is an expression identical with that associated with Santayana's later philosophy. Woodbridge's realms of being, however, do not separate functions or kinds of activities so absolutely as did Santayana. They are different conceptions.

80. John Herman Randall, Jr., "Epilogue: The Nature of Naturalism," in *Naturalism and the Human Spirit,* edited by Yervant H. Krikorian (New York: Columbia University Press, 1944), p. 366.

4

Man in Nature: The Visible World, Mind, and the Moral Order

The visible world is supreme in being the place of all that we try to understand.

Ordinary folk, and philosophers and scientists when not professional, have no doubt about all this, because the visible world is not a matter of belief.[1]

Man thinks, is an axiom. It governs and controls every attempt he makes to construe what his thinking is.[2]

The preface to morals [is] . . . : "There is no theory of the meaning and value of events which he [man] is compelled to accept, but he is none the less compelled to accept the events."[3]

Introduction

In offering a realistic metaphysical theory Woodbridge believes that human activities display, more than any other activities, Nature's qualitative richness. Moreover, he claims that a realistic metaphysical theory acknowledges that every process of inquiry, including those of the special sciences, necessarily include human activities. For Woodbridge, therefore, an acknowledgment of man's presence in Nature and an understanding of that presence is necessary to the development of an adequate metaphysical theory.

On the other hand, Woodbridge believes that a theoretical distortion of man's place in Nature leads to intellectual confusion: for example, traditional philosophical distinctions, such as appearance-reality and mind-body, become problematic because modern philosophy theoretically divorced man from his world. More specifically, taking methods and theories appropriate to the subject matters of special sciences and incorrectly applying

74

them to the subject matter of metaphysics, many philosophers of the modern period failed to clarify man's mental participation in Nature, and established instead a problematic and skeptical epistemology that attempted to explain how mind, believed to be divorced radically from Nature, could possibly experience or know Nature.

> So far as modern philosophy is concerned, the principle and generally controlling motive [for turning the natural procedure of knowing into a unique problem] is . . . the increasing prominence given to physical science in philosophical thinking. That Descartes and Locke were the distinctive personalities promoting this tendency is clear from its history. Descartes' clear and distinct recognition of the radical difference between extension and thinking, and Locke's isolation of the world of human understanding from the world of existing bodies in space, both raised the problem of the relation of thought to a world external to thought and different from it. . . . If the physical world defined in terms of extension or of more or less solid bodies moving and colliding in space is a world exclusive of thinking, and if thinking and all that goes with it is in its own terms exclusive of the physical world, then there is clearly a problem of how the physical world can be known.[4]

Developing an adequate understanding of man in Nature was a primary concern of Woodbridge; this chapter presents Woodbridge's theory of man in Nature to which his reflections led. This chapter also offers Woodbridge's criticisms of what he called the "end-term" conception of mind which he believed was a basis for the mind-body problem and related problems within modern philosophy. During this presentation his conceptions of an optically structured realm of vision, a logically structured realm of mind, consciousness, objective mind, and Nature as a moral order will be examined.

The Visible World and Its Optical Structure

According to Woodbridge, the metaphysician discovers that the primary subject matter of all scientific inquiry is Nature as man's ordinary experience of "obvious and familiar" things and their activities. Woodbridge calls this empirical subject matter of all inquiry, the "visible world."[5]

> All theories of nature find in the visible world their most conspicuous and fundamental guidance. . . . We see the stars and write astronomies, we see man and write anthropologies, but both in the same evident context and both by observation and experiment, and without what we see, both our astronomies and our anthropologies would be unintelligible.[6]

More specifically, the world as described by the physical scientist is "a heightened understanding of the world before him and not a substitute for it. . . . [It] is part of the truth of the world before his eyes, and not a substitute for that world or the source of its energy and existence."[7]

Most prominent among man's experiences of the "visible world" are those of vision; for vision reveals Nature in its most common and public structure.[8] And if the lead of Nature as visible is followed without prejudicing presuppositions, then, according to Woodbridge, Nature is discovered to have an optical, or perspective, structure: what is discovered is not a Euclidean space where, for example, parallel lines never meet, but space in perspective where parallel lines converge at the horizon. Woodbridge claims, therefore, that there is not a fixed frame of reference nor a privileged point of view within the visible world.[9] Moreover, since Nature is dynamic—visible individuals are in motion—the visible world cannot be described as being fundamentally any specific configuration. All spatial and temporal determinations are relative; Nature as a whole, therefore, is undetermined.[10]

> She [i.e., Nature as a whole] is neither big nor little; she is not cubical or spherical; she is not sometimes here, at others there; she is moving neither fast nor slowly. Yet it is clear that she is of such a character that all these discriminations are necessarily found *in their relativity* when she is analyzed and subjected to experiment. [Italics mine][11]

Nature as the visible world is the "structural unity of all possible configurations"[12] and, since Nature's optical perspectives are structurally unified, optical structure, or space, is continuous. The relationship between optical structure and individual perspectives is a kind of structural cooperation of Nature's individuals and, therefore, it illustrates the metaphysical categories of structure and individuality in their unity. The "visible world" with its optically structured space is one of the metaphysical "realms of being."

Some may object to Woodbridge's claim that Nature's spatial structure is optical on the grounds that the claim is anthropomorphic. Woodbridge's response would be that these objectors arbitrarily draw metaphysical conclusions implying the divorce of human activities, including mental activities like visual experience, from Nature.

> "Due to us" explains nothing at all. "What we do" explains much. What we do is exhibited in our lives, and what our lives are cannot be determined apart from that initial intimacy with Nature which forces us to avoid the supposition that there are independent explanations of what we do and of the world in which we do it.[13]

But an objector might continue to press his objection by pointing out that discrepancies between man's experience of the world and the world's real nature, for example, straight sticks appearing bent when in water or one moon appearing as two, indicate that human experience is not a reliable source of knowledge; mind is divorced from Nature. Woodbridge claims that if what experience shows is accepted, that is, man's bodily presence in an optically structured Nature, then all so-called empirical distortions are in fact the way things should appear given Nature's optical structure. When the optical structuring of Nature is denied, however, experience is divorced from Nature and, therefore, the credibility of empirical science is endangered.

> Our vision of Nature ceases to be a distortion of what she is and becomes rather what she is in consequence of her own inherent integration and relativity. In terms of that the so-called distortions are explained. . . . [T]o make all things different the moment *we* . . . are brought in, gives to *us* a position so privileged that a skepticism which can be only dialectically stated is its ultimate reward.[14]

Woodbridge's Emphasis on Vision

In calling the primary empirical subject matter of inquiry the "visible world," Woodbridge stresses visual experience over other kinds of experience.

> Genetic considerations revealing, as it were, a pyramiding of the senses, with touch as the base, suggest a corresponding pyramiding of experiences, as if what sight reveals were added onto or grounded in experiences more basic and more solid. . . . It is, however, not disrespectful to genetic considerations to point out that the visible world, once experience of it has begun, begins to assume possession of all existences whatsoever. However late the arrival of sight may be, without it any reading of Nature's book is very fragmentary and with it a completer reading is inconceivable except in terms of a completer vision. That is why the verb "to see" becomes an ultimate intellectual term. . . .[15]

Woodbridge holds that vision is especially important in the pursuit of scientific knowledge: more than any other kind of experience, vision is the experience of Nature as common and public. "'Come and see' is the one generally public invitation. . . . Other invitations, like 'come and touch' or 'come and taste,' are . . . invitations to private, not public experience."[16] The ability to hear and to smell, moreover, do not make available the common and the public, for, unlike vision, they are not at one and the same time experience of the world and experience of other beings with whom we share a perceivable world.

And if we speak of "public experience," what can it be if not an experience of that which lies expansed unto the eyes of all? It is the kind of experience which is shared in such a way that in that experience the sharers are identified as sharing in it. . . .[17]

According to Woodbridge, "there is cooperation in the pursuit of knowledge, an interchange of discoveries, opinions, and results."[18] Science is a public pursuit; therefore, the empirical availability of Nature as a common and public world is important to the pursuit of scientific knowledge. As he notes,

[by experimental] I have meant that . . . the various things we study . . . can all be identified by anyone who wishes to identify them, and that whatever is said about these things can be tested by anyone who will refer to the things in question.[19]

He believes that the subject matter of scientific inquiry is experienced activities. The goal of science, however, is a knowledge of the "powers," or natures, acting subjects possess and can exercise when placed in a suitable environment of objects. In order to acquire knowledge of the natures of things, scientists must be able both to identify activities with the agents that are the subjects of the activities and to identify the agents' environments of cooperating objects. Although activities are experienced through all the senses, it is only when nonvisual experiences, for example, odors and sounds, are coordinated with the seen that most activities are identified empirically with their agents.

That which so clearly lies before his eyes . . . is a vision of that region in which lie the things he feels, tastes, smells, and hears. . . .
. . . Without any light anywhere, there might be sounds and odors and the rest, but what creature could live with them as we do or think of nature as we do, we who see the bell that rings and the flowers that yield their perfume? There is little left to nature when we rob it of what it is in the event of vision. In that event, however, it is of such a character that a theory of space becomes a prerequisite in the theory of nature.[20]

Likewise, sight provides experience that is crucial to coordinate the agents of activities with their environments of cooperating objects. For "the visible world is the all-embracing world."[21]

From Woodbridge's point of view, the above discussion should not be taken as providing either arguments or reasons for the empirical superiority of visual experience. For neither the visible world nor its supremacy are matters of belief; rather, they are "obvious and familiar" qualities of man's living presence in Nature.

> The visible world is supreme in being the place of all that we try to understand. Ordinary folk, and philosophers and scientists when not professional, have no doubt about all this, because the visible world is not a matter of belief.[22]

Accordingly, Woodbridge's discussion of the visible world was a metaphysical clarification of the context of experience for every inquiry. Only those engaged in unrealistic inquiry would turn the source of inquiry, human participation in Nature, into a problem requiring a justification for the belief that man actually participates in Nature.

> Can we leave [human] life out of nature and then expect to understand what nature is? Can we turn the generator of all our problems itself into a problem and hope to say anything sensible? Have philosophers even said anything sensible about it when they have made that turning? Not making it is not immunity from follies, but it can be a prophylactic.[23]

The End-Term Conception of Mind

Given the influence on philosophical thought of physical sciences, which had been dominated for the most part by a Newtonian emphasis on mechanism, modern epistemology was launched by thinkers who used the physiological mechanisms generating mental activity as their point of departure in understanding the nature and limits of knowledge. Furthermore, there was the influence of Descartes' claim that mind is essentially different from the world known by science, the world of spatially extended bodies. According to Woodbridge, these influences were a historical basis for the notion of mind dominating modern epistemology—what he called the "end-term" conception of mind. He describes this interpretation of mind, which was first expressed in Locke's *Essay* but continued its influence through Kant into post-Kantian idealism, as follows:

> The conception of consciousness which has controlled the major portion of modern philosophy, reaching over even into the thought of such men as Huxley and Spencer, was pretty definitely fixed by Descartes, Locke, and Kant. In Locke, however, it appears to have received its simplest formulation and to have afforded the first clear and definite statement of the fundamental principles

which have characterized the idealistic development through Hegel and since. These principles are the following: (1) the only objects of knowledge are ideas; (2) all ideas are acquired; and (3) knowledge is a synthesis of ideas. It is apparent at once that we have here the germs of the idealistic doctrines of phenomenalism, of experience, and of rationally deduced, synthesizing categories.[24]

Moreover, he says:

While attempts were occasionally made, notably by Kant, to furnish evidence for the validity of Locke's principles, they have usually been presented as self-evident truths, apparent to trained philosophical reflection at least. Yet it is clear that they rest, and did rest with Locke, on an initial conception of the mind and consciousness without which their validity is far from apparent. The mind, that is, was conceived as an original capacity or receptacle, endowed with certain constitutional powers and needing the operation of some alien or resident factor to arouse it to activity. *It was the end-term of a relation,* the other term of which might be the external world, another mind, the divine being, or some unknown source of excitation. [Italics mine][25]

Woodbridge argues that when worked out the end-term conception of mind destroys itself.[26] The objects of thought are the physical bodies (man's own body included) that make up the physical world. Thought does not occur, however, until these objects of thought stimulate the sense organs of man's body and thereby excite nervous impulses which are carried to his brain. Accordingly, a physical process is antecedent to or coincident with thought. But if this physical process is taken as the point of departure from which to interpret mind, then "mind" becomes that within man which responds to this process by thinking of the world: mind becomes an end-term. "Thus we endow our bodies with an agent which, through the mediation of the body, thinks of the world of bodies."[27]

This notion of mind, however, leads to strange conclusions. For if the mind "lays hold anywhere" of the physical process generating thought, it does so in the physical organ, the brain. It would seem, therefore, that nerve processes in the brain, rather than the physical objects man believes he perceives and comes to know as the sources of stimuli, are the immediate objects of mind. But this conclusion is clearly unacceptable. Although nerve processes are the immediate occasions of thought and are somehow correlated with the mind's objects, the immediate objects of mind are never brain processes. On the other hand, since the mind is intimately associated with the brain alone, its immediate objects cannot be the exterior bodies believed to stimulate the brain. If the end-term conception of mind excludes either nerve processes or external bodies as the mind's immediate objects, what then are the objects of mind? The answer one seems led to accept is "the contents of mind itself." And in order to emphasize that these contents are not physical bodies, they are given such names as "perceptions" and "ideas":

What the mind thinks about, then, is its own perceptions or ideas. These constitute a mental world of their own in which all our thoughts and reasonings proceed. We are thus confronted with two worlds, a world of physical bodies from which the mind is wholly excluded and a world of perceptions and ideas from which the physical world is wholly excluded.[28]

If physical objects are never the immediate objects of men's thoughts and reasonings, then it is not clear what physical objects are. The holder of the end-term conception began his examination with the physical world only to lose it in the end; what was taken to be "fact" is now questionable. Even if the physical world's existence could be established, approaching the fact that man thinks from the standpoint of the physical processes involved, the argument leads to a denial of the qualitative richness of the physical world: qualities become mental perceptions, therefore, the exterior world is impoverished to the point of being explained quantitatively solely in terms of mechanical motions, vibrations, and excitations. If man is confined in all his thoughts and reasonings to his mind and its contents, however, then even an external world of mechanical relations is beyond thought. Man has a conception of a physical world, but his conception could not have come from beyond the limits of thought; therefore, man's conception of a physical world can only be a product of the mind itself. Woodbridge concludes,

It seems clear . . . that the argument which leads to this conclusion defeats itself. Starting with the physical world and its processes, it was led to assume an agent mind. It reaches the conclusion that the physical world is not after all something with which we start, but something at which we arrive. In its most condensed form, it runs as follows: The physical world requires a mind in order that it may be known, but the mind knows no other physical world than that which it constructs out of its own contents. This is scarcely intelligible.[29]

In arguing against the end-term conception of mind, Woodbridge was not attempting to disprove that mental activity is conditioned either by bodily nerve processes or by a physical world containing mechanical structures. For he was perfectly willing to accept whatever could be learned from the special sciences regarding the effects of physical processes on mental activity. Rather, the point of his argument is that inquirers must approach their subject matter realistically.

What we repeatedly need is at once the most naive and profoundest realism we can express. Especially is this needed when there is [a] question of the relation of mind to body, for here the tendency has been too prevalent to distort facts in favor of hypotheses which their makers have assumed to be necessary in view of some antecedent metaphysics of their own.[30]

Inquirers must take the subject matter of human mental activities as the point of departure, rather than the conditioning factors discovered during the course of the examination, if they hope to avoid intellectual perplexity in developing a science of mind. For, given the fact of natural teleology, factors are identified and understood relative to the activities they condition; therefore, factors conditioning human thought can be identified and understood only when considered relative to man's mental activity. Accordingly, Woodbridge claims that: *"man thinks, is an axiom. It governs and controls every attempt he makes to construe what his thinking is"* (italics mine).[31] If philosophers had taken the human mind itself (that is, the human activities of perceiving and acquiring knowledge of the world) as the point of departure in their inquiry into the nature and the limitations of knowledge, then they would have been able to examine nerve processes and the rest of the physical world as conditioning factors of the human mind without either losing mind by reducing it to an epiphenomenon of physical processes, as in materialism, or reducing the physical world to a construct of an agent mind, as in idealism. Since "man thinks" is axiomatic, the mental scientist offering a metaphysical theory of mind must return to man's empirically identifiable mental activities and, following their lead, attempt to determine what the actual facts of mind are; any attempt to replace man's mental activities as the subject matter is arbitrary.

The Human Mind as It Functions in the Human Organism and Person

According to Woodbridge, people ordinarily distinguish between a man's body and his mind, but the basis for this distinction is that they observe a difference in human activities rather than observing different elements.[32] Empirically, there is no basis for holding that the statement "Man is body and mind" refers to man as a composite of two elements: one properly called a body and another called a mind.[33]

We may . . . distinguish the mind from the body, but *back of that distinction lies the fact with which we really begin,* namely that *we think and so are minds, we walk and so are bodies.* Or if we should use a noun instead of a pronoun for the subject, then it is man that thinks and man that walks, so that man comes to be a mind and a body. [Italics mine][34]

He is, rather than has, a mind. He may be analyzed into mind and body along the lines of his activities without, however, finding mind and body to be two distinct and substantial elements of his composition. As a being he is one and undivided.[35]

Moreover, "no matter how diverse our activities may be, the one identifiable agent of them all is the same, namely, our bodily selves."[36]

If we ask what is the agent of thinking, the answer to our question is the same as when we ask what is the agent of walking. . . . The supposition of another agent of thinking besides the body ends in confusion whenever we seriously try to render it intelligible. We may believe that such an agent exists and fortify our belief with commendable arguments, but it remains something in which we believe. It is not something which we can identify nor anything which has value in metaphysical analysis. For such analysis, the thinker is, and remains, the body.[37]

On the other hand, the fact that the human body is the agent of mental as well as physical activities does not discredit the making of the distinction between the mental and the physical; for it is also an empirical fact that the same bodily agent engages in *two fundamentally different kinds of activity.*

That the body perceives, remembers and thinks, is a fact needing no proof. The consequences of its doing this, however, are such that they naturally refuse to be identified with the body itself. This, too, is in no need of proof.[38]

How, then, is man's mind to be characterized so as to be faithful to both of these evident facts of mental activity? As he did so often when confronted by philosophical perplexity, Woodbridge turned to Aristotle's analyses for guidance: the mind is a soul, or a life, of the body and, therefore, it is a kind of bodily activity or the "power" of the body to so act; accordingly, man's mind can be distinguished from his body as a kind of activity or power to act can be distinguished from the agent that acts or has the power to act. Furthermore, in addition to the human body's mental activities and powers, it behaves physically; the different kinds of bodily activities forms the basis for the distinction between the mental and the physical dimensions of human living.[39]

The soul is the body's life and in particular the life of perception, memory, imagination, and thought. And the soul as the body's life gets distinguished from the body . . . as the *life of* the body, the *exercise of* the body, or as the power of the body as over against the body as having that power. . . . It may be said that the distinction is clear enough and evident and empirical enough. The body is not the soul and the soul is not the body. All attempts to identify them seem to fail. They are in many ways incomparable.

. . . The incomparability is, however, not of a unique sort. There is the same sort . . . in general between what a thing is and what it does. . . . So it would seem that the distinction between body and soul is not a distinction between separable and discrete existences but only between agent and act, or between an agent and its powers.

. . . The position just stated is that of Aristotle. With him the soul was the outcome of the body's activity and also the body's powers. And he associated with the soul all the body's activities as a living organism. The relation between the body and soul he defined as functional, as we should say. He refused to think of the relation as in any way comparable with the relation between two bodies.[40]

Since man's mind is a "bodily function,"[41] mental activity is conditioned by the human body. For, given Nature's optical structure, the mental function of human perception is always from a perspective—the perspective of the body's spatiotemporal location relative to the other bodies within its environment; man's perception from this bodily perspective, what Woodbridge calls the "insistence of the body,"[42] and his consequent relativity of position greatly affect the structure of Nature as perceived. Furthermore, the fact that impaired sense organs limit one's ability to perceive shows that "bodily insistence" conditions perception.[43] Moreover, in such situations where "bodily insistence" is evident, the intimacy and sense of possession associated with personal experience is intensified; for, according to Woodbridge, the natural basis for this sense of intimacy and possession is the insistence of the body.[44]

Restore the body to its insistence on its own relativity amid things, then *thinking is individualized* and marks the humbler efforts of a man to inquire and comprehend. So it is that by passing from the unpossessed to the possessed, from the impersonal to the personal, and this through the insistence of the body, that we pass to many minds. They are not discovered . . . by finding them resident in bodies or, like spiritual shadows, attached to them. They are discovered out of the body's relativity. [Italics mine][45]

Although bodily insistence conditions mental activity, it is not the kind of bodily conditioning distinctive of mental activity.

Many men, . . . in so far as they are many minds, are many bodies. But these bodies are of a particular sort. Their relativity alone is not enough to define them, for all bodies have that, whether they are men or not. . . . Accordingly, while his body's relativity is responsible for the discovery of a man's mind, he will hardly take it alone as distinguishing his body from others.[46]

What distinguishes bodies capable of mental activity is bodily organization, or frame.

> Many minds are many men. But many men are many bodies of a certain sort, with a particular constitution and organized in a particular way. They interact with other bodies about them. And the peculiarity of their organization is such that they constitute highly integrated centers of communication.[47]

Woodbridge offers a general description of this distinctive bodily organization: although man is capable of being aware of a large variety of different stimuli because of the diversification of his sense organs, his nervous system and his brain enable him to react in an integrated manner whatever organ is affected and however diversified the quality of the stimulus may be.[48]

> His body is organized in relation to qualitative differences in it and in the world, and also in a manner which renders his responses to stimuli selective, coherent and unified.[49]

In offering this description, Woodbridge was not presenting a physiological account of mind; as a realist, he left that task for those to whom it legitimately belonged, physical scientists. Rather, his point was to illustrate that if the metaphysician begins with the subject matter of mental activity, he discovers it to be a distinctive bodily function and, as such, a function conditioned by the special frame of the human body, the human organism.[50] The progress of physical science in predicting and controlling mental activity by experimenting on the body's frame corroborates the discovery of the realistic metaphysician.[51]

Although the body's frame is a condition of man's mental activity, Woodbridge believes that alone it does not account for mental functioning. For all activities, including mental ones, are co-operations of a subject's frame with an environment of suitably organized things.

> Our brains and legs are instruments of different types of activity, but they can no more operate of themselves than a hammer can drive a nail of itself. They operate in connection with the rest of things, they operate in space and time.[52]

As a cooperation, the human mind is fully natural and, therefore, a scientific analysis of it requires Nature as the general context of analysis. The fact, however, that mental activity is a *bodily* function, a cooperation of frames, does not eliminate the need to acknowledge the evident differences between mental and physical activities; when the body behaves mentally, its activity displays qualities defying identification with the physical. And, since mind is natural, man's mental activities are as much a cooperation of the human organism with its environment of things as are physical activities. Therefore, according to Woodbridge, the presence of these distinctively mental qualities gives evidence that, in addition to physical structures, Nature as the field of objects conditioning human activities is structured appropriately for mental living: in addition to being a mechanically and chemically structured physical realm and an optically structured realm of vision, Nature is an intelligibly structured "realm of mind." Thus Nature displays more than one kind of structure and, therefore, more than one "realm of being."

> Now the evidence both analytic and experimental is all in favor of recognizing perception, memory, and thought as bodily functions fully as much as breathing and digestion. If we ask what it is that perceives and thinks, the answer seems to be quite clearly, the same thing that breathes and digests, and further, if we regard breathing and digesting as a cooperation with nature, so also should we regard perceiving and thinking. If digestion implies a chemical constitution to nature, then thinking implies a logical constitution.[53]

Mental Activity and Its Objects

Although acknowledging the human mind as a bodily function accounts for the distinction between mental activity and the human body as the agent of the activity, it cannot wholly account for the distinction between the mental and the physical as different kinds of activities. Yet Woodbridge believes that everyone readily makes the distinction, for the body's mental behavior displays qualities that resist being identified as physical. Woodbridge concludes that the characteristic structure mental activity makes available to man, not the human body, is the basis for defining the qualities distinctive of mental activities in a manner that yields an understanding of the essential difference between the mental and the physical.

> *When we attempt to define the mind, we are led ultimately to consider, not an individual agent or being which thinks, but the realm of being* in which thinking occurs. . . . Although we may . . . call ourselves minds, we should be under no illusion that thereby we had discovered in our bodies something different

from them which could properly be called a mind. We discover in them no mind at all. And yet they think. To explore this fact carries us beyond ourselves to what we think about, to the realm of being in which our thinking is an event and to which our bodies belong. Then it is that this realm of being discloses itself as so connected that we can discover what one fact or event in it implies in terms of other facts and events. *We discover ourselves to inhabit* a realm of being which has a logical structure. That I take to be the discovery of the essential nature of mind. [Italics mine][54]

One human activity is walking, and when someone describes what was done when a man walks, or what was done in this kind of activity, he does so in statements like, "He walked (moved) from here to there." The description of this kind of activity requires determination of change of place and rate of change of the bodily agent relative to the place and time of other individuals; it requires spatiotemporal limitation. On the other hand, when one describes what was done when a man perceived, remembered, imagined, thought, or knew, spatiotemporal determinations seem strangely inappropriate. Rather, in these cases, one is forced to consider the objects of the activities, the objects of thought: What was done when the man perceived? He perceived a star (as it existed millions of years before his time).[55] What was done when the man imagined? He imagined what society might be like in 1984. What was done when the man remembered? He remembered the good times he had as a child. "We think about the North Pole and the other side of the moon."[56] As Woodbridge says, "What is a thought unless there is something thought about?"[57]

Although mental *activities,* like all activities, endure only for a limited time, as *mental* activities, the objects they make available to man are not temporally limited in the manner of physical activities; mental objects are often spatially and temporally removed from the time of the mental act and the place of the thinker or perceiver. As Woodbridge says,

thinking is so bound up with the objects of thought that we find ourselves dealing with their world in every attempt to deal with its. It seems idle, therefore, to say of the mind: "Lo, it is here, or lo, it is there." . . . [W]e think beyond [i.e., the objects of thought are beyond] our body's place and our life's duration.[58]

Although in the definition of mental activity the emphasis falls on the nature of mental objects, Woodbridge does not allow this emphasis to dissolve the distinction between the human *body's* mental *act* and the *mental object.* For without this distinction, how could the spatiotemporal *remoteness* of mental objects be acknowledged?[59] An adequate description of mental activity implies, therefore, that the space-time relations between the human organism's mental act and its mental object(s) are also accessible to mind: "Since we think beyond our body's place and our life's duration, there is no intelligible divorcing of time and space from the realm of mind."[60] Mental activity, by making spatiotemporally remote objects available, makes space and time accessible to man. Accordingly, although the subject matter with which mental science begins is a kind of bodily activity, the structure distinctive of the objects of mental activity, as opposed to the spatiotemporally limited human body, is the defining characteristic of mind.

The analysis leading to the above distinction between the mental and the physical exemplifies natural teleology: for, although factors are identified and understood relative to the activities they condition, activities are identified and understood relative to their uses. Likewise, mental activities are defined relative to their use, making the spatiotemporal, or physical, dimension of Nature's objects available to man.

> Although our days are numbered and our steps measured, we can think of times when we neither were nor shall be, and of places far beyond the possible tread of our feet. *Thinking finds no limits in time or space.* To say this is not necessarily to indulge in rhapsody, although rhapsody has often been provoked by saying it. *We are noting an obvious and commonplace fact. . . .*
> This fact is taken here as defining in some measure the domain or realm in which thinking goes on [i.e., the realm of mind]. [Italics mine][61]

Mentally, man is freed from spatial and temporal limitations in a manner which he can never be physically free.

Human Thinking and Ideas

Although mental activity is a function of the body, its distinctively mental quality is neither identifiable nor definable apart from the fact that Nature's objects constitute not only a physical realm but also a mental realm. Moreover, the ability of physical scientists to control mental *activity* by means of the manipulation of physical factors does not discredit the fact that, in addition to physical conditions, the mental structures of Nature's objects condition the occurrence of *mental* activity. For example, intelligent human action—employing knowledge of the world for the effective use of the physical world—implies that Nature is intelligibly structured. Woodbridge claims, therefore, that if the mental scientist follows the lead of the subject matter of mental activity, he will discover that Nature's individuals structurally cooperate not only spatiotemporally, or physically, but also logically.

If we turn to explore what we think about and let thought be led on by its objects, then we discover that thinking is coextensive with its subject-matter. It is bodily activity and depends on the body for its vigor and sustaining, but it comprehends the body and very much more. It has many limitations readily traceable to the body, but it has also a limitation not so traceable at all. . . . We discover, that is, that there is in the realm of being a structure. . . . which . . . opens to us the reaches of time and space and what they contain. This structure can not properly be described as physical. It is logical. Accordingly, if mind means anything else than a thinker, we have taken it to mean the logical structure of the realm of being which we explore when we think. In this sense the mind is not *a* being or *an* agent or *an* existence. It is rather the implication of all beings, agents, and existences, revealing something basic about the realm of being itself.[62]

Nature is not only a spatial realm of vision and a temporal realm of matter but also a logically structured "realm of mind."

Since activities are identified and understood relative to their uses and, therefore, mental activities are understood relative to the objects they make available to man, and since knowing is a mental activity providing known objects, Woodbridge believes that the metaphysician should examine objects as known to acquire an understanding of the general nature of the logical structure of the world: although knowledge is derived from experience, experience is not knowledge; to experience an object is not as such to know it. The bare existence of a subject matter, therefore, is not an adequate substitute for a science of it. "Knowing things is not being them, nor is their existence knowledge of them."[63] Moreover, if the experience of existing objects is not itself a knowledge of them, then a so-called "conscious" correspondent or some other form of representation of existing objects is not as such knowledge.

Possession of a counterfeit of reality is no nearer to knowledge than the possession of reality itself. . . . The counterfeit may resemble its original and be comparable with it point for point and we may be conscious of this resemblance, but even then knowledge may still be far away, for without taking over the burden of this perplexing doctrine, each of us knows well enough that the consciousness of the resemblance of a photograph to its original is knowledge neither of the one nor the other. At best it is knowledge of the resemblance between them.[64]

Woodbridge uses the term 'idea' for the object as known in order to distinguish it from the same object whose existence is merely experienced. "Ideas are in no sense like perceptions."[65] Yet "to know a thing is to have an idea of it."[66] Although knowledge of objects, or ideas, is acquired from experience, since ideas and experience differ, he concludes, given all the experience we have or can have, an idea—unless we arbitrarily make it such by a definition to start with—is never a copy, image, likeness, resemblance, counterfeit, presentation or representation of anything whatever. Likenesses are things like photographs, paintings, drawings, models. They are expressed in lineaments comparable with the things they are like. Ideas are not so expressed. They are expressed, when we write or speak, in propositions. And a proposition is never, in any sense, like the thing it propounds. Its effect is not photographic but communicative. It conveys ideas and effects knowledge.[67]

Being Conscious and the Myth of Consciousness

According to Woodbridge, although experience and knowledge differ, their difference should not be allowed to encourage the misinterpretation of "consciousness" as a veil or some other kind of substance that must be pierced in order to know directly existing objects.

> Tear away any veil of consciousness supposed to hang between us and the things we know and knowledge is not thereby brought into being. Or stretch it tight, make it opaque, paint on it a picture of that it screens us from and then add on what we will, we have not even then exhibited knowledge.[68]

Man directly perceives existing objects and yet he must admit that his experience, though direct, is not knowledge. Yet "consciousness" is often interpreted as a subjective substance,[69] implying thereby that consciousness is radically divorced from the world of objects and, therefore, that man can neither perceive nor acquire knowledge of existing objects. Woodbridge worked at solving this "problem of consciousness" for many years, for he believed its solution would remove much of the theoretical basis for the end-term conception of mind implicit in modern philosophy.[70] He attempted to solve the problem through a reclassification of the ontological status of consciousness: early on, for example, he believed that if consciousness is conceived to be a relation rather than an end-term of a relation, the problem might be solved.[71] He finally concluded, however, that any attempt *to solve the problem* of consciousness was doomed to failure, for any such attempt presupposed the interpretation of consciousness that was the basis for the problem. In 1936, he wrote,

> in retrospect, the controversy [does consciousness exist] wears for me a different look than it had at the time of its activity. Then it seemed that all that we mortals mean when we use the word "soul" was at stake. Now it seems that we were tricked, allowing ourselves to be influenced more by forms of speech than

by what we were talking about. What is *consciousness*? What is it *to be conscious*? These two questions might have been more generally suspected to be
identical, if we had not been so much obsessed by the disjunction: consciousness must be either a *stuff* or a *function*. . . .
     . . . the problem of consciousness is at least equivocal. It may be . . .
called an artificial problem, one, that is, that arises from the manner of its
statement rather than from the exigencies of subject-matter. . . .
     . . . As a stuff, consciousness has been made to look like a superstition; as
the function of some sort of stuff, I doubt if it fares any better.[72]

Rather than attempting *to solve* the problem, he eventually got over it;[73]
and, according to Woodbridge, the way to get over a problem, which is as
such unsolvable, is to ignore the problematic theories of the subject matter
and begin again realistically with the subject matter itself. And, when the
empirical subject matter called 'consciousness' is identified, what it is "to be
conscious" is simply:

seeing, hearing, tasting, smelling, feeling; thinking about what we see, hear,
taste, smell, and feel; and expressing the result in language of some sort. That is
what being conscious is, and no philosopher has ever delivered anything
more.[74]

From the realistic vantage point of the genuine subject matter, i.e. the
empirically evident fact that man perceives, inquires into, and comes to
know existing objects, Woodbridge claims that the "problem" of consciousness is shown to be a spurious problem. *Rather than solving the problem, he
believes that his realism allowed him to get over it.* Moreover, problematic
interpretations of "consciousness" assume the very facts they seek to
discredit: for even these theories are interpretations and, as such, presuppose consciousness as the subject matter being interpreted; that is, according to Woodbridge, they presuppose the unproblematic fact that man
perceives, inquires into, and comes to know his world.

Thinking about a surrounding world in which we find ourselves alive, awake,
active, planning, and telling ourselves and others about it—that is what it is to
be conscious. And this is quite literally a principle, a beginning and not an end,
a start and not a finish. . . . Abolish being conscious and there is nothing to
talk about. Being conscious is the source of common sense, society, religion,
art, and science. . . . Since being conscious is the admitted source of all our
problems and of their solutions—a genuine principle—in what sense can it itself
be a problem . . . ?[75]

"Consciousness," or its cognates, may be used as simply another name for the mental activities of perceiving or knowing existing objects. It may also be used as another name for the mental activity of inquiry. While using it consistently in any of these ways would be harmless of itself, the use of the term 'consciousness,' being grammatically a noun, too often had encouraged *the reification* of mental activities into a subjective substance. By 1926, therefore, Woodbridge chose to avoid the use of the term 'consciousness' in his development of a theory of mind. Because of his realism, Woodbridge believed that he had "gotten over" the use of "consciousness" as an explanatory notion; therefore, his realism functioned for him as an "Occam's Razor" of sorts.

> It may be insisted that consciousness must exist before there can be knowledge. . . . We have, nevertheless, to insist with equal energy that the body must first exist and the world too. We do not reach knowledge simply by multiplying existences.[76]

The Logical Structure of the World

If the use of a conception of consciousness is unnecessary—indeed, harmful—to a clarification of the difference between experience and knowledge of existing objects, then how can this difference be clarified? As shown above, Woodbridge believes that objects when known are ideas and as such are distinguishable from the same existing objects when only perceived. What then is an idea; what is its distinguishing characteristic? Woodbridge's answer is, "an idea is an object in its logical connections."[77] When the objects of Nature are known rather than merely perceived, they are discovered to possess a radically different structure in addition to the spatiotemporal structures—whether mechanical, chemical, or biological—they possess as physical beings.

> Mind as logical structure is discoverable. There is a coherence in things which is found out by thinking. This coherence is something quite different from spatial juxtaposition, temporal succession or mass accumulation.[78]

While he uses the term 'logical' to distinguish mental structure from other kinds, he does not limit its meaning to "formally logical."[79] Rather, the discovery of objects as ideas is the discovery of "a structure by virtue of which one fact or event . . . may lead our thinking on to other facts and events which are involved."[80] Moreover, he believes that, as inquirers follow these logical relations from facts and events to other facts and events, they discover "a genuine coherence among the things we think about."[81] This coherence of objects in their mental connections is knowledge of objects, or ideas. "It is that which language tries ultimately to express."[82] And these mental structures are neither subjective forms by which the human mind structures its world nor fictions created by the mind in order to explore its world; rather, scientific inquiry *discovers* them to be a characteristic of the world itself. Accordingly, Woodbridge uses the term 'objective' in referring to the world as logically structured, as a world of idea objects, an "objective mind."

> Mind as logical structure is objective. By affirming its objectivity we mean that it has to do with the make-up of the world in which we think. . . . [I]t is not something which we create, but something which we discover. It is of the essence of things.[83]

Although the ontological difference between the logical relations of objects and their other kinds of structure must be respected, their logical structure makes the others available to human thought and is the objective source of their intelligibility. For example, logical structure is the objective basis for the intelligibility of Nature's spatiotemporal dimension:

> We seem forced to affirm the relativity of all bodies, not only because we observe it, but also because we are constrained thereto by the logic of events. For it seems quite clear that in a world where there was no logic of running, Achilles could not run.[84]

Furthermore, this logical structure is the objective basis determining the adequacy and inadequacy of scientific theories.

> We may think about anything. . . . We may think foolishly, insanely and incorrectly. If, however, our thinking is to be wise and sane and correct, it is not the body which makes it so, but a genuine coherence among the things we think about.[85]

For the scientific inquirer, the logical structure of his subject matter is "absolute"; that is, the discovery of the ideas of objective mind terminates inquiry, for the goal of scientific inquiry, knowledge of Nature, has been attained.

Structure is really a discovery and a discovery of an absolute kind. That is, the inquiries which lead to the discovery of structure terminate absolutely in that discovery. . . . Such knowledge is in the highest sense explanatory, because it leaves nothing to be explained. By that I do not mean that it puts an end to all intellectual interest or that the discovery of structure is not progressive. I mean rather that did we know the structure of things thoroughly, all our intellectual interests would become practical and inventive. Science would become dogmatic while art would flourish.[86]

Although important differences exist between kinds of relations, mind cannot be divorced from the physical world, because, according to Woodbridge, it is *the same objects* that being logically related are ideas and being spatiotemporally related are physical things. *"Ordo et connectio idearum idem est ac ordo et connectio rerum."*[87] Woodbridge is a logical realist.

What then, are ideas? We may now say that an idea is an object in its logical connections. It is in no sense image, copy, likeness; in no sense one kind of existence set over against another kind, demanding comparison between the two in order that there may be knowledge. *Nor is it the object's presence,* not even if we describe that presence as a presentation to or in consciousness. *For we may see objects and yet have little or no idea of what they are.* . . . To have knowledge, something more and something quite different is necessary. Objects must effect a specific kind of leading on. They must evoke affirmations and denials. They must generate propositions. And our contention is that *they do this, not by being first transformed into something like them or into something which implies them, but by being themselves already involved in a set of logical connections which we follow out and discover.* . . . In terms of the realm of mind, ideas are its logic particularized and focused in objects.

Objective mind is thus a system of ideas. It is not, however, a system which is parallel with the physical or interacts with it. Nor is it identical with the physical, or, with the physical, an aspect of something still more fundamental. It were better to say that *it is a system of the physical, that system in terms of which things may become propositions,* be reduced to formulas and admit affirmations and denials. *Knowledge finds in it its objective ground and the possibility of its verification.* [Italics mine][88]

According to Woodbridge, whether an existing object is perceived or known, it is the same existing object; the only difference between an object as perceived and as known is that, when known, the object's spatiotemporal and logical structures, which it possessed before becoming known, are discovered through its logical structures.[89] For Woodbridge, neither existence, perception, nor knowledge creates a radical dichotomy in Nature.

Objective Mind and Objective Idealism

Woodbridge's "objective mind" is similar to the views of objective idealists, for he took objective idealism quite seriously. Recognizing these similarities, Woodbridge used terms associated with objective idealism — 'realm of mind,' 'objective mind,' and 'absolute' — in developing his theory of mind; and yet, he interpreted these terms in such a way as to distinguish his own position. For objective idealists, objective mind is the objectification of the cosmic Subject, or Mind. Although idealists claim that science discovers objective mind, since it is an externalization of Subject, according to Woodbridge's theory, the objective idealist's conception of "objective mind" is not genuinely objective.[90]

His use of 'absolute' should also be distinguished from that of objective idealists. For Woodbridge, the structures of objective mind are only cognitively absolute: the goal of inquiries, the acquisition of specific bodies of knowledge, is *perfectly, or absolutely, accomplished* in the discovery of Nature's structures. Seen cognitively, therefore, structure is only contextually absolute: according to Woodbridge, Nature is a pluralism of many subject matters possessing many structures that require many different sciences rather than a Subject with an essentially monistic structure requiring one Science for its adequate articulation.

Moreover, Woodbridge rejects the objective idealist doctrine that the relations constituting reality are also axiologically absolute. For Woodbridge, although the discovery of structure provides an explanation of the factors conditioning behavior, its discovery neither determines what should be done nor justifies what is done. Furthermore, as a metaphysical pluralist, Woodbridge rejects the essentially monistic theory of natural history held by objective idealists; that is, he opposes the view that natural history is the evolution of mind from a plurality of many subject matters articulated by many sciences supporting many moral forms to Mind's eventual Self-discovery as Absolute Mind identical with one Absolute Science expressed morally in one Absolute Community.[91]

> I am in entire agreement with idealism in its claim that questions of knowledge and of the nature of reality can not ultimately be separated, because we can know reality only *as* we know it. . . . That we really do know it, I would most emphatically claim. Still further, I would claim that what we know about it is determined, not by the fact that we can know in general, but by the way reality, [Nature,] as distinct from our knowledge, has determined. These ways appear to me to be ascertainable, and form . . . a section of metaphysics. But the metaphysics will naturally be realistic rather than idealistic.[92]

The Moral Order

While Woodbridge believes that his metaphysical science of mind had accomplished its task — to show that human cognitive functions are entirely natural and, therefore, to undercut the problematic mind-body and mind-nature dichotomies — he acknowledges that human living indicates that man not only behaves physically and mentally within the context of Nature but also that mankind is concerned for and devoted to ideals, or ideal possibilities, which as such transcend the context of Nature. Since science assumes Nature, whether spatiotemporally or logically, as the context for analysis, science cannot completely define human life;[93] for man also defines himself relative to his ideals, or his nature-transcending projections. Man is, therefore, a "super-natural" as well as a natural being.

> The problem of the relation of many minds to one another, so far as it is definable analytically, is the problem of the relation of many bodies and not of a juxtaposition of isolated souls. So far as it is more than this, it is not a metaphysical matter, but a matter of society, morals and religion.[94]

Woodbridge regarded Nature also as a basis for man's pursuit of and devotion to ideals, what he called man's "pursuit of happiness"; even the super-natural has its natural basis. Because Nature's structures are knowable and natural knowledge can be used in man's "pursuit of happiness," Nature satisfies the conditions necessary for the intelligent promotion of human ideals. Therefore, although Nature apart from man's ideals is a realm without moral values, she may be characterized as a "moral order" in light of her support of the human super-natural quest. Given the importance of Nature to man's pursuit of ideals, some of the qualities that Woodbridge believes compose Nature's "moral order" will be examined.

One such quality is Nature's own teleology. Natural teleology is the order in events making each significant for subsequent events. Because of natural teleology, Nature's structures are discoverable; and since already actualized structures maintain the quality of possibility, once her structures are discovered, future events can repeat relationships like those already known to be characteristic of Nature. Therefore, a knowledge of natural order can be reliably used to promote human ends. Man takes what he learns of Nature's means, through an investigation of her teleology, and uses them for his ends. Accordingly, the unintentional purposefulness of Nature becomes intentional purposefulness with man; Nature's teleology becomes intentionally effective.

Both natural goods and bads exist, for some natural occurrences satisfy, while others frustrate, natural human needs. Nonetheless, since chance is as much a characteristic of natural processes as is necessity, apart from human ideals, Nature shows no preferences; she does not offer humanity moral standards. Moreover, since chance is a genuine natural quality, Nature presents human beings with opportunities for the free exercise of choice and, therefore, for making moral discriminations. Without knowledge of Nature, however, man would not be able to bring about the goods he has chosen. Accordingly, mankind is under the "natural obligation" to submit it to the scientific disciplines that yield knowledge.

Nature does not provide ideals that function as moral standards and religious sanctions in human living; therefore, the super-natural dimension of human living must be distinguished from its natural dimension. Since, however, Nature provides man with opportunities for the free choice of ends and for the knowledge necessary to the effective expression of choices, she is the basis for her own human transcendence. According to Woodbridge, therefore, while Nature is not the "text" for man's moral and religious living, she is the "preface to morals"; she is a "moral order."

> To be obliged to accept events, to work with them and adjust them in order to live well, and to do this without being compelled to accept a theory of their meaning and value, is something very real and very concrete. . . . It is this compulsion which makes men make morals and which makes them religious.[95]

> There is . . . [in] Walter Lippmann's *A Preface to Morals* a sentence which as *the* preface to morals has no rival whatever. . . . "There is no theory of the meaning and value of events which he is compelled to accept, but he is none the less compelled to accept the events."[96]

Summary

Woodbridge claims that the primary subject matter of all scientific inquiry is Nature as man's ordinary experience of things and their activities, that is, the "visible world." Science is a public pursuit; therefore, man's visual experiences of the visible world are more important than other kinds, for vision is the experience of Nature as common and public.

Moreover, man's experience is a completely reliable source of knowledge. Even perceptual problems—for example, optical illusions—do not show human experience to be unreliable; rather, things always appear as they should given the conditions under which they occur and are experienced. Judgment errs not because experience is deceptive but because man makes judgments before discovering all the conditions, especially the fact that his own presence affects his experience.[97] Woodbridge claims to recognize the significant influence of man's presence within the context of empirical inquiry, and he generally criticizes other philosophers for their failure to respect man's presence in Nature.

An example of this neglect, according to Woodbridge, was the development within modern philosophy of a theoretical divorce of man and his world. Taking methods and theories appropriate to the subject matters of special sciences and misapplying them to the subject matter of metaphysics, many philosophers of the modern period distorted man's mental participation in Nature by developing a problematic and skeptical epistemology that attempted to explain how mind, conceived as an "end-term" divorced radically from Nature, could possibly experience or know Nature. A realistic inquiry into the nature of mind, however, avoids problematic theories such as the "end-term" conception by acknowledging the authority of the genuine subject matter of mind, mental activities, rather than allowing interpretations to prejudice inquiry: "man thinks" is axiomatic when inquiry seeks facts about the mind.

Woodbridge argues that, when inquiry follows the lead of the mental subject matter of mental activities, human mind is discovered to be a bodily function. Although the acknowledgment of human mind as a bodily function accounts for the distinction between mental activity and the human body as the agent of the activity, this acknowledgment cannot account for the distinction between the mental and the physical as different kinds of activities. While mental activity is a bodily function, its distinctively mental quality is neither identifiable nor definable apart from the fact that Nature's objects, the very objects that mental activities such as perception and knowledge make available to man, constitute a mental as well as a physical realm; Nature is not only a spatial realm of vision and a temporal realm of matter but also a logically structured "realm of mind."

When known, Nature's objects are themselves logically connected. Therefore, Woodbridge called the world discovered in human knowledge — the world as logically structured idea objects — "objective mind." And although his conception of "objective mind" (and his "realm of mind") are somewhat vague, as is evident in Woodbridge's inability to decide whether Nature is actually or only potentially an objective mind (or a "realm of mind") apart from man's mental activities,[98] his essential position is clear: while Nature is not known apart from the presence of human beings, human knowing does not determine the nature of the objects known; that determination is objective to and, therefore, independent of human knowing.

In addition to being a realm of vision and a realm of mind, Nature inclusive of man is a "moral order." According to Woodbridge, human living indicates that man not only behaves physically and mentally within the context of Nature but also pursues the realization of ideals, ideal standards that Nature herself does not provide. Therefore, man in his pursuit of ideals transcends the context of Nature; he is a "supernatural" as well as a natural being. Since, however, Nature supports man's supernatural quest for ideals by providing him with opportunities to choose freely the ends that serve his ideal interests and the knowledge necessary for the effective expression of these choices, Nature is the basis for the "supernatural," that is, her own human transcendence; as such, Woodbridge called her a "moral order."

Harry Costello tells a story that illustrates some major points of this chapter. His story is about Woodbridge attending a Bertrand Russell lecture at Columbia University. According to Costello's recollection, this is Woodbridge's account of the lecture:

> Russell lectured to us about what we perceive when we perceive a penny. He pulled a penny out of his pocket and held it up for us to see. We gazed at it hypnotically. He turned it over and whirled it around. We followed his every move. He explained that the penny was really a series of little elliptical flat disks, each two-dimensional, which ran out toward us like buttons on a wire. In fact, there were rows of disks running out in all directions. The collection of these was the penny. He told us the penny we saw was much smaller than the penny he saw. I confess it did not look smaller to me than pennies usually are. But suddenly things grew worse. We were in six-dimensional space. Each of us, he told us, knew three dimensions of this space, and in it was a two-dimensional flat disk. This was our 'hard datum,' our penny. Other people had other three-dimensional spaces, too, in the six-dimensional space, and each of them had a little brown disk, his own precious 'hard datum,' which was his private penny. And we had somehow to get together and correlate these disk-like pennies. The collection of all of them was the only really-real penny. Though just how we were to correlate so many things we did not possess, he did not explain. Instead of that, he gave the penny a final twirl in the air and put it in his pocket, at which we all gasped. For just what it was he was putting in his pocket had by this time become an ineffable mystery.[99]

From Woodbridge's point of view, Russell's difficulty in explaining how mind can experience and know Nature and the resulting perplexities of his audience shows the confusions that result when methods and theories appropriate to special kinds of inquiry are prejudicially applied to the different subject matter of metaphysics, an important part of which is man's mental participation in Nature. In contrast to the unrealistic reductive analyses of such epistemologists, Woodbridge believed that pragmatists were engaged in realistic inquiry that respected contexts and subject matters and, therefore, clarified mental activities. Even so, as will be shown in the next chapter, Woodbridge criticized the pragmatists for their eventual loss of realism and the confusion that followed.

NOTES

1. Frederick J. E. Woodbridge, *An Essay on Nature* (New York: Columbia University Press, 1940), p. 65.
2. Frederick J. E. Woodbridge, *The Realm of Mind* (New York: Columbia University Press, 1926), p. 56.

3. Frederick J. E. Woodbridge, *Nature and Mind: Selected Essays of Frederick J. E. Woodbridge* (New York: Columbia University Press, 1937; reprint ed., New York: Russell and Russell, 1965), p. 471.

4. Ibid., p. 283.

5. The "visible world" is not only the primary subject matter but also the general context of inquiry. Occasionally, however, when Woodbridge wanted to emphasize the general context of inquiry rather than the primary subject-matter, he used the phrase 'universe of discourse.'

6. Woodbridge, *Nature and Mind,* p. 290.

7. Ibid., p. 289; also see, Woodbridge, *Essay on Nature,* p. 72.

8. Woodbridge, *Essay on Nature,* pp. 60–61.

9. Ibid., pp. 87–90.

10. Woodbridge's analysis of the visible world emphasizes the individual places of optical perspectives in the continuum of space, therefore, he emphasizes space rather than time. Nonetheless, he acknowledges that Nature as experienced is dynamic: space is not separated from time. He holds, therefore, that while metaphysical analysis may distinguish spatial from temporal qualities, it must not radically divorce one from the other. "It is an error to think of space and time independently. One must think of them together as space-time. And that is precisely what we ordinarily do and what we actually observe" (ibid., p. 170). Woodbridge's analysis of the temporal dimension will be examined below in Chapter 6.

11. Ibid., p. 96. Space, therefore, "is not a container, but is the system of being contained" [Frederick J. E. Woodbridge, "Papers, 1884–1940" (Woodbridge's unpublished correspondence, diaries, essays, and lecture and reading notes, Columbia University, Special Collections), lecture notes entitled "Nature Beheld," undated, p. 3.].

12. Woodbridge, *Essay on Nature,* p. 100.

13. Ibid., p. 104.

14. Ibid., pp. 102–4.

15. Ibid., pp. 62–63.

16. Ibid., p. 62.

17. Ibid., p. 61.

18. Ibid., p. 209.

19. Woodbridge, *Nature and Mind,* p. 352.

20. Ibid., pp. 289–92.

21. Woodbridge, *Essay on Nature,* p. 63. Woodbridge also emphasizes vision over the other kinds of experience because he holds that Nature's "time-scheme" is most evident in vision: "Nature's time-scheme or structure, *so obviously displayed in the visible world* as the unified or integrated bracketing of events in their relative duration or whiling, is the source of our knowledge of time and history" [ibid., p. 147 (italics mine)].

22. Ibid., p. 65.

23. Woodbridge, *Nature and Mind,* p. 275.

24. Ibid., pp. 322–23.

25. Ibid., pp. 323–24.

26. Woodbridge, *Realm of Mind,* pp. 12–18.

27. Ibid., p. 12.

28. Ibid., pp. 14–15.

29. Ibid., pp. 17–18.
30. Ibid., pp. 115–16.
31. Ibid., p. 56.
32. Ibid., p. 3.
33. Ibid., p. 4.
34. Ibid., p. 5.
35. Ibid., p. 94.
36. Ibid., p. 45.
37. Ibid.
38. Ibid., p. 112.
39. Woodbridge acknowledges the ambiguity in the usage of the term 'body.'

> The body is, perhaps, the chief source of complication. For we use the term not only to denote ourselves as physical in distinction from ourselves as mental, we use it also to denote our bulk, the assemblage of the head and trunk and limbs. This body occupies space, endures in time, has cubical contents, and is built in a definite way. As such, it is not strictly *the* body in distinction from the mind, but *a* body in distinction from other bodies, other bulks, other things which occupy space and endure in time. [ibid., pp. 8–9]

In order to avoid problems resulting from this ambiguity, in my exposition of Woodbridge's theory of mind I will reserve, when possible, the use of the term 'body' to denote man's "bulk" and use the phrase 'the physical' (as well as 'the mental') to denote a dimension of human living. Man's "body" displays individuality while 'the physical' and 'the mental' are different ways in which man cooperates with the rest of Nature and, therefore, they exhibit the category of structure.

40. Woodbridge, "Papers, 1884–1940," "Lectures on Metaphysics: Spring 1928–29," pp. 59–60.
41. Ibid., p. 62.
42. Woodbridge, *Realm of Mind*, p. 95.
43. See, ibid., pp. 95–96. Furthermore, according to Woodbridge, "relative position, naturally conditioning our vision, leads on . . . to condition our thoughts" (Woodbridge, *Essay on Nature*, p. 91).
44. See Woodbridge, *Realm of Mind*, pp. 96–97.
45. Ibid., p. 97.
46. Ibid., pp. 98–99.
47. Ibid., p. 103.
48. Woodbridge, *Nature and Mind*, pp. 366–67, 370–71.
49. Woodbridge, *Realm of Mind*, p. 102.
50. "Organism" is being used here in the Aristotelian sense.
51. See, for example, Woodbridge, *Realm of Mind*, pp. 107–09.
52. Ibid., p. 24.
53. Woodbridge, "Papers, 1884–1940," "Lectures on Metaphysics," p. 62.
54. Woodbridge, *Realm of Mind*, pp. 1–2.
55. According to Woodbridge, experience is not the same as knowledge. Therefore, the perception of a star is not itself a knowledge of the extent of the star's space-time remoteness from the perceiver.
56. Woodbridge, *Realm of Mind*, pp. 21–22; cf. Woodbridge's different examples, ibid., pp. 21, 29.

57. Ibid., p. 4.
58. Ibid., p. 24. Woodbridge warns against turning this fact into a problem.

Others . . . have converted it into a problem, asking how it is possible for our thinking, which is a present fact, to refer to facts which are not present. I have no desire to convert it into any such problem, for when I do, I can find no solution of it. All solutions with which I am familiar take the fact for granted and then speedily forget that they have done so. They run somewhat as follows: I think of a past event; now my thinking is in the present and its object in the past, there is a time interval between them; this interval is bridged by the reference of the present event to the past event, the former is the representative of the latter; the present event thus transcends itself either because it is its nature so to do, or because the ground of its transcendence is time. *Such an argument appears to me only to affirm that I, who am here and now, think about what is neither here nor now. If it is offered as a solution of a problem, it perplexes me. I am perplexed, for example, about that time interval. Is it also an object of my thinking? If it is, how is my thinking of it explained by the solution?* It is not explained by stoutly insisting that a present event transcends itself and represents a past event, for that is only to insist that as a matter of fact we do think about the past. The Kantian position appears to be more profound, since there is something quite genuine in the claim that all spatial and temporal thinking presupposes time and space. It is only the nature of the presupposition which is troublesome. Kant made it a mystery which an impressive vocabulary could do little to alleviate. *In the end it appears to mean no more than the fact that thinking finds no limits in time or space. Although we are here and now, we think about events and facts remote.* [ibid., pp. 22–23 (italics mine)]

59. Failure to make the distinction between mental *act* and the mental *object* would allow statements like "He (now) perceives a star as it existed millions of years ago" and "He (now) knows what occurred in 399 B.C. in Athens" to degenerate into the exceptionally odd claims, "He (a presently existing person) perceives a star a million years ago" and "He (a presently existing person) knows an occurrence in 399 B.C. Athens."
60. Woodbridge, *Realm of Mind,* p. 24. Woodbridge, however, does not want his position to be confused with Kant's.

Kant dealt with what I have called the realm of mind, and insisted that space and time belong to it, but I can make nothing of the doctrine that that realm is a compound of what the mind contributes and what something else contributes. So when I say that time and space are in the realm of mind and that realm in time and space, I do not at all imply that the mind is responsible in any way for time and space. I do not imply that time and space are in any sense mental or forms of sense perception. I fear I have no idea of what an *a priori* form of sense perception in the Kantian sense could possibly be. For me the realm of mind is analyzable, but it is not analyzable into factors which once came, or ever do come, together to compose it. [ibid., p. 28]

61. Ibid., pp. 22–23.

62. Ibid., pp. 45–46.

63. Ibid., p. 57.

64. Ibid., p. 58.

65. Woodbridge, "Papers, 1884–1940," "Lectures on Metaphysics," p. 62.

66. Woodbridge, *Realm of Mind*, p. 60.

67. Ibid., pp. 60–61. Although the proposition is the principle form of communication of ideas in inquiry, other kinds of linguistic vehicles also convey ideas. Moreover, in addition to language, other kinds of vehicles, according to Woodbridge, carry ideas.

> Ideas are expressed in propositions. They are not only so expressed. They are expressed in gestures, as when deaf-mutes communicate . . . and no sound breaks that silence to stir thought by the spoken word. They are expressed in the tension of the eyes, in the tell-tale look of the face, in the knitting of the brows, in strains in the head and in what we call nervous processes in the brain. The variety of the form of their expression and communication is innumerable. [ibid., p. 62.]

Yet ideas are not like any of these vehicles; the distinction between ideas and things is genuine.

> It is an impressive fact that they are communicated and expressed in so many different ways. It is still a more impressive fact that they are wholly indifferent to any specific mode of conveyance. . . . This fact proves conclusively that the mode of expression, although it carries an idea from one thinker to another, is not itself an idea at all. . . . We face again the fact that ideas are in no sense likenesses of anything. They are rather that which can be translated from one mode of expression into another radically different mode and from one language into another without losing themselves or ceasing to be what they are. [ibid., p. 64.]

68. Ibid., p. 59.

69. Woodbridge writes, "the existence of consciousness as something substantive has been doubted, but not the existence of conscious response" ("Papers, 1884–1940," notes entitled: "Nature Beheld," p. 1).

70. See, for example, Woodbridge, *Nature and Mind*, pp. 326–27. He worked at solving the "problem of consciousness" for twenty-two years (1904–1926). The importance he placed on the discovery of a solution is shown by this statement of 1906:

> That problem has been the central and controlling problem of modern idealism. Our philosophy has become so disturbed and disorganized by it, that we can not hope to find our way about with confidence and freedom until the problem has been reckoned with. We can hardly dismiss idealism cavalierly as a great mistake. [ibid., p. 335]

71. See, for example, ibid., p. 335.

72. Ibid., pp. 418–19, and p. 426.

73. The expression "we don't solve problems, we just eventually get over them," which was a popular epigram among the philosophers at Columbia, originated with John Dewey (Herbert Schneider, conversations, Summer, 1977). Woodbridge gave his own interpretations to Dewey's expression; for Woodbridge believes that there are intellectual problems, for example, the end-term conception of human mind and consciousness as a subjective substance, that cannot be solved but can only be overcome by applying *the principle of realism* in inquiry.

74. Woodbridge, *Nature and Mind*, p. 420.

75. Ibid., pp. 420–21.

76. Woodbridge, *Realm of Mind*, p. 59.

77. Ibid., p. 85.

78. Ibid., p. 47. See his discussion of the differences between mechanical, chemical, biological, and mental structures, *Nature and Mind*, pp. 150–52.

79. See, for example, his discussion of a "logic of events," Woodbridge, *Realm of Mind*, p. 98.

80. Ibid., p. 46.

81. Ibid.

82. Ibid., p. 47.

83. Ibid., p. 49. He writes, "the implications taken up in the judgment must, therefore, be real implications" (*Nature and Mind*, p. 71). See, ibid., pp. 59–60. Also, Woodbridge apparently believed that the relation of cause and effect is one of the more (perhaps the most) pervasive types of "logical" relation. See, for example, *Realm of Mind*, p. vii. An example of a scientific equation that could be interpreted as the expression of a causal relation is "$F/M = A$." This equation can be expressed in the form of an implication: Any change in the force applied to a thing and/or in the thing's mass *implies* that the magnitude of the thing's acceleration is in direct proportion to changes in the force applied and in inverse proportion to changes in its mass.

84. Woodbridge, *Realm of Mind*, p. 98.

85. Ibid., p. 46.

86. Woodbridge, *Nature and Mind*, pp. 155–56.

87. Woodbridge, *Realm of Mind*, p. 82. He writes, "I wish to emphasize the fact that the relation of meaning which is so prominent among the things is just as much *a relation between them* as is space or time" (Woodbridge, *Nature and Mind*, p. 339).

> Note that when objects become representative of each other it is *of each other* that they become representative, but not of anything else. They are not ideas which represent things, or phenomena which represent noumena, or things in the body which represent things outside, or states of consciousness which represent an external world. It is each other that they represent, [ibid., p. 310.]

Along with Aristotle's *De Anima*, 431 b 20, Woodbridge quoted Spinoza's *Ethics*, "Homo Cogitet" (Book II. Ax.2), on the title page of *The Realm of Mind*. In quoting Spinoza above, as well as both he and Aristotle on the title page, Woodbridge acknowledges a belief he shares with them: that a realistic inquiry into the fact of mental activity would lead the metaphysician to discover that in Nature there is a realm of mind, or mental structure, as well as a physical realm. For Woodbridge's interpretation of Aristotle on this point, see, for example, his *Aristotle's Vision of Nature*, p. 47. Cf. J. H. Randall, Jr.'s, exposition in *Aristotle*, pp. 103–4.

88. Woodbridge, *Realm of Mind*, pp. 85–87. Harry Costello in his essay within *Naturalism and the Human Spirit* writes: "When someone raised the question one day whether there is ever such a thing as imageless thought, Woodbridge replied that the real question is whether there is any thought which is not imageless" [ed. Y. H. Krikorian (New York: Columbia University Press, 1944), p. 308]. Again, Woodbridge insists that one does not think with images of Nature's individuals but with the implications of Nature's things or events themselves.

89. While Nature is intelligible apart from man's presence, Woodbridge never made it entirely clear whether her intelligibility is only the potential to be logically structured or whether she is actually logically structured apart from human presence. See ahead, n. 98. I believe that for Woodbridge it is more likely the latter case.

90. See, for example, Woodbridge, *Nature and Mind*, pp. 75–76.

91. See, for example, ibid., pp. 154–57.

92. Ibid., p. 63.

93. Woodbridge warns against the attempt to present a scientific account of the "supernatural" dimension of human living.

> Wisdom advises that we leave it for poetry and religion to express. . . . I can not escape the conviction that there is a monstrous absurdity in turning it into subject-matter for so-called scientific inquiry. [*Realm of Mind*, p. 131.]

94. Ibid., p. 92.

95. Woodbridge, *Nature and Mind*, p. 476.

96. Ibid., p. 471.

97. Ibid., p. 392. Woodbridge holds that man's experience of the things of his world is completely reliable. Error does not exist because man's perceptions mislead him. Rather, error exists because man, while still in a state of ignorance regarding the nature of a particular subject matter, makes judgments regarding his experience of it in order to act. Experience is reliable and, therefore, is adequate as the source for a scientific knowledge of Nature. Experience of itself, however, is not knowledge. Inquiry's process from experience to knowledge involves a special kind of mental activity—the making of judgments regarding what factors conditioned the occurrence of the experienced subject matter and the testing of these hypotheses. The source of error is not experience, for if it were it would be impossible to correct error through an acquisition of empirical knowledge. Neither error nor the process of inquiry that eliminates it would exist except that man interprets subject matters.

98. Although Nature is intelligible apart from man's mental presence, Woodbridge never made it entirely clear whether her intelligibility is only the potential to become logically ordered, that is, with relations of implication, when mentally active human beings are present or whether, apart from human mental activity, she is logically ordered. For textual examples of the former position, see *Nature and Mind*, pp. 75–76; for the latter, see ibid., p. 171.

99. Harry Todd Costello, "The Naturalism of Frederick Woodbridge," *Naturalism and the Human Spirit*, pp. 300-301.

5

The Realist Among Unrealistic Empiricists

Many of us have become pragmatists in one sense or another,
but few of us claim to be pragmatists in the sense that we have
found in pragmatism a philosophy of human living, a theory
of knowledge, or the key which unlocks the mind.[1]

A conclusion I am led to by reading the writing of Professor
Dewey . . . [is] that nature is essentially dialectical. . . .[2]

Introduction

As was noted in the Preface, Woodbridge was one of the principal figures
responsible for originating and developing both American realism and naturalism, and even pragmatism; yet he was critical of the views of other
leaders within these movements, such as Charles S. Peirce, William James,
and John Dewey, for what he believed to be their lack of realism and naturalism. Accordingly, Woodbridge's criticisms, though largely ignored, provide important insights from inside these movements. This chapter presents
his criticisms of pragmatism, especially the thought of Peirce, James, and
Dewey.

According to Woodbridge, although pragmatism had originally shown
promise, pragmatists had not respected its inherent limitations: what had
begun as a realistic demand to respect contexts through maintaining respect
for the authority of the subject matter of inquiry, had itself ceased to do
so — a fact evident in pragmatists having been drawn into controversies such
as that regarding the nature of truth.

In his criticisms of the pragmatists' loss of context, Woodbridge illustrates many of the principles of his philosophy discussed in previous chapters,

106

that is, his realistic method, the naturalism-humanism implied thereby, and more specifically, his realistic theory of language and metaphysical science of mind. Hence, this chapter serves two vital purposes: it provides not only a critical inside view of American philosophical movements but also a clarification of Woodbridge's own philosophy as he seeks to critically appraise the positions of others.

Language in Inquiry: Realistic Versus Dialectical

In addition to the other functions of language,[3] Woodbridge believes that it performs a necessary operation within scientific inquiry: language functions "informatively" as the instrument through which interpretations of subject matters are formulated and communicated.[4] Like all activities, the informative linguistic function is conditioned by natural factors; therefore, its efficient use in inquiry requires knowledge of the factors conditioning its use. He says, for example, that language is

> the use of the power of one thing to stand for or represent another thing. There is representiveness in nature for anyone who can discover it. We have made use of it. . . . And having found that out, we have developed a technique for it. . . .[5]

A factor of great concern to Woodbridge was society: the terms and grammatical forms used in the different linguistic functions are socially determined conventions;[6] and the terms and forms of a vernacular convey meanings common to a community.

> Words . . . have both denotation and connotation. They are names of something or other and they have meanings. As names they may be considered conventional and arbitrary. . . . As meanings they guide the thought of him who uses them. . . . In all discourse it is what words mean, what they carry the thought to, that is of importance. Their carrying power can not be a matter of individual preference if we are to hope to understand each other. It is not a matter of individual experience. It is a matter of historical experience. . . . [I]t is just the mind of the past and not any experience of ours which has given us the major categories of all our thinking.[7]

Woodbridge acknowledges the value of language to preserve the knowledge and culture of one generation for the next; for each generation benefits from the accumulated scientific knowledge of past generations and from the record of the effects of their cultural aspirations.

Because of the influence vernacular has had on human judgment, according to Woodbridge, the inquirer's vernacular is an important factor conditioning how efficiently he uses informative language. The inquirer participates in genuine scientific inquiry, taking advantage of knowledge already available in tradition without being prejudiced, if he maintains the realistic distinction where the meaning of the concepts of hypotheses and the adequacy of hypotheses are determined by their use in the examination of extra-linguistic subject matters rather than by linguistic convention.[8]

> We ought not to let language itself deceive us in this matter. Here we are dealing with something quite different from the conventional vernaculars of mankind. We are dealing with what all of them, as they are developed more and more in the interest of communication and the pursuit of knowledge, try to express.[9]

"The articulation of things, or, as I prefer to say, articulation in nature, is precisely what we try to discover in the pursuit of knowledge and to express in language."[10] Unless the inquirer maintains a realistic attitude, however, inquiry degenerates into "dialectic," or pseudo-inquiry.

One form of "dialectic" is what Woodbridge called the "dialectical play of words," where unrealistic inquirers become so preoccupied with the linguistic instrument of inquiry that they ignore the instrument's end, knowledge of subject matters: the "subject-matter may be refined and to such a point that we seem to be talking about language only, but this is a delusion."[11] Referring to Hobbes's *Leviathan,* Woodbridge warns against this unrealistic interest in the *words* of language apart from their use in the analysis of extra-linguistic subject matters:

> "Words are wise men's counters, they do but reckon by them; but they are the money of fools." The folly of taking words as other than counters to reckon with is abundantly illustrated in human discourse. We try to avoid it by inventing new counters which tend to make the reckoning more effective and to keep it from *degenerating* into a *dialectical* play of words which the articulation of language permits—as if one were entitled to say that the nonexistent must exist in some way if its existence in any way is to be denied. [Italics mine][12]

Woodbridge believes that the "dialectical play of words" is accompanied usually by another unrealistic preoccupation with the grammatical forms of a vernacular: we "should observe the . . . effect of language rather than the *grammatical dialectic of words.* Playing the parts of speech off against one another does not advance knowledge" (italics mine).[13]

Woodbridge gave numerous instances of the intellectual perplexities resulting from an inquirer's "dialectical play of words." For example, he points out that philosophers "have invented subsistence for the round square, believing that since the thing can be named, it must somehow be. The power of words is great."[14] Elsewhere he notes the intellectual influence that conventionally determined syntax can have on the unwary.

"Move" indicates something which objects do, not something which they are. We may speak of them as *in* motion or *at* rest, but the "in" and the "at" do not indicate new objects which themselves either move or rest. Physicists as a rule avoid such an indication. *Their language sometimes suggests it* as when they speak of the transfer of motion from one object to another, of the gain or loss of motion, or different amounts of motion, etc. *Such language decries only those who are more influenced by the grammatical construction of sentences than by the effects of linguistic usage.* Motion does not move; rest does not rest. These elementary facts are of primary importance in preserving sanity. . . . [Italics mine][15]

The reification of ways of behaving and functioning into transcendent and, therefore, mysterious substances and agents, such as mind as an end-term and consciousness as a subjective substance, is promoted by the "dialectical play of words."[16] More generally, preoccupation with forms of expression rather than with their use in inquiry encourages the confusion of contexts and subject matters characteristic of the displacement of one science's subject matter (for example, that of metaphysics) with another's (for example, that of acoustics).

Our forms of expression are apt to trick us. When, for example, I say that sounds are vibrations of air I may trick myself and others into saying that vibrations of air are sound. The obvious fact, however, is that one who knows what sounds are, who can identify them as subject-matter for examination, can understand what it means to say that sounds are vibrations, while one wholly unfamiliar with sounds can not possibly understand what it means to say that vibrations of air are sounds. This homely illustration may be generalized. . . . [Our] understanding of the familiar world in which we live is an extension of our familiarity and not the attainment of a substitute for it.[17]

While the power of language to prejudice human judgment is a principal reason for the degeneration of realistic inquiry into dialectic and the "dialectical play of words" is a common form of dialectic, Woodbridge believes that any divorce of the meaning or adequacy of the method of inquiry from the context of its use to discover the natures of extra-method subject matters yields dialectic in its many forms—cognitive arbitrariness, preferential reductionism, and intellectual controversies yielding opinion rather than knowledge. Moreover, for Woodbridge, the "dialectical play of words" is not dialectical because of the inquirer's preoccupation with language per se, for language use is as proper an empirical subject for scientific inquiry as any other and, as such, the language scientist must be as occupied with his subject as any other scientist in order to avoid dialectic. Rather, it is dialectical because inquirers have allowed language to replace their subject matters as the object of their examinations; more generally, their dialectic is a confusion of the contexts and subject matters of inquiry. Logical positivists, for example, trespassed on the domain of metaphysics, replacing the subject matter of metaphysics with that of more specific sciences, such as the science of language; the positivists were unrealistic empiricists.[18]

Although Woodbridge did not fully develop a theory of language, nonetheless, implicit in his criticism of dialectic is an indication of what his metaphysical theory of language would be: as in his realistic metaphysical theory of mind (for language as it functions within inquiry is a cognitive mental function), he holds that when language functions informatively within inquiry, it cannot be metaphysically defined and, therefore, understood apart from the natural subject matters to which it refers. This is the meaning of Woodbridge's claim that the nature of scientific language is to be understood relative to its effects: "it conveys ideas and effects knowledge."[19]

Shall we . . . say that the articulation of language can never be the articulation of things without running the risk of falling into a dialectic which destroys any reference of language to anything but itself?

But I find little satisfaction in dialectic. . . .[20]

The accessibility of the world to language or the fact that the world can be talked about is the ground of the world's intelligibility. This is, of course, only saying again that the *basis of intelligibility is the world* as a world that can be talked about. [Italics mine][21]

We go from things to formulas, from what they are in this evident character to what can be said about them, and find that *the latter can not maintain itself with stability and success without their co-operation.* Language as a living and natural communication with nature is something quite different from a superficial articulation of words, conventionally playing over things, and requiring a leap over a gulf if it is to find contact with existence. [Italics mine][22]

Accordingly, "the use of language as a tool is never free from its use in the context of Nature."[23]

The Promise of Pragmatism

Since Woodbridge believes that dialectic can be avoided only where the meaning, and the adequacy, of the concepts of inquiry are determined by their use in the study of subject matters, it is not difficult to understand why he writes, "many of us have become pragmatists in one sense or another. . . ."[24] For he is in complete agreement with pragmatism as a method of clarifying "ideas," that is, conceptual meaning in inquiry.[25]

> Pragmatism originally appeared as an attractive name for a method of clarifying our ideas, "a new name for some old ways of thinking," as James himself phrased it. Ideas, we were advised, can be clarified by finding their meaning in the procedure in which they are employed. We were cautioned against meanings independent of procedure or supposedly antecedent to it. Arbitrary definitions were to confess the fact that they were arbitrary and were not to be allowed to encourage dialectic. . . . Freedom and flexibility in thinking, the habit of seeing how ideas are generated and modified by following the lead of subject-matter . . . —such as these were the aims which pragmatism professed to further.[26]

More specifically, when pragmatism is understood to be a method of clarifying the concepts of inquiry, the pragmatists and Woodbridge agree that,

> ideas, concepts, categories, definitions and the like, no matter what meanings may be given to them independent of their use in the exploration of some subject-matter, have a discoverable meaning in every such exploration. They have a meaning when they are at work which can be discovered from the way they work. . . . Seen in the light of the procedure in which they are involved, they gain in precision, definiteness, and effectiveness.[27]

Moreover, since pragmatism contends that linguistic meaning is determined by its use in inquiry, according to Woodbridge, pragmatism implies that inquirers should not mix their universes of discourse; that is, they should not participate in the unrealistic practice of the confusion of contexts characteristic of one science's displacement of the subject matters of another.

> Meanings derived from context . . . often lead thought to conclusions which can not be understood unless in terms of their operating meaning. We are, as a consequence, repeatedly confronted with statements, conclusions, and beliefs

which mean one thing in their own context and quite a different thing, or nothing at all, when transferred to another context.[28]

Pragmatism not only encourages a respect for differences in contexts
but Woodbridge also believes that pragmatic analysis can be used to reveal
instances of the confusion of contexts, thereby aiding in the elimination of a
source of intellectual perplexity. For example, in his book *The Nature of the
Physical World,* A. S. Eddington distinguishes two tables, the table of ordinary human experience upon which he writes and the same table as described
by the physical sciences, that is, numerous elective changes rushing about
vast stretches of emptiness.[29] The seeming oddity of being able to write on
the same table as that described by the physical sciences is eliminated when
pragmatic analysis reveals Eddington's confusion of the contexts of the
physical sciences with that of metaphysics, the obvious and familiar field of
man's vital cooperation with his natural environment. With the acknowledgment of this difference of contexts, one can see that the "scientific table"
is never the table *upon which one writes.*

> The table we write on, when explored, leads to the discovery of a table to which
> writing on is quite irrelevant as an expression of what it is. . . . I must take
> both tables as equally genuine. But I can not take the discovered table as iden-
> tical with the table from which it is derived. Making them identical seems
> always to lead to saying about the familiar table what is said about the unfamil-
> iar, and this results in something paradoxical and bizarre. . . . I must, at least
> pragmatically, keep my two tables from merging into one, if I am not to lose
> either of them or sanity.[30]

In general, Woodbridge believes that many of the attempts to clarify concepts of the physical sciences for "the intelligent reader"—concepts like
space, time, motion, mass, and matter, which are intelligible within the contexts of these sciences—by offering interpretations in terms of the different
context of the familiar world of everyday experience are misguided and
essentially unintelligible.

> What their authors have to say about space and time can not be said in terms of
> the space and time with which the intelligent reader is familiar. . . . Yet many
> of the illustrations, and often the crucial illustrations, that are given to him to
> help him understand, are illustrations in terms of *his* space and time and not in
> terms of *the* space and time of the physical world. . . . The fact is that just such
> illustrations are used. They promote confusion instead of clearness. They create
> the suspicion that there is confusion in the minds of those who use them. . . .

... The very fact that we speak of the *physical* world ought to warn us that the ideas which go to make it up ought to be made clear, not by illustrations drawn from another world, but in terms of the procedure which is employed in discovering the physical world. . . . I should have to use pragmatic analysis to make these unintelligibilities clear.[31]

Woodbridge's agreement with the pragmatists is not limited to their method of clarifying ideas. Occasionally, he characterized "experience" in a manner similar to those offered by pragmatists. He writes, for example, "our experience, with all its ups and downs, its impulses, instincts, and desires, its hopes and fears, its joys and sorrows, has been disciplined into increased effectiveness."[32] Moreover, he believes that the pragmatic description of how we think and inquire is essentially accurate:

Take any problem which one has to work out in his own experience and trace it from the point where it originates to the point where it disappears and is a problem no longer, then, surely, one finds that he has followed the leading of what certain facts have suggested until the facts are found in which these suggestions terminate. That is the way the lost man finds his way home. That is the way the planet Neptune was discovered. Consequently, I have said the doctrine of pragmatism, thus limited, appears to occasion no particular difficulty.[33]

He does not object to their description of how in the individual's experience the concepts composing beliefs become functionally distinguished.

Facts, thus, give rise to ideas in the situations in experience where reorganization becomes necessary; and ideas lead to new facts when the reorganization is effected. Such appears to be the doctrine of pragmatism regarding the instrumental relation between facts and ideas, and the functional continuity of experience.[34]

Furthermore, Woodbridge believes that the pragmatic theory of the biological *genesis* of mental functioning in human organisms, where inquiry is a form of vital adaptation, and judgment within inquiry is instrumental to the solution of vital problems, contributes to the genetic continuity of mind and Nature:

The insistence that logical processes are both mental and vital has done much to take them out of the transcendental aloofness from reality in which they have often been placed, especially since Kant. So long as thought and object were so separated that they could never be brought together, and so long as logical processes were conceived wholly in terms of ideas set over against objects, there was no hope of escape from the realm of pure hypothesis and conjecture. . . . They have insisted . . . that logical processes are not set over against their content as idea against object, as appearance against reality, but are processes of reality itself. Just as reality can and does function in a physical or a physiological way, so also it functions in a logical way.[35]

"The distinction between facts and ideas discloses, thus, according to pragmatism, not two distinct and exclusive orders of existence, but a functional and instrumental relation within experience itself."[36] Because of the contributions pragmatism has made as a method toward the elimination of dialectic and as a biological-psychological description of the genesis, processes, and functions of mental activity toward the removal of the theoretical mind-Nature dichotomy, Woodbridge said of pragmatism, "There was promise in it."[37]

A Critique of the Philosophies of William James and C. S. Peirce

Although Woodbridge believes that the pragmatic method is appropriate for clarifying the meaning of concepts, he disagrees with the implications that some of the pragmatists draw from it:[38] some have identified pragmatism with the belief that the practical effects of the concept of an object constitute the whole of the conception of that object. If by this is meant that the expected experimental effects of behavior combine to form the *whole* of the inquirer's conception of an object as subject-matter, then, according to Woodbridge, William James has rightly identified pragmatism with the doctrine of nominalism.[39] Woodbridge claims, however, that whether the pragmatic method is taken as *the* method of inquiry, as it is by pragmatists, or is used in the clarification of the concepts employed in contextual analysis, as is the case for himself, it does not imply nominalism. For even the nominalist cannot identify the conception of a subject matter with expected experimental effects without referring to (and, therefore, including at least implicitly within the conception) *the fact that this subject matter leads to* these *expectations.*

If . . . we are to understand by such an abuse of speech, that we are to identify the ideas of an object [as subject matter] with what that *object* leads us to expect, must we not distinguish between the object and its leadings, and consequently demand that this distinction be a part of our whole conception of the object.[40]

In other words, the anticipated practical effects of the conception of a subject matter is not the *whole* of that conception for two reasons. First, the meaning of the conception must include at least an implicit reference to something other than practical effects, a reference to the *bare* fact of the *extra*-conceptual *presence*—and therefore, the extra-linguistic presence—of the subject *matter* (i.e., the Aristotelian "thisness") leading to these expectations. Even James, claiming to be a nominalist, accepts this.[41] Secondly, in addition to a reference to the presence of the subject matter, any conception of a subject matter must include, at least implicitly as a part of its meaning, that it is the extra-conceptual *subject's* possession of a *nature* (i.e., the Aristotelian "whatness") that forms *the basis for* the expected practical effects. Woodbridge's position is obviously that of a realist in regard to the ontological status of universals; for him, realistic and, therefore, scientific inquiry into any subject matter implies logical realism. On the other hand, if pragmatism implies that the *whole* of the conception of a subject matter is its practical effects, then it implies that the language of inquiry is meaningful apart from any reference to the natures of extra-linguistic subject matters. If this is James's view, then, according to Woodbridge, James, as well as others holding this position, are guilty of an abuse of the realistic principle and, therefore, guilty of the folly of a "dialectical play of words."

Woodbridge also criticizes C. S. Peirce for his lack of an attitude of realism (and Peirce, it may be recalled, considers himself to be a realist in regard to universals). He quotes Peirce as follows:

"Different minds may set out with the most antagonistic views, but the progress of investigation carries them by a force outside of themselves to one and the same conclusion. This activity of thought by which we are carried, not where we wish, but to a foreordained goal, is like the operation of destiny. No modification of the point of view taken, no selection of other facts for study, no natural bend of mind even, can enable a man to escape the predestinate opinion. This great law is embodied in the conception of truth and reality."[42]

According to Woodbridge, realists believe that, "if we all work [i.e., inquire] long enough and industriously enough, we shall all approach or reach one and the same conclusion. Nearly every one believes that."[43] It does not appear, however, that Peirce intends merely to state the obvious and commonplace. For, as a pragmatist, he had "identified the existence of force [the "force" outside ourselves which carries investigation to one conclusion] with what we know of its effects."[44] Woodbridge believes, therefore, that Peirce attempts "to identify things with relations, existence with meaning. . . ."[45] For Peirce, pragmatism implies objective idealism. Accordingly, Woodbridge says of Peirce's statement,

[T]he realistic quibbler will undoubtedly ask, Is the whole conception of that force *outside our minds* which will thus eventually and necessarily carry us all to one and the same conclusion, and which is embodied in the conception of truth and reality, nothing but the "one and the same conclusion" to which it so carries us?[46]

Although Peirce may allow that along the way—that is, throughout the history of inquiry—inquiry has incorporated a realistic distinction between the inquirer's linguistically expressed hypotheses and the extra-linguistic referents which are the basis for their adequacy and significance, the pragmatic method implies for Peirce that ultimately, or eventually and necessarily, this distinction dialectically dissolves into the one, perfect and meaningful community—"firstness" and "secondness" resolve their one-sidedness in the continuity of "thirdness." Woodbridge holds that this idealistic reduction of the realistic distinction to meaning or relation, though ultimate, yields dialectic: "speech becomes confused and thought loses in clearness."[47] Moreover, although humanity may eventually attain unanimity of values through, for example, religious indoctrination, Woodbridge believes that "one and the same conclusion" will never be reached *scientifically* by dissolving, even ultimately, the very realistic distinction that makes scientific inquiry possible.

Pragmatism's Loss of Context

Although pragmatism had originally shown great promise, according to Woodbridge, pragmatists had not respected the inherent limitations of their position. What had begun as a demand to *respect contexts,* had itself ceased to do so—a fact especially evident when pragmatists find themselves drawn into a fruitless controversy regarding the general nature of truth.

What is truth? Those who stay for an answer are pretty sure to stay for a quarrel. Pragmatism tried to alter the question, to ask instead for samples of truths or for a consideration of the adjective rather than the noun. But unhappy and unfortunate phrases got in the way. The slogans of pragmatism were perilous. When it was claimed that an idea is true because it works, the rejoinder was ready and well-nigh inevitable that an idea works because it is true. "Working" was something that had to be defined, but the best of definitions never seemed competent to settle the question. . . . Undoubtedly there is something suspicious about any identification of the truth of ideas with their effectiveness. . . . Beliefs are obviously effective when they are not true, and no "long run" of their effectiveness seems adequate to remove them from suspicion. . . . It ought not to be said that the opponents of pragmatism were successful. . . . To equate truth with consistency or with the agreement of ideas with objects, was as perilous as to equate it with effectiveness, especially when a pragmatist was one's opponent. There were nasty questions to answer. How are ideas found to be consistent? How are they found to agree with objects? The answer seemed to be: Is pragmatism true because it works or does it work because it is true? The answer was, in other words, to renew the controversy.[48]

As long as the pragmatists limited themselves to the context of their own specific subject matter, that is, the mental processes whereby vital problems are solved, "truth" was not held to be an essence, which as such could be defined independently of the contexts of inquiries into subject matters; rather, it was *the solving* of problems within specific "situations," or contexts, *through concepts* acquired by following the lead of the relevant facts.

> The pragmatic doctrine of the relation between facts and ideas *should be confined to those situations* in experience where problems are in actual process of solution. . . . [T]he doctrine of pragmatism, *thus limited,* appears to occasion no particular difficulty.
> And yet we are having, both here and abroad, a most valiant and vigorous debate about truth. . . . I think *it never would have existed if pragmatists had rigorously adhered to the limitations* suggested by Professor Dewey, and if their opponents had taken greater pains to understand these limitations. Problems are, it seems to me, raised and solved in the way Professor Dewey has shown. . . . To ask if the solutions are true is to ask if the problems have been solved. They either have been solved or have not. . . . [Italics mine][49]

When pragmatists allowed contextually relative processes of *verification* to be reified into the elusive substantive of "truth," the resulting controversies were in principle unsolvable; for every attempted solution, for example, truth as either effective, consistent, or as agreeing conceptions, presupposed the misunderstanding of truth as an essence definable apart from the contexts of inquiries, a misunderstanding that formed the basis for the problem. For Woodbridge, the way to get over an unsolvable problem is realistically to return to the subject matter.

> [The controversy] wore itself out. The unfortunate consequence was that it left pragmatism to be remembered mainly as a controversy . . . a debate without an issue. Tired of trying to tell what truth is, the combatants turned to a more promising occupation, that of trying to tell what other things are.[50]

Conflicting Philosophies of Mind

According to Woodbridge, pragmatic inquiries into the subject matters of the genesis, processes, and functions of mental activity were helpful as long as they limited themselves to the specific contexts of these biological and psychological subject matters. With their loss of context, however, they took procedures and concepts appropriate to these special sciences and unrealistically applied them to the general context and primary subject matter of Nature in general; they had trespassed on the domain of the metaphysician. More specifically, Woodbridge's development of a realistic metaphysical science of mind is fundamentally at odds with pragmatists who generate a metaphysical theory of mind out of biological and psychological sciences.[51] For a realistic metaphysical science of mind, Woodbridge claims, the fact that man thinks is axiomatic. Accordingly, when, for example, the mental activity of knowing is clarified, the realist begins with the fact that man knows rather than with the factors conditioning man's knowing, such as the psychological and biological factors emphasized by pragmatists and others.

> Knowledge is first *knowledge,* and only later a set of processes for psychological analysis. That is why, as it seems to me, all psychological logicians, from Locke to our own day, have signally failed in dealing with the problems of knowledge. The attempt to construct knowledge out of mental states, the relations between ideas, and the relation of ideas to things, has been, as I read the history, decidedly without profit. Confusion and divergent opinion have resulted instead of agreement and confidence. . . .
> . . . The situation would be worse for psychology than it is, if that vigorous science had not learned from other sciences the valuable knack of *isolating concrete problems and attacking them directly, without the burden of previous logical or metaphysical speculation.* [Italics mine][52]

In regard to turning a biological theory into a metaphysical account of the mental activity of knowing, Woodbridge says,

> nothing is clearer than that there is no necessity for knowledge to issue in adjustment [or adaptation]. And it is clear to me that increased control of experience, while resulting from knowledge, does not give to it its character. . . . Knowledge works, but it is not, therefore, knowledge.
> . . . Is the biological account of knowledge correct? . . . Can we, to put the question in its most general form, accept as an adequate account of the logical process *a theory which is bound up with some other specific department of human knowledge?* It seems to me that we can not. [Italics mine][53]

Moreover, for realistic metaphysics, activities are defined from the point of view of their uses; therefore, the nature of mental activities such as knowing are clarified by their effects, i.e., making available known objects. Accordingly, if human thought is to be metaphysically understood, then thought cannot be divorced from its natural objects, that is, from the context of Nature.

The conflicting philosophies of mind held by Woodbridge and the pragmatists are evidenced by their different views regarding experience. For instance, beginning with a psychological-biological account of consciousness and mental acts in his *Psychology,* William James's conception of "pure" experience works toward a metaphysical conception of experience that, possibly because of his psychological-biological orientation, is never entirely free of subjectivism. Woodbridge appears to have been thinking of James when the former explains why he does not use 'experience' to refer to the general context and primary subject matter of metaphysics.

> I have . . . studiously avoided the term experience because it has come to imply that the world of experience is one world set over against and discontinuous with another world which is not the world of experience; that the former is something which somehow experiences or knows the latter, without, however, being in any way *the* latter. . . . Such implications I wish wholly to avoid. If experience is taken in a naive and unsophisticated way, *without recognizing on our part any obligation to speculate about its origin, its nature, its validity, or its relation to what is not experience* [italics mine], then all I have said amounts to saying that the realm of experience is the realm of mind, and this realm is a realm of being. But in affirming that it is a realm of being, I do not imply that it is cut off from or set over against the realm of being generally.[54]

As opposed to those whose conception of experience theoretically divorce experience from the world man seeks to know, Woodbridge's realistic metaphysics argues that the nature of human experience cannot be defined adequately apart from the objects perceived; therefore, human experience cannot be divorced from Nature as a "visible world."[55]

Moreover, when limited to psychological-biological contexts, Woodbridge does not reject the pragmatist's attempt to describe how distinctions functionally arise in human experience. With a loss of context, however, Woodbridge warns that even functional distinctions are likely to be taken more absolutely than their special scientific contexts warrant; therefore, they may degenerate into ontological distinctions that seem to imply a radical divorce of the individual mind from the world. Over against such a confusion of contexts, realistic metaphysics serves as a corrective agent by making it evident that,

> the universe which we investigate is, in a very genuine sense . . . a sort of total object of thought, the totality of which seems to be in no wise impaired by any

of the distinctions discovered or set up within it. The mind which is studied in psychology as a determinate form of being exists in this universe of inquiry alongside other determinate forms of being from which it is distinguished.[56]

Their conflicting philosophies of mind are also illustrated in contrasting views regarding the mental activity of inquiry. Inquiry as a form of adaptation and judgment within inquiry as instrumental to the solution of problems are unobjectionable as theories describing the biological genesis of mental functioning within human organisms. When, however, pragmatists drew metaphysical conclusions from these interpretations, their theories led to intellectual confusion, according to Woodbridge.

> It must indeed seem strange if thinking itself should not be the result of evolution, or that, in thinking, parts of the world had not become adjusted in a new way. But while I am ready to admit this, I am by no means ready to admit some of the conclusions for . . . metaphysics which are often drawn from the admission.[57]

Within a biological context, it would be reasonable to conceive of inquiry as a kind of vital adaptation and, therefore, of knowledge (the goal of inquiry) as beliefs that aid adaptation. If, however, this biological conception of knowledge is allowed to become a metaphysical definition without regard for the shift in contexts, then it is liable to lead to what Woodbridge believes is the metaphysically unfortunate conclusion that knowledge is adaptive beliefs irrespective of whether or not these beliefs are faithful to the objective natures of things.[58]

Likewise, when "judgment" within inquiry is examined from a biological point of view, then its interpretation as being instrumental to the solution of an organism's vital problems may be quite accurate. If taken metaphysically, however, Woodbridge believes that this biological thesis could lead to the intellectually confused belief that *the* goal of judgment in inquiry is the solution of vital problems rather than a knowledge of Nature.

> It is claimed that, instead of revealing anything independent of the judging process, judgment is just the adjustment and no more. It is a reorganization of experience, an attempt at control. All this looks to me like a misstatement of the facts. . . . When I make any judgment, even the simplest, I may make it as the result of tension, because of a demand for reorganization, in order to secure control of experience; but the judgment *means* for me something quite different. It means decidedly and unequivocally that in reality apart from the judging process, things exist and operate just as the judgment declares.[59]

More generally, because the pragmatists lost their psychological-biological contexts, according to Woodbridge, they tended to make metaphysical claims about human living, knowledge, and mind which were as such dialectical, yielding intellectual confusion and controversy rather than understanding.

> The pragmatic doctrine of the relation between facts and ideas leads to confusion only because its limitations are not observed. Because ideas function in experience as the hints which lead to the production of new facts, we have heard the astonishing doctrine that the whole of experience is the product of the efficiency of ideas. Because it is the function of belief to issue in action and thus find verification, we have had it suggested that the objects of belief depend on our believing in them. Because knowledge as a process in experience is instrumental, some have rushed to the conclusion that knowledge affords no account of what our world is like, but only a convenient means of satisfying our wants. How far pragmatists reject these remarkable doctrines is hard to discover. That they indicate sources of great misunderstanding is, I believe, clear.[60]

Critique of John Dewey

Dewey and Woodbridge were colleagues in the philosophy faculty of Columbia University from 1905 to 1930. And one need only visit the philosophy library at Columbia to acquire some impression of their extraordinary influence in shaping the intellectual milieu of that great department, for prominently displayed to one side of the rear of the philosophy library is the portrait of John Dewey; on the other side hangs that of F. J. E. Woodbridge. While each possessed a distinct personality reflected in different philosophical styles (Dewey was the prolific author who gave humanistic naturalism to the world, while Woodbridge was more inclined through a personal, Socratic encounter to direct his students' attention toward Nature), one would expect some philosophical agreement, given their mutual influence in establishing a humanistic-naturalistic climate at Morningside Heights. Even so, there were important and profound differences.[61]

Having been perplexed from time to time by Dewey's claims,[62] Woodbridge says that he could not figure out what Dewey was doing, but with Dewey's writing of *How We Think,* he realized finally that all Dewey had been doing was describing how we think.[63] And as long as Dewey's claims are limited to the psychological-biological context of how the mind functions in the human organism's responses to the "exigencies of living," Woodbridge believes that Dewey's judgments are reasonable and helpful. Within this context of a description of the mind's practical functioning, for example, Dewey's attempt to substitute courage and hopefulness for the "quest for certainty" was reasonable.[64]

Professor Dewey has had an eminently practical effect. . . . [His] pronounce-
ment has had on many minds the effect of a genuine liberation from obstacles
which warped their thinking and clogged their action. It proposes to substitute
courage for uncertainty and hopefulness for fear. That is a very practical substitution. . . . The soul is not to be cured of uncertainty and fear by becoming
certain and courageous. It is to be made immune to its vices by means of . . .
an alignment revised in view of the exigencies of living.[65]

Within this context, where "life with its exigencies is fundamental" to the
understanding of mental functioning, Woodbridge believes that Dewey's
analysis of reflective thinking and, consequently, his description of a mental
procedure for the efficient overcoming of vital problems — his logic of intelligent practice — were helpful.

He has shown us in a wholly convincing manner that . . . we must begin with
the concrete operations of intelligence as these promote more satisfactory living, and not with some antecedent scheme of things which is supposed to explain
or justify these operations. Life with its exigencies is fundamental. . . .[66]

In his respect for the fact that life's crises are fundamental to an analysis of
both efficient and inefficient mental functioning and in his acknowledgment that mind functions more efficiently when led by the vital problems to
be solved than by theoretical preconceptions which can prejudice inquiry,
Dewey displayed realism within the context of his inquiries and his realism
had encouraged a like attitude in others.

The attempt to bring intelligence to bear on life in the manner described, is an
attempt which is, and can be, made, without first having solved any antecedent
problem whatever. . . . Problems do not exist to be solved before we can live:
they arise in the process of living, and in that process are solved and resolved.
Professor Dewey has driven that fact home with untiring persistence. . . .
As a consequence, he has made many of us intolerant of any other attitude. . . .
Life with its exigencies is fundamental, and this fundamental can not be explained by any solution of life's problems, nor deduced from any antecedent
system of things which our ingenuity may devise.[67]

If Dewey had been able to maintain his realistic attitude and to bring
into his later metaphysical inquiries what had been learned from his earlier
mental science without allowing it to prejudice his examination of what
Woodbridge considers to be the different subject matter of metaphysics,

presumably the results would have been most beneficial to metaphysics. Perhaps it was such an expectation that encouraged Woodbridge to influence Dewey to engage in metaphysical reflection and to write *Experience and Nature*.[68] Woodbridge, however, eventually writes of Dewey's philosophy,

> [I]t is . . . a philosophy with a doctrine of experience and nature which admits of a positive and progressive development in its own terms, which stands, as I have said, on its own bottom; but which, in spite of this, is made to depend on a dialectic. . . . We should expect, as I see it, a metaphysics which is wholly inferential. We have, instead, a metaphysics which is a matter of preference. And this preference . . . implies that nature is essentially dialectical. . . .[69]

To Woodbridge it appears that within *Experience and Nature* and *The Quest for Certainty* Dewey had taken the substitution of courage for certainty, which for practical purposes is justifiable within the context of his science of mind, and, without *realistic* respect for the shift of contexts from that of psychology to that of metaphysics, had given this substitution an unwarranted ontological basis.

> The shift involved [from certainty to courage] is naturally described [by Dewey] as a shift from the theoretical to the practical. And I suspect that the major difficulties found in construing the philosophy of Professor Dewey arise from attempts to justify that shift on theoretical grounds. It is difficult for me to think that Professor Dewey himself does not attempt to provide such a justification. . . . I seem at times to be asked to substitute courage for certainty on the ground that there is no certainty, and hopefulness for fear on the ground that there is nothing of which to be afraid. In such moments I find myself involved in a dialectic of theories of knowledge and existence. I become myself a controversialist, and find myself leaving the solid ground of experience.[70]

Moreover, in his development of a theory of intelligent mental procedure, Dewey had become at times more preoccupied with his argument against an "antecedent reality," or what Woodbridge called, "antecedent objects," to which intelligence must conform than with the establishment of the relation between intelligence and vital problems. That Dewey stressed within *Experience and Nature* and *The Quest for Certainty* the theoretical issue of antecedent objects rather than the exigencies of life, as if the former rather than the latter justified intelligent mental activity, led Woodbridge to conclude that Dewey's polemic showed his loss of realism, a confusion of contexts in his unwarranted shift from a psychological to an ontological basis for understanding mental activity.[71]

Whether or not reflective thinking implies an antecedent reality to which knowledge must conform to be successful . . . is a question to be settled by inquiry fully as much as any other. To make it a wholly illegitimate question [gives] to Professor Dewey's thesis a character extraordinarily difficult to construe. . . . *I can not find that the problem of their existence has to be settled first* before validity can be claimed for the thesis. Yet I am forced to believe that Professor Dewey thinks that such a settlement is essential. [Italics mine][72]

Woodbridge knows that Dewey affirmed both the existence of antecedently existing objects and that inquiry is often initiated with them. Woodbridge, therefore, searches for some clarification of Dewey's denial of antecedent objects and finds it in Dewey's statement, *"only the conclusion of reflective inquiry is known"*;[73] although inquiry is initiated with antecedent objects, only eventual objects are known. According to Woodbridge, whatever justification there is for Dewey's statement is provided by the practical context of his earlier science of mind.[74] For within the situation of intelligent response to vital problems, objects are primarily *the objectives* of a reflective mental process that attempts to transform the less valuable, for example, alienated or unharmonious, antecedent objects of problematic situations into the more valuable objects of unproblematic situations; within this practical context, ideas, or concepts, are primarily instruments for the successful reorganization of experience rather than for the disclosure of the structures of objects. While this psychological-biological context justifies the belief that knowledge of subject matters is subservient to their transformation into more valuable objects, according to Woodbridge, it cannot account for Dewey's statement that only the object as transformed is known; for knowledge of subject matters alone provides adequate data for their transformation. Accordingly, Woodbridge believes that Dewey's statement reveals his loss of context.

Why . . . play eventual objects over against primary subject matter, making of the former reconstructions of the latter, and making these reconstructions the objects of knowledge? I am quite ready to agree that it is the important business of knowing so to deal with subject-matter that more satisfactory objects are substituted for less satisfactory, and that, thereby, greater security, control, and happiness are secured; but I fail to see how this warrants the statement that "only the conclusion of reflective inquiry is known." *That statement seems to me to come from another source.* [Italics mine][75]

If Dewey's statement that only eventual objects are known is not justified by the practical context where "life with its exigencies are fundamental," then what was his basis for making this statement? In his criticism of *Experience and Nature,* Woodbridge provides an answer:

Do what things are and the ways they operate depend on the eventuation of inquiry? Must we conclude that they do so depend because intelligence does, as a matter of fact, participate in the order of events, and so operate that more satisfactory objects are substituted for less satisfactory? . . .

The questions are not asked to try to convict Professor Dewey of contradictions. They are asked because one reader at least finds *no clue to an answer to them except in the [Dewey's] dialectic,* and that clue leaves him in the dialectic. *The best he can do is* to conclude that existence is essentially dialectical. . . . [Italics mine][76]

Woodbridge suggests that Dewey's dialectic, that is, Dewey's method *divorced from* the practical context of *its being subservient to* the solution of vital problems, is the basis for Dewey's statement. And as this statement indicates, Dewey's method is no longer a description of *how we think* in acquiring the knowledge necessary to the solution of life's problems; it has become definitive of the very nature of knowledge,[77] not a psychological-biological description of intelligent mental functioning but a metaphysical theory of the ontological status of mind.

In light of Woodbridge's critique, Dewey's other claims, his seeming rejections of any certainty and of antecedent objects, have the same unrealistic, dialectical basis. As long as life with its crises and problems is fundamental and, therefore, intelligent method is subservient to dealing efficiently with vital problems, then the discovery through inquiry (rather than the wish-fulfilling presumption) of permanent and stable structures in experience provides the knowledge needed in meeting life's challenges. On the other hand, however, where sustaining method has become an end unto itself, permanence and stability, even that of the structures of objects, can be seen as threats to the perpetuity of method. Again, in criticism of *Experience and Nature,* Woodbridge says,

Why, then, should inference to anything permanent and unchanging be forbidden? . . . I do not find . . . that Professor Dewey rejects them because there is not evidence for them. He seems, rather, to argue them into illegitimacy. The ground of the argument seems to be . . . the conviction that any recognition of the permanently fixed or unchanging is bad. . . .

. . . If it is, then I am forced to conclude that dialectic is a better sample of nature's processes than any other. . . . I find no help whatever in terms of that practical procedure which marks the development of securer knowledge.[78]

When method is no longer a means to the end of an acquisition of knowledge of subject matters but is itself the end of inquiry, and when concepts within inquiry are no longer instruments for the disclosure of the nature of subject matters but are instruments for the preservation of a methodological reorganization of experience, then, according to Woodbridge, "experience appears to be . . . not something which is justified by its fruits, but which is justified by a dialectic which determines what experience is like."[79] That Woodbridge entitled his critique of *Experience and Nature* "Experience and Dialectic" suggests a belief that Dewey's preoccupation with method over against subject matter had driven Dewey perilously close to divorcing mind from Nature metaphysically by theoretically replacing Nature with dialectic as the primary context of mental functioning. (Given Woodbridge's critique of Dewey's *Experience and Nature,* it is interesting that Dewey had originally planned to entitle this book *Experience and the Idea of Nature* but changed it to its published title out of regard for Woodbridge.[80]) Woodbridge believes that the excesses of unrealistic philosophies of mind should be corrected by the elaboration of a realistic metaphysic of mind which would exhibit the fact that the general nature of human mental functioning cannot be understood when theoretically separated from Nature, that is, the fact that mental functioning discloses a world of visible and intelligible objects.[81]

Method and Education

In 1929, Woodbridge anticipated later criticisms of the so-called "technological crisis" in his criticism of allowing method to be divorced from the goal it serves: when man loses sight of the ends which his methods, or tools, were developed to realize, he runs the risk of being tyrannized by his own instruments. Such a possibility exists, for example, in education when educators become so preoccupied with the institution of education or their instructional techniques that they neglect educational goals.

> We live in an age in which the tool has almost passed from being a servant to becoming a master. Tools now make other tools with increasing elimination of the human factor, until many of us wonder if we are not becoming tools ourselves, instruments in a mechanism which is using us, rather than our using it, a mechanism, too, which if rudely disturbed may leave us floundering in inconvenience or misery. This bondage is not only practical, forcing us to follow lines of least resistance wherever we go, in our clothing, our eating, our drinking, our being merry; it is also moral, elevating the virtues of efficiency, method, dispatch—the doing of it now—over those other virtues which, like temperance, justice, and courage, flower only after considered and reflective procrastination. It has taken much intelligence for men to learn the use of tools. It would be a strange consequence of their success, if intelligence thereby became unnecessary. The ideal of a foolproof world or a foolproof system of education calls for critical examination in our moments of leisure.[82]

More specifically, Woodbridge believes that when methods of inquiry are no longer subservient to their subject matters, then the result is arbitrariness rather than knowledge—an arbitrariness that may express either a content of purely technical values, for example efficiency, or the biases of those using the methods. From a Woodbridgian point of view, as long as pragmatism was genuinely realistic, it contributed to the humanization of education;[83] however, with an unwarranted emphasis on method, pragmatism encouraged in education and elsewhere the arbitrariness of personal bias rather than knowledge.

> There are many . . . consequences of the educational revolution. Most of them follow from a radical change in emphasis involved, the change from an emphasis on subjects to an emphasis on persons. . . .
>   . . . Respect for persons is what the old education neglected. It would be a pity, would it not, if the new should neglect respect for learning? Which, after all, is the more important? Education seems to be brought face to face with that question at the last. . . . Let me remind you, however, that Plato wrote a piece called the *Meno* in which he observed that you can teach a slave geometry but you can not teach the sons of Pericles virtue. I have wondered much what the Son of Apollo meant by that observation. I have reached the conclusion that what he meant was this, that education is on solid ground when that which is taught controls those who learn, as was the case with the slave, and it is not on such solid ground when those who learn control that which is taught, as was the case with the sons of Pericles. . . . Perhaps by making what we study more important than ourselves, we find ourselves unexpectedly important in the accomplishment of our pilgrimage.[84]

Woodbridge believes that procedures of inquiry and learning cannot be perfected apart from a realistic commitment to the authority of subject matter.

Summary

Within scientific inquiry language functions "informatively" as the instrument that formulates and communicates interpretations of subject matters. Moreover, the terms and grammatical forms of language are socially determined conventions that convey meanings common to a community. According to Woodbridge, inquirers can take advantage of these meanings without prejudicing inquiry if they maintain the realistic distinction where the subject matter rather than convention is authoritative in determining the meaning and the adequacy of the concepts of hypotheses. If a realistic attitude is lost, scientific inquiry degenerates into "dialectic," or pseudo-inquiry.

According to Woodbridge, although pragmatism had originally shown

promise, pragmatists had not respected the limitations inherent to pragmatism: what had begun as a realistic demand to respect contexts through
maintaining respect for the authority of the subject matter of inquiry, had
itself ceased to do so. For example, the pragmatist's inquiries into the subject matters of the genesis, processes, and functions of mental activity were
helpful as long as they limited themselves to the specific contexts of these
biological and psychological subject matters. With their loss of context,
however, they misapplied procedures and concepts of their special sciences
to Nature in general and, therefore, made metaphysical claims about
human living, theory of knowledge, and mind which, according to Woodbridge, yielded intellectual confusion and fruitless controversy rather than
understanding.

Of the pragmatists, Woodbridge was especially critical of his friend and
colleague at Columbia University, John Dewey. According to Woodbridge,
Dewey's substitution of "courage" for "certainty" and his arguments against
inquiry's goal being knowledge of an "antecedent reality" are justifiable
within the context of Dewey's psychological-biological subject matter of the
human organism's mental response to vital crises. Woodbridge claims, however, that Dewey's statement that only the object as transformed is known
shows that Dewey's method is no longer merely a psychological-biological
description of mental functioning but has become a metaphysical theory.
For example, Harry Costello recalls Woodbridge saying of Dewey,

"I ask Dewey from time to time some simple question, such as, 'Is there not
something about the past that never again changes? Surely the state before
change begins cannot itself also change.'" I [Costello] said, "What did he
answer?" "Answer!" Woodbridge replied, "Dewey defined and distinguished
and qualified, in such a maze of dialectic, that not only I did not get any
answer, I didn't even know where my question went to. And do you know,
when he gets that way, he thinks he is being empirical."[85]

According to Woodbridge, for Dewey, the role of mental functioning,
including experiencing, in the preservation of method had become more
basic to an understanding of mind than the fact that mind provided experience and knowledge of Nature. Dewey's naturalism had been jeopardized by
his loss of realism where a preoccupation with method over against subject
matter had driven him close to divorcing mind from Nature by displacing Nature with dialectic, or method, as the primary context of mental
functioning.

The following chapter provides further criticisms of pragmatism in light
of Woodbridge's theory of time and his philosophy of history.

NOTES

1. Frederick J. E. Woodbridge, *Nature and Mind: Selected Essays of Frederick J. E. Woodbridge* (New York: Columbia University Press, 1937; reprint ed., New York: Russell and Russell, 1965), p. 215.

2. Ibid., pp. 238-239.

3. Other linguistic functions distinguished by Woodbridge are the expressive and the directive; see, *Essay on Nature* (New York: Columbia University Press, 1940), pp. 227-228.

4. See above, "Language and Contextual Analysis," in Chapter 1.

5. F. J. E. Woodbridge, "Contrasts in Education," three lectures given under the provisions of the Julius and Rosa Sachs Endowment Fund, Bureau of Publications, Teachers College, Columbia University, 1929, pp. 10-11.

6. Woodbridge, *Essays on Nature,* p. 218.

7. Woodbridge, "Contrasts in Education," pp. 47-48.

8. Language use is empirically observable and, therefore, it can also be examined scientifically. When language becomes the subject matter of scientific inquiry, according to Woodbridge's view, language as subject matter is extra-linguistic relative to the language functioning informatively within inquiry.

9. Woodbridge, *Essay on Nature,* p. 233.

10. Ibid., p. 216.

11. Frederick J. E. Woodbridge, "Papers, 1884-1940," (Woodbridge's unpublished correspondences, diaries, essays, and lecture and reading notes, Columbia University, Special Collections), Phi Beta Kappa lecture entitled: "Language," undated, p. 2.

12. Woodbridge, *Essay on Nature,* p. 215.

13. Ibid., p. 252.

14. Woodbridge, "Papers, 1884-1940," essay entitled: "Ideology," undated, p. 13.

15. Ibid.

16. See, for example, Frederick J. E. Woodbridge, *The Realm of Mind* (New York: Columbia University Press, 1926), p. 4.

17. Woodbridge, "Papers, 1884-1940," "Claims of Science," p. 11.

18. Woodbridge says of logical positivism, "it seems absurd to most of us to affirm that language communicates language or that an analysis of grammar or syntax can of itself reveal whether sentences have meaning or not" (*Essay on Nature,* p. 244). Perhaps he was thinking of Rudolf Carnap's *The Logical Syntax of Language* wherein Carnap says that philosophy is logical analysis of logical syntax. [Trans. by Amethe Smeaton (London: Routledge and Kegan Paul Ltd., 1937), p. 332]. Furthermore, according to Carnap,

The logical analysis of philosophical problems shows them to vary greatly in character. As regards those object-questions whose objects do not occur in the exact sciences, critical analysis has revealed that they are pseudo-problems. The suppositious sentences of metaphysics . . . are pseudo-sentences; they have no logical content, but are only expressions of feeling . . . . [Ibid., p. 278]

19. Woodbridge, *Realm of Mind,* p. 61.

20. Woodbridge, *Essay on Nature,* p. 216.

21. Woodbridge, "Papers, 1884–1940," lecture entitled: "Metaphysics, 1932–33," p. 7.

22. Woodbridge, *Nature and Mind,* pp. 294–95.

23. Woodbridge, *Essay on Nature,* p. 219.

24. Woodbridge, *Nature and Mind,* 215.

25. Woodbridge uses 'idea' to refer to both objective logical structures and the meaningful content of hypotheses in order to emphasize the continuity of discourse as it functions in realistic inquiry and the intelligibility of natural subject matters. Since, in most instances, "conceptural meaning" can be used to refer to the latter use and since he holds that the realistic distinction between interpretation and subject matter must be maintained during inquiry, while 'idea' will be reserved for reference to the logical structures of objects, henceforth, when possible, I will use 'concept' to refer to units of the meaningful content of language, especially the interpretations of informative language.

26. Woodbridge, *Nature and Mind,* p. 215.

27. Ibid., p. 220.

28. Ibid., pp. 220–21.

29. See A. S. Eddington's own description of these two tables in his book, *The Nature of the Physical World* (New York: Cambridge University Press, 1929, pp. ix–xiii).

30. Woodbridge, *Nature and Mind,* pp. 227–28. According to Woodbridge, A. N. Whitehead's use of concepts like "community" and "society" in his characterization of the inorganic world also involves a confusion of contexts (ibid., p. 221; he referred specifically to Whitehead's *Symbolism,* p. 62). Woodbridge says pragmatic analysis "seems to be poignantly recommended when rocks become social . . ." (ibid., p. 228).

31. Ibid., pp. 222–24.

32. Woodbridge, "Contrasts in Education," p. 10.

33. F. J. E. Woodbridge, "Pragmatism and Education," *Educational Review* (October, 1907):236.

34. Ibid., p. 235. Also see, Woodbridge, *Nature and Mind,* pp. 161–63.

35. Woodbridge, *Nature and Mind,* p. 72.

36. Woodbridge, "Pragmatism and Education," p. 234.

37. Woodbridge, *Nature and Mind,* p. 215.

38. Woodbridge, "Pragmatism and Education," p. 237.

39. Ibid., p. 231.

40. Ibid.

41. See, for example, William James, *Pragmatism and Other Essays* (New York: Washington Square, 1963), p. 109.

42. Woodbridge, "Pragmatism and Education," pp. 231–32.

43. Ibid., p. 232.

44. Ibid., p. 231.

45. Ibid.

46. Ibid., p. 232.

47. Ibid., p. 231.

48. Woodbridge, *Nature and Mind,* pp. 216–17.

49. Woodbridge, "Pragmatism and Education," p. 236. He attributes this limitation to the situation, or context, of inquiry to John Dewey and cites Dewey's article "The Control of Ideas by Facts" in the *Journal of Philosophy, Psychology, and Scientific Methods* (Vol. IV, p. 257) in support of this claim.

50. Woodbridge, *Nature and Mind*, p. 217.

51. Woodbridge does not claim that the pragmatists intended to develop a metaphysics of mind; rather, from his point of view, this is what in effect they did. For example, he says of them,

> The basal problem of logic becomes, undoubtedly, the metaphysics of knowledge, the determination of the nature of knowledge and its relation to reality. It is quite evident that this is just the problem which the current tendencies criticized have sought, not to solve, but to avoid or set aside. Their motives for so doing have been mainly the difficulties which have arisen from the Kantian philosophy in its development into transcendentalism, *and the desire to extend the category of evolution to embrace the whole of reality, knowledge included.* [Ibid., p. 75 (italics mine)]

52. Ibid., pp. 61–62. Here Woodbridge only identifies pragmatism explicitly with biological tendencies (see, ibid., p. 64); however, he also associated pragmatism with the psychological.

53. Ibid., p. 69.

54. *Woodbridge, Realm of Mind*, p. 41; in addition, see the rest of his critique of what he calls the "prevailing philosophies of experience" (ibid., pp. 39–41). A few pages later, he criticizes James for his belief that,

> in our consciousness existence or parts of it is somehow counterfeited, so that we internally possess some similacrum of the greater outer world. As James once put it: "Our images of things assume a time- and space-arrangement which resembles the time- and space-arrangements outside." [Ibid., pp. 57–58]

55. Woodbridge does not conceive of "experience" as being passive as, for example, a spectator passively observing the world, but as the active cooperation of human organism and environment: "Experience is then our active participation with the rest of things" (ibid., p. 63).

56. Woodbridge, *Nature and Mind*, p. 162. In the text he quotes George Santayana's *Life of Reason* (Vol. I, pp. 124–25); nonetheless, it is clear that his criticism is not directed solely, or even primarily, against Santayana's philosophy. He says of his Santayana quotation, "it is to be emphasized that what now follows is neither criticism nor exposition of the quoted passage . . ." (ibid., p. 161). Accordingly, I take this quotation to be a point of departure for his criticism of anyone who, having lost his psychological context, metaphysically concludes that individual mind is divorced from the rest of Nature. And, since he had already been critical of the metaphysical repercussions of the pragmatists' loss of psychological-biological contexts, it is very likely that his criticism was partly directed towards the pragmatists. An example of a pragmatist's description of the functional discriminations of experience is that of John Dewey in his *Experience and Nature* [2nd ed. (Chicago: Open Court Publishing Company, 1925), p. 196], although Dewey's functional analysis was an

attempt to overcome ontological dichotomies, for example, the subject-object dualism, which he despised (see, for example, ibid.).

57. Woodbridge, *Nature and Mind*, p. 66. Woodbridge associated this "evolutionary view" that he criticizes with, among others, the pragmatists (ibid., p. 64).

58. See, ibid., pp. 66–67.

59. Ibid., p. 68. From the realistic point of view, Woodbridge claims one can see that it is the action resulting from the judgment made in inquiry rather than the judgment itself that is the instrumental factor (ibid., p. 69).

60. Woodbridge, "Pragmatism and Education," p. 237.

61. Other commentators have emphasized the similarities more than the differences between their thought. See, for example, Patricia Ann Heuser, "Woodbridge, Critic of Modern Philosophy" (Ph.D. dissertation, Columbia University, 1950), p. 43; and Hae Soo Pyun, *Nature, Intelligibility, and Metaphysics: Studies in the Philosophy of F. J. E. Woodbridge* (Amsterdam: B. R. Grüner, 1971), pp. 24–27.

62. Many of Woodbridge's criticisms of pragmatism examined earlier in this chapter were in part against John Dewey.

63. Herbert W. Schneider, conversations, June, 1977 and January–June, 1979.

64. While Woodbridge does not specify a justifiable reason for the substitution of courage for certainty beyond meeting the "exigencies of living," a reason that complements his point is as follows: in order for the human mind to be flexible enough to meet "intelligently" and, therefore, effectively life's crises and problems, one must avoid giving in to the desire for the security of certainty.

65. Woodbridge, *Nature and Mind*, pp. 230–31.

66. Ibid., p. 232.

67. Ibid., p. 232.

68. Herbert W. Schneider, *A History of American Philosophy*, 2nd ed. (New York: Columbia University Press, 1962), p. 474.

69. Woodbridge, *Nature and Mind*, pp. 238–39.

70. Ibid., p. 231.

71. In the article from which most of Woodbridge's critique of Dewey is drawn, "Experience and Dialectic," Woodbridge shifts without explanation from the phrase "antecedent reality" to "antecedent objects" (*Nature and Mind*, p. 233). Although Dewey would reject "reality" prior to intelligence because he was anxious to disassociate himself from idealism, he would not have claimed the non-existence of objects prior to intelligent activity. Although it is difficult to justify Woodbridge's having made such a shift without explanation, I do not believe that he ever seriously believed that Dewey rejected the existence of objects possessing structures prior to intelligent activity; for he acknowledges Dewey's belief in such objects several times (see, for example, "Pragmatism and Education," p. 235 and quotation, *Nature and Mind*, p. 317). Rather, Woodbridge is using his criticism of Dewey's discussion of antecedent objects as a point of departure to get at what he believes is the basic problem in Dewey's metaphysics.

72. Woodbridge, *Nature and Mind*, p. 233.

73. Ibid., p. 234; Woodbridge cites p. 182 of Dewey's *The Quest for Certainty*.

74. See, for example, Woodbridge, *Nature and Mind*, p. 234.

75. Ibid., p. 234.

76. Ibid., p. 235.

77. Dewey himself realized that his analysis of method was not just a description of how we think but had become a theory of the nature of knowledge. This is indicated

by Dewey's having told Herbert Schneider soon after the publication of his *Logic: The Theory of Inquiry* that this book presented his theory of knowledge (Herbert Schneider, conversations).

78. Woodbridge, *Nature and Mind*, pp. 237–38. He cites page 72 of *Experience and Nature* as an example of the textual basis for his statements.

79. Ibid., p. 239.

80. Herbert Schneider, conversations.

81. The reader who is interested in a further understanding of the differences between the philosophies of Woodbridge and Dewey is urged to read Sterling P. Lamprecht's clear and, I believe, helpful discussion of their different empiricisms. Lamprecht says,

> The central insistence in the former [Woodbridge] is on the primacy of subject-matter; the central insistence in the latter [Dewey] is on the primacy of method. Neither, however, ignores the other element requisite for an adequate empirical theory of knowledge. . . . Yet the difference of emphasis or approach in the two men is more than terminological and leads to considerable differences in the end. [*The Metaphysics of Naturalism* (New York: Appleton-Century-Crofts, 1967), pp. 39–40.]

Elsewhere, he criticizes one form that the empiricist tradition took beginning with Locke and continuing in Dewey: "This excessive attention to method seems to me to have led the empirical tradition astray" (ibid., pp. 38–39). Regarding Dewey, he continues,

> It is surely fair to see in Dewey a continuance of that phase of the empirical tradition in which subject-matter is resolved into means for pursuit of method. Even if the fact of subject-matter is acknowledged, that fact is overlooked save so far as it promotes the continued exercise of inquiry. However brilliant Dewey's analysis of empirical method may be, his statements stand as a truncated empiricism. [Ibid., p. 54]

Reflecting his sympathy with Woodbridge, Lamprecht concludes,

> If empiricism is to develop soundly, if its predilection for methodology is not to lead to merely effete dialectics, it must be more ready to see each of its methodological devises and distinctions as disclosures of the nature of that subject-matter which makes the methodology workable. And this means that empiricism should become frankly an appeal to the authority which subject-matter may exercise over thinking and a respect for the theoretical knowledge of that subject-matter which experimental methodology may really gain. [Ibid., pp. 58–59]

82. Woodbridge, "Contrasts in Education," p. 12.

83. Although it was an early article (1907), see Woodbridge's description of pragmatism's contributions to educational practice in "Pragmatism and Education," pp. 237–40.

84. Woodbridge, "Contrasts in Education," pp. 48–50. Here Woodbridge does

not name pragmatism in his critique of the "new education." Given the important role of pragmatism, especially Dewey, in shaping "progressive education" and the nature of Woodbridge's critique, I believe that he is criticizing, at least in part, pragmatism, and more specifically, Dewey.

85. Costello, "Naturalism of Frederick Woodbridge," *Naturalism and the Human Spirit,* p. 296.

6

History and Historical Comprehension

He is not freed from the past who has lost it or who regards
himself simply as its product. In the one case he would have no
experience to guide him and no memories to cherish. In the
other he would have no enthusiasm.[1]

The historian is himself an historical fact indicating a selection, a distinction, and an emphasis in the course of time. His
history is naturally colored by that fact. Other histories he can
write only with an effort at detachment from his own career.
He must forget himself if he would understand others; but he
must understand himself first, if he is successfully to forget
what he is. He must know what history is. . . .[2]

Introduction

Woodbridge holds that the subject matter for every science is natural historical processes; accordingly, Nature is not only a spatial realm of vision and
a logical realm of mind but also a temporal realm of matter. He believes,
therefore, that the metaphysician should provide a theory of time and a
philosophy of history. Moreover, Woodbridge was a student of the history
of philosophy, and he encouraged this historical interest in many of his students at Columbia.[3] For these reasons, Woodbridge devoted considerable
reflection to the subjects of time, history, and the historian's activity. The
present chapter presents a summary of those reflections.

In the development of his theory of time, Woodbridge is especially critical of philosophers who misrepresent time through its spatialization. In
opposition to the spatialization of time, Woodbridge affirms that the present
alone is active.

Woodbridge distinguishes the special sciences of historians from other sciences on the basis of a difference in subject matter: although the occurrence of activity is historical and, therefore, every subject matter of a science is historical, only some things have a "progressive" or temporal nature, therefore requiring special historical sciences for their study. In his metaphysical analysis of the historical subject matters of historians, Woodbridge distinguishes several categories, some borrowed from his more general metaphysical theory and some specific to the temporal nature of historical subject matters: "careers," "purpose," "selection," "pluralism," and "historical continuity" or "evolution." Having drawn these distinctions, Woodbridge uses them to clarify the historian's activity and to criticize other interpretations that are rejected as being nonrealistic or reductive.

In addition to an exposition of the above, this chapter presents Woodbridge's important distinction between scientific histories of human careers and nonscientific "histories of human interests." Woodbridge believes that a confusion of these two kinds of human histories is the basis for many of the misrepresentations of time, of the historical nature of natural processes, and of the activities of historians.

As already noted, Woodbridge's thought has been influential, especially through his students at Columbia. His theory of time and philosophy of history have also shaped subsequent thought. For example, Corliss Lamont acknowledges his indebtedness to Woodbridge's theory of time.[4]

Theory of Time

Since, according to Woodbridge, the subject matter of every science is dynamic, cooperative activities, subject matter is always natural historical processes. Therefore, although he claims, like Aristotle before him, that the goal of science is the adequate linguistic expression of the structure of subject matters and that these structures are "logical,"[5] the dynamically structured subject matter being investigated, rather than formal logical criteria, determines the adequacy of these logical expressions.

> Nothing is ever understood until it is intelligibly expressed. It is needless to say, therefore, that education should make much of language. . . . I mean discipline in adequate expression.[7]

> Nature as evidenced in our living . . . is history with eventuality through and through. It will not let itself be coerced into any formal system and without it any formal system loses all intelligible meaning beyond its own algebraic coherence. . . . Life and existence can not be deduced from systematic discourse because that discourse is a systematization of what is first said about acknowledged life and existence.[8]

Since Nature's processes are historical, it is fitting that the philosopher qua metaphysician should examine this historical dimension *as* historical and develop a philosophy of history.

Woodbridge rejects philosophies of history, such as those of Augustine and Hegel, where events are understood to fulfill a cosmic plan or goal.[9] Since metaphysic's subject matter is the most general one, if its goal were to discover a history, this history would be of the cosmos as a whole. According to Woodbridge, however, the cosmos *as a whole* is neither historically nor in any other manner determinable; for, as such, there is nothing beyond it relative to which the Whole is determined and all qualities of historical processes are relative determinations. Woodbridge claims, therefore, that the goal of metaphysics is to discover the categories descriptive of Nature's historical processes when these processes are taken individually rather than collectively.[10]

> The world [or Nature] has no history. . . . The world is a collective idea which we can frame because we can group things and because things are grouped in nature. To extend the art of grouping, however, until we have the idea of a group from which no fact remains uncollected, and then to suppose that there corresponds to this idea an object of which we may ask, Has it a beginning in time, an extent in space, a history or an evolution? is to enter the realm of illusion. No; the world as a useful concept must be used distributively. It must mean, Take any item you like, but not, Take all items together. It must be regulative and not constitutive.[11]

By including in a metaphysical description only traits common to any or every individual historical process *as* historical, Woodbridge believes that a metaphysical description of Nature's historical processes yields Nature's "temporal order" rather than *a* history. Accordingly, in addition to a theory of the visible world and a metaphysical science of mind, another species of metaphysical science is a philosophy of history, which, as metaphysical, becomes a theory of time;[12] Nature's activities in context display three kinds of cooperation that lead metaphysically to the acknowledgment of three natural realms: the spatial realm of vision, the logical realm of mind, and the temporal realm of matter.

In *The Purpose of History*, Woodbridge criticizes the customary conception of time as divisible into past, present, and future. According to Woodbridge, this temporal division has often been interpreted spatially. For example, philosophers have claimed that human experience, being incomplete and unfinished, projects on reality—which in itself is complete and, therefore, changeless—the appearance of temporal succession; that is, what is in reality spatial, appears temporal.[13] Therefore, the temporal distinctions of past, present, and future are not indicative of genuine ontological differences. Other philosophers who have not conceived reality to be finished and complete, nonetheless, have spatialized time. They have claimed that the nature of every activity is already completely determined by previous occurrences; the past is taken to be the cause of the present and, through the present, the future. Since the past is alone effective, according to their conception, the present is merely the transition point where already determined events occur. In summary, Woodbridge says of these conceptions,

> [T]hese philosophies . . . gain whatever force they have principally from the fact that they think of time in terms of space. They . . . thus behold time spatially with all its parts co-existent as the points on the line. Events are then conceived to move from the past through the present into the future, just as a pencil point may pass from the beginning of the line through its middle point to the end. But, unlike the pencil point, they can not go backward. . . . The present is but the transition point of their going.[14]

Although the interpretation of events as dates and places is advantageous in some instances, for example, in constructing calendars, making clocks, and developing a science of mechanics, according to Woodbridge, time is not anything like a line already drawn and the present is not like a point passed along the line. The false interpretation of reality as finished and complete reifies the past and the future into something like co-existent localities, as if the passage of the pencil along the line were its traveling from one place (the past) to another (the future) in very much the same manner as one might travel from New York to Boston. But if the past and the future are like localities to be departed from and arrived at, then one is presented with the perplexing possibility of being at the present time in the past or at the present time in the future. Yet "Boston is already there to go to, but the future is not anywhere to go to. And New York is there to leave, but the past is not anywhere to leave."[15] And "it is quite clear that to-day is neither past nor future, that it is neither yesterday nor tomorrow, and that if we go anywhere we must start to-day."[16]

Woodbridge claims that similar conceptual perplexities arise with the belief that the past completely determines the present and the future. If, for example, the cosmos is known with sufficient completeness, then, according to this belief, both the natures of what will eventually exist and the moment of their existence should be knowable prior to their occurrence. In other words, according to Woodbridge, if one knows sufficiently the antecedents of one's future acquisition of knowledge, then one would in effect know what will be known even before the occurrence of actually knowing it. As Woodbridge points out, however, "the antecedents of my present knowledge are not my knowledge, ... I have not been able to discover any wisdom or profit in putting my present knowledge into its antecedents in order to explain how that knowledge originated. . . ."[17] Woodbridge believes that the two spatial interpretations of time illustrate what is generally true of such conceptions: they encourage the theoretical confusion of past, present, and future; they rob Nature of her changes and, therefore, of the genuineness of her dynamism and productivity.[18]

Woodbridge, therefore, concludes that "time is not like a line already drawn. It is more like a line in the drawing."[19] Neither Nature's future ends nor her past of already actualized structures in themselves are effective; only the present coincidence of individuals possessing appropriate frames and agency produces activities; therefore, the present alone is active: "It is all that we mean by activity or eventuality."[20] The present should not be reified into some thing that comes out of the past or goes into the future;[21] it is not the so-called specious present, a "vanishing point between past and future."[22]

Nor, for that matter, is the present even an event. Rather, the present is *all* of Nature's cooperative activities, or events, as still active; it is her historical processes in their dynamic relatedness.[23] Accordingly, "it is not, so to speak, in the same line or dimension with [the past or the future] . . . . It is the *drawing* of the line, but in no sense is it a part or point of the line itself."[24] Nonetheless, because every activity, however novel, conforms to the structural limitations left in its environment by past actualizations, the present is "continuous" with the past.[25] Since, however, only the present assemblage of individuals is active, temporal continuity is not an effect of the past but, rather, is the result of an active, often novel, present's realization of past structural possibilities.[26]

Woodbridge suggests, therefore, that the past is "matter"—not "matter" as conceived by materialists who believe it to be both the cause and the determination of every event, but matter *as material* whose structures limit but neither cause nor determine its use by the active present.[27] Rather than rigidly conforming to the past, Nature's present transforms her past within the limits of the structural possibilities past materials provide.

All time-processes . . . appear to be, when we attentively consider them, processes which supplement, complete, or transform what has gone before. They are active conservations and utilizations of the past as material. They save what has happened from being utterly destroyed, and in saving it, complete and develop it.[28]

Although the fact of an occurrence cannot be changed and, therefore, to this extent the past is dead and cannot be transformed, the past as material for further development can be transformed. "Yesterday as yesterday is gone forever. Its opportunities are over and its incidents dead. As an historical yesterday it lives as material for to-day's employment."[29] In the latter sense, therefore, the present can be said to be the cause of the past; "the line, instead of growing into the future, grows into the past—continually more and more of it is drawn."[30]

Since the present uses the past as material, according to Woodbridge, "time is . . . constantly rounding out things, so to speak, or bringing them to some end or fulfillment."[31] The movement of time, therefore, is purposeful and displays "natural teleology." Although Nature's historical processes display purposes, this does not imply that the ends of processes *as ends* are productive. For, assigning agency to "final factors" can lead to the confused belief that future ends produce whatever occurs. But the empirically evident fact of change discredits the belief that final factors are also efficient and, therefore, sufficient of themselves to have already accomplished every possible purpose.[32] Rather, if the present is the active transformation of past materials, then the future is "not yet done, but only possible";[33] the future *as future* is "open."

> The future of the line is not the place on the paper or in the air which by and by the line may occupy. *Its future is a genuine future,* a possibility as yet nowhere realized. It is the part of the line which always will be, but never is; or, better, it is that part of the line which will have a place and a date if the line continues to be drawn. [Italics mine][34]

Thinking of time as a line in the drawing rather than as a line already drawn avoids much of the conceptual confusion that attends the spatialization of time. For as Woodbridge notes,

> it serves to point out that past, present, and future are not like parts of a whole into which an absolute or complete time is divided. They are more like derivatives of the time process itself in the concrete instances of its activity.[35]

Like the logical and spatial structures of Nature, her temporal structure is a dimension of cooperative activities rather than a frame antecedently prepared for their occurrence.[36] (Indeed, "the fact that time seems to be a dimension and not a frame of existence makes it impossible to assume a time order filled in independent of other orders" like the spatial order.[37]) Accordingly,

> past, present, and future are adjectives before they are nouns. They qualify events before they qualify time, and only after they have been allowed to qualify time are they turned into nouns, *the* past, *the* present, and *the* future, as if they were original divisors or divisions.[38]

"A line being drawn" is not a perfect analogy, however, for it still carries misleading spatial connotations, for example, a linear interpretation of time. Woodbridge says, "time may be styled a dimension of nature, but it is not a linear dimension."[39] A more accurate description of time is a realistic statement of what every changing or growing thing generally displays: the movement of time is a movement "from the possible to the actual, from what may be to what has been."[40] In light of this definition, Woodbridge believes the derivative concepts of "past," "present," and "future" can be more accurately defined: while the past is the actual and the future is the possible, the present "is the concrete, definite, and effective transforming of the possible into the actual."[41]

Thus, Woodbridge claims that a realistic metaphysical theory of time shows that "everything that grows or changes manufactures a past by realizing a future";[42] therefore, the theory clarifies the fact that every event, that is, every cooperative activity or historical process, is jointly retrospective and prospective. Moreover, although man's intentional and intelligent uses of past materials to realize chosen futures is not the only example of Nature's time scheme, it is perhaps the clearest.[43]

> Starting with nature as eventual, with every event jointly retrospective and prospective, our being in a nature of that sort is itself jointly retrospective and prospective being. . . . Why, I repeatedly ask myself, is it worthwhile making miracles of our knowledge of the past and our hopes of the future when the only way to do so is by supposing that our temporal being is not a sample of what temporal being is?[44]

> Human experience is one kind of history, namely, history conscious of itself, the time process deliberately at work.[45]

A realistic theory of time shows that the past is all man has to work with and that he must either intentionally transform it or simply continue to live in it as dictated by Nature. Since this theory displays the historical qualities of continuity and purpose, it also shows that the past is knowable and that this knowledge reveals future possibilities. With its presentation of the facts of an active present and an open future, the theory shows that knowledge can be used deliberately to transform the past into a more desirable future. Woodbridge believes, therefore, that an adequate theory of time is of serious practical consequence.

> He is not freed from the past who has lost it or who regards himself simply as its product. In the one case he would have no experience to guide him and no memories to cherish. In the other he would have no enthusiasm.[46]

Historical Science and the Dual Purpose of Human Histories

Although *in its occurrence* the activity of every thing is historical, not everything has a "progressive" or temporal *nature,* what Woodbridge calls a "career."[47]

> There may be things the nature of which is only historically definable, the nature of which is, we may say, just their concrete history. A grain of wheat in its chemical and physical composition is a thing quite different from what we call a seed. . . . [T]he nature of a thing may be progressive. Time may enter into its substance. . . . That some natures are progressive seems certain; that all are seems doubtful. And that, I suspect, is why we find the distinction between the organic and the inorganic so natural and so helpful.[48]

Since time is a factor entering into the natures of some subject matters and not others, it is the realistic basis for the distinction between those special sciences that are "historical" sciences and those that are not. Although many historical sciences, for example, biology and psychology, study living subject matters, some do not, as is shown by the non-living, yet essentially historical nature of geology's subject matter.

Among the historical sciences are those of the individuals who write about "human histories" in order that human careers might be "remembered and understood." Since "undoubtedly man is a part or instance of nature,"[49] in their attempt to present an accurate "record" of human occurrences and a correct "understanding" of human careers in Nature, these historians (e.g., archaeologists and anthropologists) attempt to discover the truth about the natural careers of man.[50] As historical, human nature is scientifically definable; according to Woodbridge, however, the fact that man writes histories is evidence of a dimension of human life that continually evades scientific definition. For, in his writing of histories, man defines his own natural history and the histories of others; and, by his defining them, man can transcend them.

> All time processes are histories, but man only is the writer of them, so that historical comprehension becomes the significant trait of human history. To live in the light of a past remembered and understood is to live, not the life of instinct and emotion, but the life of intelligence.[51]

What is distinctive of human careers, therefore, is that they are "history conscious of itself,"[52] "the recovery of the past with the prospect of a future."[53] Past and present actions conform to scientifically discoverable natural laws;[54] but the distinctive human motivation for lawful activities is not natural, the perpetuation of what is or what has been, but supernatural, the transformation of Nature as it exists through a future realization of ideal human interests.[55] Since it is distinctive of human careers that they are intentionally lived, according to Woodbridge, the human historical sciences cannot offer a completely adequate understanding of them; the human sciences need to be supplemented with histories of another kind. Rather than presenting human careers as the exhibition of natural laws, this latter kind of history would present them as the revelation of the supernatural; that is, it would narrate the drama of man's struggle to transform Nature according to his ideals. Woodbridge says, "I may even now invoke the Muses to my aid, but Clio first, and, afterwards, Calliope."[56] While the latter type of history is not a science, it adds to the human sciences what Woodbridge calls "historical comprehension." Woodbridge believes, therefore, that a complete understanding of human careers requires many histories of man, the collection of which serves a dual purpose, one scientific the other dramatic.

> Human history is human history only. The hopes and fears, the aspirations, the wisdom and the folly of man are to be understood only in the light of his career. . . .
>
> . . . [W]hat is not human should not be taken as the standard and measure of what is human. Human history can not be wholly resolved into physical processes nor the enterprises of men be construed solely as the by-product of material forces. . . . [In] refusing to anthropomorphize matter, we ought not to be led to materialize man. We should rather be led to recognize that the reasons which condemn anthropomorphic science are precisely the reasons which commend humanistic philosophy. . . . So we may conclude that the pluralism of history . . . does not . . . make human history a presumptuous enterprise for them that *write it not in the language of nature, but in the language of man.*
>
> . . . His history . . . must be written *also in terms of aspiration.* [Italics mine][57]

Even though histories that aspire to "historical comprehension"—what may be called "histories of human interests"—are not sciences, Woodbridge believes that they are not as such arbitrary. Although the historian of human interests freely chooses the ideals he desires to exhibit, once those ideals are chosen and applied to Nature's processes, the historical interconnectedness of Nature's events in their actual ability to frustrate or contribute to the realization of man's ideals becomes the historian's subject matter.[58] Nature provides, therefore, a basis whereby one history of human interests can be judged to be a more accurate understanding of historical facts than another.[59] Although histories of human interests do not imply the dissolution of the metaphysical distinction between Nature and the supernatural, that they exhibit the role of human transcendent ideals in shaping human history in Nature contributes to a much richer metaphysical conception of Nature than the special sciences alone would suggest.[60]

> Man is a part or instance of nature, governed by nature's laws and intimately involved in her processes. But he is so governed and involved not as matter without imagination. . . . Nature is not what she would be without him and that is why his history can never be remembered or understood if he is forgotten. He can not be taken out of nature and nature be then called upon to explain him.[61]

Moreover, the historian's *choice* of an ideal to exhibit historically is not entirely arbitrary; for what interests really motivated humanity and therefore actually shaped human affairs in Nature are not determined by the historian's personal interests. Like realistic scientists, the wise historian seeks detachment from the interests of his own personal career in order to be faithful to his subject matter, the interests of mankind. An understanding of the general nature of history and the uniqueness of the human historical career encourages wise detachment, for it is necessary to acknowledge that one's historical career as a human being is defined partly by supernatural interests in order to avoid jeopardizing inquiry.

> The historian is himself an historical fact indicating a selection, a distinction, and an emphasis in the course of time. His history is naturally colored by that fact. Other histories he can write only with an effort at detachment from his own career. He must forget himself if he would understand others; but he must understand himself first, if he is successfully to forget what he is. He must know what history is. . . .[62]

This understanding of history and of the human career is also helpful to scientists. For in light of the transcendent dimension of his career, man clarifies his tendency to lose the realistic scientific attitude through prejudicial preferences. An adequate understanding of the general nature of history and, more specifically, the nature of human history will assist in maintaining the important distinction between natural science (whether historical or nonhistorical) and the history of human interests.

The Career, Purpose, Selection, and Pluralism of Natural Histories

Because Nature consists of cooperative activities and every activity in its occurrence is historical, Woodbridge's metaphysical theory of time is an

important part of his general metaphysics. Some things, however, have progressive or temporal *natures*. Accordingly, in addition to Woodbridge's
metaphysical categories, his lectures on *The Purpose of History* developed
additional terms, such as, 'pluralism,' 'continuity,' and especially 'career,' to
express the uniquely temporal nature of what he called "natural histories,"
which are the subject matter of the historical sciences.

Woodbridge calls progressive or temporal natures "careers." Since a
thing's career requires "time" for its realization, the thing's cooperation with
its environment is progressive—requiring many cooperations at various
stages in its development with a changing environment. The goal of the historical sciences is to discover Nature's careers.

> Facts march on in time, but not all at the same speed or with the same endur-
> ance; they help or impede one another's movement; . . . their careers overlap
> and interfere; so that the result is a failure for some and success for others. The
> march is their history.
>
> . . . The seeds which we buy and sow in the spring are not simply so many
> ounces of chemical substances. They are also so many possible histories or
> careers in time, so many days of growth, so much promise of fruit or flower.
> Each seed has its own peculiar history with its own peculiar career. The seeds
> are planted. Then in the course of time, soil and moisture and atmosphere and
> food operate in unequal ways in the development of each career. Each is fur-
> thered or hindered as events fall out. Some careers are cut short, others
> prosper. Everywhere there is selection. Everywhere there is adaptation of
> means to ends. The history of the garden can be written because there is a
> history there to write.[62]

The historical possibilities of any stage of a developing career are evident only when realized at a later stage. Like other kinds of activities, therefore, natural histories display the "converging of means upon a specific
end," what Woodbridge calls "purpose."[64] Moreover, the ends of natural
histories are not as such effective, means alone are effective; therefore, the
purposes of natural histories are what he calls "natural teleology."[65]

> It seems clear, therefore, that there is purpose in history. But "purpose" is a
> troublesome word. It connotes design, intention, foresight, as well as *the con-
> verging of means upon a specific end*. Only in the latter sense is it here used. . . .
> [Italics mine][66]

Although many natural careers have definite beginnings and endings, in
other instances, just when a career seems to have been fulfilled and to have

become a finished part of the past, some turn of events shows its further development. And since a career's end clarifies its means, each additional development of a career enables the historian to better understand it. Human histories in particular defy completion of their careers. The historians of human history, therefore, must continually write new histories. Although an accurate "record" or chronicle of past events need not change— for past events as such do not change—Woodbridge believes that the "historical understanding" of careers can continue to grow so long as the careers in which events participate continue to develop.

The accuracy of the record is not the truth of history. We are well assured, for instance, that the Greeks defeated the Persians at the battle of Marathon in 490 B.C. The record on that point is not seriously questionable. . . .

. . . From the accessible records of the battle of Marathon we can understand with tolerable success the immediate antecedents and consequences of that great event. But in calling the event great we do not simply eulogize its participants. We indicate, rather, that its antecedents and consequents have been far-reaching and momentous. Greece, we say, was saved. But what are we to understand by that salvation? To answer we must write and rewrite her own history, the history of what she has been and is; and with every fresh writing the battle of Marathon becomes better understood. It becomes a different battle with a different truth.[67]

Moreover, a career can develop beyond the stage where either itself or its effects *produce* consequences, for even after its effects become a part of the inactive past, they remain as materials which influence, rather than produce additional uses.[68] For example, the work of an historian is itself an historical fact that, through his use of historical material, is under the material's influence. His writing, therefore, is itself a further development in the career he studies. Accordingly, Woodbridge claims that the truth of historical understanding, especially of human careers, is a progressive truth; it is different for different ages in the development of a career.[69] Since Nature is dynamic and her processes display natural teleology, Nature requires the historian to write new histories in order to gain historical understanding of her careers.[70]

We discover history backward, but write it forward, and properly so, because Nature's teleology is thereby illuminated and the causes of past events are better understood. . . .[71]

According to Woodbridge, the "means" that cooperate in the development of natural careers are not all equally effective; they contribute in different ways. And since natural histories are purposeful, the different contributions of means can be discovered by following the lead of the activities they produce; that is, given the different uses of means, they appear to have been "selected" for different roles in the production of activities. As a general quality of natural histories, "selection" is not intentional.

> The things that have happened have not all contributed to these results in the same measure. Some have contributed more, some less. . . . This appears to be true generally. Every history is a particular career in the development of which some facts, persons, and events have been more significant than others so that the termination of the career at any time is like an end that has been reached or a consequence to which its antecedents are peculiarly appropriate. That is the sense in which history is purposeful and selective.[72]

Since natural histories are not only purposeful but also selective, Nature places the historical scientist under the necessity of discovering the different contributions of her means and past materials in order to acquire either scientific knowledge or historical understanding.

> Selection is, consequently, not a device which the historian has invented; it is imposed upon him by his own purpose to preserve the memory and promote the understanding of what has happened. The procedure of the historian is not arbitrary, but necessary. It is imposed upon him by the character of the facts with which he deals.[73]

Woodbridge believes that natural histories are "selective" not only in the different contributions of means to careers but also in that not all things are relevant to a particular career. The latter implies, according to Woodbridge, a pluralism of natural histories.[74] While "pluralism" is a general trait of Nature, it is especially characteristic of the variety of human histories.

> Always there is a particular career and particular incidents appropriate to it. Any career may be as comprehensive as desired, but the more inclusive it is the more restricted it becomes. The history of Milton contains details which the history of English literature will omit; and the history of the cosmos shrinks to nothing when we try to write it. . . .
> There are thus many histories . . . distinguished from one another by the incidence of choice or emphasis.[75]

In addition, Woodbridge claims that a philosophical implication of "pluralism" is that "to no one history can absolute superiority or preference be assigned."[76]

There is no considering of history absolutely at all. For history is just the denial of absolute considerations. It is the affirmation of relative considerations, of considerations which are relative to a selected career. There is no other kind of history possible.[77]

Those who attempt to understand Nature through the organization of all her events around either a cosmically significant event, for example, through ascribing universal significance to the birth of Jesus, or a cosmic goal, such as the evolution of Absolute Mind, or even a cosmic past, which determines all subsequent history, are engaged in theoretical reductions of Nature's rich pluralism of different histories to just one preferred kind of history (e.g., religious, idealistic, or materialistic). Evolutionary theories that either moralize natural history (e.g., the theories of Bergson and Alexander), or interpret human moral interests as a nonefficacious epiphenomenon (e.g., Spencer), are also instances of this reductionism.[78] While the inquirer must avoid anthropomorphic science, he must also reject the equally reductive and one-sided views of Nature that deprive man of qualities distinctive of human histories.

If no history can claim preëminence over any other, it is true also that none can be robbed by any other of its own distinction and character. . . .

Yet men have been prone to write their own history as if it were something else than a human enterprise, as if it were something else than the history of humanity. Those who seek to read their destiny from the constellations ascendent at their birth are generally called superstitious; but those who seek to read it from the constitution of matter, or from the mechanism of the physical world, or from the composition of chemical substances, although no less superstitious, are too frequently called scientists. But "dust thou art and unto dust thou shall return" is an essential truth only about the history of dust; it is only an incidental truth about the history of man. One learns nothing peculiarly characteristic of humanity from it. It affords no measure of the appreciation of poetry, of the constitution of a state, or of the passion for happiness.[79]

According to Woodbridge, respect for the differences in careers, especially the uniqueness of man's supernatural dimension, is essential to the historian's proper functioning.

Historical Continuity and Evolution

In addition to natural teleology, selection, and pluralism, another general trait of natural histories that is important for an historian's adequate performance is Nature's historical "continuity." Activities conform to the structural limitations, or possibilities, already present in the context of their occurrence; therefore, the structural possibilities established by present activities, whether similar or different, are nonetheless *continuous with* previous ones. According to Woodbridge, therefore, natural histories display the quality of "continuity."

> Things with histories . . . are not now what they will be, but what they will be is always continuous with what they are, so that we must think of them stretched out, so to speak, in time as well as in space. . . . The results reached at any time are such as complete those which have gone before. . . .[80]

> The continuity of history is the continuity of the results of the conversion of the possible into the actual. . . . It comprises all that has been accomplished . . . and existing for continued modification or use. As such, it has its own structure, its own uniformities, and its own laws. To them every modification made is subject. That is why everything "connects on from what lies at hand," and why everything we do . . . points backward to what our ancestors have done.[81]

However novel an activity, it conforms to and, therefore, is continuous with the already present structural possibilities of its context. Accordingly, although careers often have definite beginnings, they are continuous with the past nonetheless. Woodbridge, therefore, defines the nature of continuity as "the possibility of precise and definite distinctions."[82] While careers can be analyzed without going further into the past than their beginnings, since Natures' processes are continuous, these beginnings are never absolute; the historian can always go further into the past in search of additional structural possibilities to which subsequent events have conformed. Earlier the difficulty of *finally ending* the history of careers was noted; now Woodbridge acknowledges his belief that they cannot be *absolutely begun*. For example,

> we may begin the history of philosophy with the Greeks, with Thales of Miletus, but the question has been repeatedly asked, Was not Thales a Semite? Did he not derive his ideas from Egypt and Babylonia? And whence came philosophy itself? Was it not the offspring of religion which preceded it, so that, before we begin its history, we must pass, as Professor Cornford suggests, from religion to philosophy? Then what of religion itself? What were its antecedents and whence was its descent? So the questions multiply. . . . History, being continuous, has neither beginning nor end.[83]

The fact that histories are continuous is an additional reason for the rejection of philosophies that attempt to give history a universal meaning on the basis of either a cosmically significant origin or climax. "There is not an absolute first or last in history taken as a whole. . . ."[84]

Having defined 'evolution' to be only "historical continuity,"[85] Woodbridge raises the important question of what the continuity or evolution of history can explain.

> What have been the antecedents of any given fact? These antecedents the continuity of history explains in that it makes them clear. It may also make clear what the consequences of a given fact have been or may be. But this explanatory value is a derivative of the preceding or an enlargement of it, through our habit of looking at consequences as derived from their antecedents, and of basing our expectations of what may happen upon our observations of what has happened. Further explanatory value in the continuity of history it seems difficult to find. . . .[86]

Although limited, the explanatory value of continuity is considerable. Given the fact of historical continuity, activities frequently realize structures that are similar to previously realized structural possibilities; therefore, the past indicates the natures of future activities.

> Finished events, finished sequences of events, the past—there is the source of understanding events and of instruction for the future. An unfinished event, an unfinished sequence of events, leaves us helpless. We must have the past as a period ended in some way or other if we are to have events in changeless character with their interdependence fixed. Not until a man is dead can the tale of his life be written.[87]

Nature's continuities, therefore, "beget the vision of an ordered world and help to frame rules which are applicable in the control of nature."[88]

The continuity or evolution of history does not explain *the origin* of an historical career. For, according to Woodbridge's theory of time, the past is inert; only present individuals possessing appropriate frames and agency produce activities; the present alone is active and productive. If, therefore, the historical scientist wants to discover the origin of a career, rather than limiting his inquiry to the career's past as if it alone determined the career's occurrence, he must either appeal to the contemporaneous experience of the age he studies or experiment in order to determine how factors cooperated in the career's initiation.

> *To explain the origin of anything . . . we can not trust to the continuity of history alone.* That continuity may carry us back to the beginnings of beliefs and

institutions which have persisted and been transmitted from age to age; it may reveal to us experimental factors which have shaped beliefs and institutions, but which have long since been forgotten; but *it can never, of itself, reveal the experimental origin of any belief or institution whatever. That is, in principle, the limitation by which the explanatory value of historical continuity is restricted.* To understand origins we must appeal to the contemporaneous experience of their own age, or to experimental science. [Italics mine][89]

Woodbridge contends that too often inquirers under the influence of evolutionary theory have not respected the explanatory limitations of continuity. Rather than acknowledge that the present alone is active, their disregard for any principle other than historical continuity or evolution in their study of natural histories showed their metaphysical bias that the past determines all subsequent events.

It was principally the doctrine of evolution or development as set forth by biologists, anthropologists, and historians that made the fact of continuity convincingly apparent and freed philosophy from the necessity of attempting to explain it. . . . The doctrine of evolution thus wrought a real emancipation of the mind.

But this freedom has been often abused. Relieved of the necessity of explaining continuity, philosophers, biologists, historians, and even students of language, literature, and the arts, have been too frequently content to let the fact of continuity do all the explaining that needs to be done. To . . . trace the descent of ideas, institutions, customs, and forms of life, . . . [has] been for many the exclusive and sufficient occupation, to the neglect of experimental science and with the consequent failure to make us very much wiser in our attempts to control the intricate factors of human living. . . . And this . . . has sometimes taken the form of metaphysics. If we wish to know the nature of things or to appraise their worth, we are told to contemplate some primitive cosmic stuff from which everything has been derived.[90]

Given Woodbridge's views regarding continuity and his theory of time, which characterized the past as material for the transformation of the active present, his understanding of the historian's task was radically different from what he believed to be the misconceptions of evolutionists. If the historian seeks to understand past events and careers from the perspective of their significance for his own age, then, in accordance with Woodbridge's theory of time, the historian must show the manner in which the past was used as material by later agents in the production of its current significance. If, however, the historian wants an understanding of past events and careers in the perspective of their time rather than his, then through a disciplined exercise of his imagination, he must seek to display these past events in the temporal status of their original occurrence—*not as past* events that have had a subsequent historical development, *but as present* active transformations of their own past.

> When we speak of history our minds turn naturally to the past. We think of what [for example] men have done. . . . Of course we know that it was all once something quite different. . . . The past we study was once not past at all. It was an active present, alive with vitality, existing for its own sake and not for ours. . . . To recover the past, therefore, involves something more than digging into it. We must try to make history something more than a museum of antiquities with specimens catalogued and arranged upon the walls of memory. We must try to recover its vitality, to make it rise from the dead and live again. We must try to see it, not as the past for us, but as a present for itself, with a past of its own and a future as unknown, as uncertain, as precarious, and as dreamy as our own. . . . [Those] historians who begin their histories somewhere in the past and try to show how the past produced what followed . . . seem to have the queer notion that the past produced the present. . . . *The present produces the past.* . . . There are, for example, no buildings until after they are built. So an historian, if he wants to understand a building, must do more than find an antecedent building. He must find a builder who did something to the building he found, lived in it, made it over, or tore it down and built a new one. . . . *History is not the study of the past made, but the study of it in the making.* [Italics mine][91]

There were some evolutionists, for example, Bergson and to some extent pragmatists like Dewey, who acknowledge the fact that only the present is active but, failing to respect fully Nature's historical continuity, neglect the extent to which the present, though active, must nonetheless conform to the structural possibilities of past materials. For example, over against those whose emphasis on present creativity had fostered a progressive educational philosophy, which encouraged freedom for students from the limitations of traditional academic disciplines, Woodbridge claims that schooling requires in part critical (rather than blind) submission to the traditional if students are to use it as material for the improvement of their intelligence.[92]

> The new education involves a break with the past which, intellectually considered, is as violent and radical as a break could be. The revolution presupposes that our mentality, so to speak, is free; but it is anything but free. It may be free in its spontaneous exercise, but it is not free face to face with the material with which it has to deal. Take geometry, for example. How shall we teach it? Shall we teach it in the tradition of Euclid or in some other way? And, after all, what is geometry? I am quite sure that we must answer that it is a piece of historical intellectuality. There is nothing in the subject-matter with which geometry

deals which forces us to treat that subject-matter as Euclid treated it. His technique is by no means the only technique. It happens, however, to have been the technique on which all later developments have been based. In other words, the mentality represented by geometry is a product of history. It may be acquired without a knowledge of that history, but it has to be acquired if the great contributions to mathematics are to be understood. In this matter we have no intellectual freedom at all. Of course, any boy can see that the angles at the base of an isosceles triangle are equal without having first to cross the *pons asinorum,* but he must cross that bridge if he is to go far on a geometrical journey. . . .

I have used geometry and mathematics as an illustration because they illustrate the point obviously. They make it quite clear that we are not free to introduce into them any kind of mental attitude we choose. Unless we accept the long established attitude we embark on a voyage into waters not yet charted and for ports not yet known. Now, what is true of mathematics is true of well-nigh everything else.[93]

Moreover, Woodbridge believes that evolutionists (e.g., emergent evolutionists like Alexander) who claim that the natural evolution, or continuity, which is generally characteristic of natural histories, displays *natural progress,* are confused regarding the genuine nature of continuity. For Woodbridge, continuity refers to the fact that every event conforms to the structural limitations of its past. Continuity implies, therefore, that every occurrence is under the restraints of natural laws; as continuous, no event is exceptional. While events can become natural goods or bads relative to their use in later occurrences, because of Nature's continuity, all these uses are historically relative. There are, therefore, no *natural* absolute norms relative to which natural goods and bads can be ranked according to better and worse; Nature provides no standards of "progress."[94]

For historical continuity . . . does not of itself disclose progress or any standard by which progress may be estimated. It teaches no lesson in morals. . . . And the reason for this is simple. History is continuous, and, therefore, there is no point, no date, no occurrence, no incident, no origin, no belief, and no institution, which can claim preëminence simply on account of its position. If men were once superstitious because of their place in history and are now scientific for precisely the same reason, we can not therefore conclude, with any intelligent or rational certainty, that evolution has progressed from superstition to science, or that science is better than superstition. Values are otherwise determined. The continuity of history levels them all.

Yet there may be laws of history. . . . [S]uch laws would not be indications of progress. They would indicate rather the conditions under which progress is or can be made. For laws are expressions of the limitations under which things may be done. They show the forms and structures to which actions conform. But whether these actions are good or bad, upward or downward, progressive or retrogressive, they do not show. For decline no less than progress is in conformity with law, and the continuity of history is indifferent to both.[95]

Since there are no natural standards of historical progress, Woodbridge claims that the source of these standards is man's supernatural ideals relative to which he determines his own progress and the progress of other historical careers.

> To improve nature involves the doing of something which nature, left to herself, does not do, and, consequently, that nature herself affords no indication of progress and no measure or standard of it. . . . [Likewise] progress implies some improvement of history, so that to judge that there has been progress is . . . to judge that history has measured up to a standard *applied to it*. . . .
>   Yet . . . man makes moral judgments. . . . Accordingly his history then might reveal both progress and the criterion of it. But it would do so not simply because it is a history, but because it is a history of a certain kind. Man makes progress because he can conceive what progress is, and use that conception as a standard of selection and as a goal to be reached. [Italics mine][96]

Woodbridge's conception of historical continuity implies the same conclusion indicated earlier by his analysis of historical pluralism: realistic respect for the significant differences among historical careers, especially the difference between natural careers and the unique supernatural quality of human careers, is essential to the historian's proper use of his historical subject matters.

Historical Comprehension and the Life of Reason

Because man in his pursuit of happiness seeks to use knowledge of Nature to realize ideals, according to Woodbridge, man has need of a new form of historical "comprehension." In addition to a scientific knowledge of Nature, man needs "histories of human interests" that promote an understanding of the practical consequences of holding alternative values. He gains such an understanding from the discovery of the manner in which events have either frustrated or contributed to the historical realization of the human institutions, beliefs, ideas, customs, and life styles that display past human ideal aspirations. Woodbridge believes that this historical study can promote the "life of reason."[97] For if the human interests to be historically displayed are chosen with care and are accurately displayed, then an understanding of the practical consequences of holding alternative values can encourage a harmony of man's ideal aspirations and his natural situation.

And if this attempted harmony inspires man to attempt to transform Nature so as to perfect without loss his natural situation, then he is living a "life of reason." He has moved from simply living toward an attempt to live well; his life has become an art of living, the perfecting of his natural existence.

> His life is not only a life of nutrition and reproduction, or of pleasures and pains, but a life also of hopes and fears. And when hope and fear are not blind, but enlightened, his life is also a life of reason, for reason is the ability to conceive the ends which clarify the movements toward them.[98]

> His animal enjoyments . . . are idealized and transformed into a vision of what they might be freed from the material grossness which clogs them. Man then begins to conceive ideal love and friendship, and an ideal society. . . . the purpose of his history is . . . to use the materials of the world so that they will be permanently used in the light of the ideal perfection they naturally suggest.[99]

Summary

Since, according to Woodbridge, Nature is a temporal as well as a spatial and logical realm, the metaphysician should provide a theory of time and a philosophy of history.

Woodbridge criticizes philosophers who misrepresent time through its spatialization. For example, whether the past and the future are represented as somehow like co-existent localities to be departed from and arrived at or the past is thought to determine completely the present and the future, conceptual perplexities results. Woodbridge proposes, therefore, that time is more like "a line in the drawing" than "a line already drawn," for, unlike the more spatialized conceptions of "a line already drawn," thinking of time as like "a line in the drawing" illustrates the fact that the present alone is active. According to Woodbridge, however, "a line being drawn" is not a perfect analogy, for it still carries misleading spatial connotations. Therefore, Woodbridge prefers to describe time as the movement from the possible to the actual: while the past is the actual and the future is the possible, the present is the "effective transforming of the possible into the actual."

According to Woodbridge, what distinguishes the sciences of historians from other special sciences is that the historical sciences study things that have a "progressive" or temporal nature. Woodbridge distinguishes categories appropriate to the metaphysical analysis of the special historical subject matters of historians, that is, "career," "purpose," "selection," "pluralism," and "historical continuity" or "evolution," and uses them to clarify the historian's activity and to criticize other interpretations of this activity. For example, those who believe that historians can understand Nature through the organization of all her events around either a cosmically significant event, a cosmic goal, or a cosmic past fail to acknowledge "pluralism" as a category, for they reduce Nature's rich historical diversity into just one preferred kind of history. Moreover, neither those who believe that the past determines the present and the future nor those who hold that the present is free from past influences understand the "continuity" of Nature's historical careers; for, given Nature's continuity, the present, though active, must nonetheless conform to the structural possibilities of past materials. The belief that natural progress can be attributed to Nature's historical careers is also inconsistent with historical continuity. More positively, according to Woodbridge, Nature's pluralism shows that respect for career differences is essential to the historian's proper functioning. Along with "natural teleology," Nature's continuity implies that, while Nature's historical careers have beginnings and endings, they are not absolute and, therefore, historians can acquire additional historical understanding of careers by discovering influences before careers began or after they end.

Among the things with a progressive nature, or career, are living things. And since human beings are living beings with progressive natures, historical sciences, such as archaeology and anthropology, are needed to acquire scientific knowledge of human histories. Woodbridge claims, however, that since man is not only a natural being with a natural career but also a supernatural being with the supernatural career of seeking to realize Nature-transcending ideals, the human historical sciences need to be supplemented with nonscientific "histories of human interests" that narrate the drama of man's struggle to transform Nature according to his ideals. Woodbridge holds that recognition of both kinds of historical study would encourage realistic inquiry, for to acknowledge that man's historical career is defined partly by supernatural interests would help him avoid interests that prejudice inquiry.

The following chapter presents Woodbridge's views regarding man's supernaturalness.

NOTES

1. Frederick J. E. Woodbridge, *Nature and Mind: Selected Essays of Frederick J. E. Woodbridge* (New York: Columbia University Press, 1937; reprint ed., New York: Russell and Russell, 1965), pp. 146–147, and *Purpose of History* (New York: Columbia University Press, 1916; reissued, Port Washington, New York: Kennikat Press, 1965), pp. 88–89.

2. Woodbridge, *Purpose of History*, p. 51.

3. According to Sterling P. Lamprecht, "he was a leader, possibly *the* leader, in the movement in the United States in the twentieth century which made the history of philosophy one of the major philosophical disciplines." [Sterling P. Lamprecht, *Our Philosophical Traditions: A Brief History of Philosophy in Western Civilization* (New York: Appleton-Century-Crofts, Inc., 1955), p. 486.]

4. For examples of Woodbridge's influence on Corliss Lamont's thought, see Lamont's *Freedom of Choice Affirmed* (New York: Horizon Press, 1967), pp. 100–1; pp. 124–25.

5. See above, "The Logical Structure of the World," in Chapter 4.

6. Dewey, being more interested in the nature of the vital process of scientific inquiry, or in the psychology of knowing, than in the structure of scientific knowledge, emphasizes the eventfulness of experience rather than its structures. Woodbridge's emphasis on the structure of knowledge, especially its logical structure, when contrasted with Dewey's emphasis could give the impression that Woodbridge does not respect sufficiently the fact of the world's dynamic quality. While there were these different emphases, Woodbridge does respect the genuineness of dynamism. In his science of mind, he emphasizes logical over dynamic structures because he believes that a realistic analysis of his subject matter indicates the logical to be metaphysically distinctive of mind. He believes, moreover, that although the other types of structure could not be reduced into the logical, the logical is discovered to express the intelligibility of the other types.

7. Frederick J. E. Woodbridge, "Contrasts in Education," three lectures given under the provisions of Julius and Rosa Sacks Endowment Fund, Bureau of Publications, Teachers College, Columbia University, 1929, p. 11.

8. Woodbridge, *Nature and Mind*, pp. 292–93.

9. Woodbridge, *Purpose of History*, p. 3.

10. For a more thorough discussion of this point, see above, "From History to Science of Existence," in Chapter 2.

11. Woodbridge, *Nature and Mind*, p. 141.

12. See Woodbridge, *Purpose of History*, p. 49.

13. Ibid., pp. 34–35.

14. Ibid., pp. 36–37.

15. Ibid., p. 37.

16. Ibid., p. 38.

17. Woodbridge, *Nature and Mind*, p. 137.

18. See, for example, Woodbridge, *Purpose of History*, pp. 35–36.

19. Ibid., p. 38.

20. Ibid., p. 39.

21. Frederick J. E. Woodbridge, *An Essay on Nature* (New York: Columbia University Press, 1940), p. 142.

22. Woodbridge, *Purpose of History*, p. 39.

23. This is the meaning of his saying,

> *the* present, being the bracketed unity of all existing whiles, has not an independent while of its own; it is not itself an event. It does not come out of the past and go into the future . . . or from one place to another or from nothing to nothing. Events in their relative duration diversify it, but no event of the kind it displays either starts it or stops it. [Woodbridge, *An Essay on Nature*, p. 142]

24. Woodbridge, *Purpose of History*, p. 39.

25. See, for example, ibid., p. 81.

26. For a discussion of continuity, see "Historical Continuity and Evolution," later in this chapter. Woodbridge says of historical processes: "They are not now

what they will be, but what they will be is always continuous with what they are. . . . (ibid., p. 46).

27. Woodbridge holds a very unusual conception of the nature of "matter." Matter is not some original material that constantly maintains the same qualities, nor is it of itself the so-called "building blocks" of the universe. Rather, matter is the already actualized continuity brought about by the transformations that Nature's processes have so far undergone; it is the stability of structures that the transformations of the past have achieved (Woodbridge, *Purpose of History,* pp. 34 and 82). Matter is the already actualized *inert* structural systems to which all activities now conform.

28. Woodbridge, *Purpose of History,* p. 34.

29. Ibid., p. 32.

30. Ibid., p. 39.

31. Ibid., p. 34.

32. Woodbridge, *Nature and Mind,* p. 125.

33. Woodbridge, *Purpose of History,* p. 39.

34. Ibid.

35. Ibid., p. 40.

36. Woodbridge, *Nature and Mind,* p. 293. For Woodbridge, the fact that Nature's structures are a dimension of her existent individuals did not imply that the category of structure could be reduced to either the category of activity or the category of individuality. These categories maintain their ultimacy.

37. Woodbridge, "Papers, 1884–1940," lectures entitled "Lectures on Metaphysics, Spring, 1928–29," p. 41.

38. Woodbridge, *An Essay on Nature,* p. 140. He says in regard to Nature's events being primary and the distinctions of "past," "present," and "future" being derivative,

it is clear that past, present, and future can not be construed as a one-dimensional framework independent of the events that happen and with which those events are correlative. Bergson's analysis of this matter seems to be decisive. We may and do think of the past in such a framework. We can date and locate events in the past as before or after any given event in the past, but this can be done only after the events have happened, and every event that happens is an addition to the past. The past is, however, the sum of events that have already happened and as such can not have a temporal status like that of events in their happening. The past as conserved is not identical with the historical past but with existence in its dynamic character. Something similar may be said of the future. Sometimes it seems that the best we can do is to say that the past is not and the future is not and only the present is. This seems very much like saying that past and future are consequences of there being anything at all. One thing seems pretty clear, namely that a supposed dividing point between past and future is not the date or locus of any event, but that event makes whatever division there is. [Woodbridge, "Papers, 1884–1940, "Lectures on Metaphysics, Spring, 1928–29," pp. 50–51.]

39. Woodbridge, "Papers, 1884–1940," "Lectures on Metaphysics, Spring, 1928–29," p. 70.

40. Woodbridge, *Purpose of History,* p. 39.

41. Ibid., p. 39.

42. Ibid., p. 40.
43. Woodbridge, *Nature and Mind,* p. 293.
44. Ibid.
45. Woodbridge, *Purpose of History,* p. 40.
46. Ibid., pp. 88-89.
47. For his notion of "career," see, for example, *Purpose of History,* pp. 47 and 49.
48. Woodbridge, *Nature and Mind,* pp. 143-44.
49. Woodbridge, *Purpose of History,* p. 56.
50. In regard to his use of historical "record" and historical "understanding," see, for example, ibid., pp. 18-19.
51. Ibid., p. 57.
52. Ibid., p. 40.
53. Woodbridge, *Nature and Mind,* p. 146.
54. Woodbridge, *Purpose of History,* p. 56.
55. For example, in "Contrasts in Education," Woodbridge says,

> what he does is to make nature an object of inquiry and thereby turn her into the servant of his purposes. He is not content to take nature as he finds her. He insists on making her over. And he justifies doing this by reasons drawn from his own imagination. He makes some sort of a philosophy of life. That is why nature and human life are antithetical. [p. 17]

56. Woodbridge, *Purpose of History,* p. 31.
57. Ibid., pp. 54-57.
58. Henceforth, when I want to refer to Woodbridge's conception of the peculiarly human histories that narrate the drama of man's struggle to transform Nature according to transcendent ideals, I will use the phrase 'histories of human interests.'
59. See, for example, ibid., pp. 18-19.
60. In addition to being intelligible, when the presence within Nature of human careers exhibiting a supernatural dimension is acknowledged, then the conception of Nature *must allow,* even if it *cannot explain,* her own transcendence. For example, Nature must be a realm wherein it would be possible for a being to envisage possibilities. The metaphysical distinction between Nature and the supernatural is not dissolved, however, for while possibilities can function in human experience as ideal standards, or absolutes, as such, they never exist in Nature (see, for example, ibid., pp. 75-79).
61. Ibid., pp. 56-57.
62. Ibid., p. 51.
63. Ibid., pp. 45-56.
64. Ibid., p. 47.
65. For a more thorough discussion of Woodbridge's metaphysical category of "natural teleology," see above, "From Evolution to Natural History" and "Natural Teleology and Mechanism," in Chapters 2 and 3 respectively.
66. Woodbridge, *Purpose of History,* p. 47.
67. Ibid., pp. 18-19.
68. See, for example, ibid., p. 32 and n. 38 above.
69. Woodbridge, *Purpose of History,* pp. 14-18. While the truth of historical understanding is different for different ages in the development of some careers, a

career's history can be written either from the contemporary perspective of its present significance or, by the disciplined exercise of the historian's imagination, from the perspective of any earlier developmental phase, including the period of its origin.

> He may seek to recover the sense, so to speak, of past contemporaneity, transplanting us in imagination to days no longer ours and to ways of feeling and acting no longer presently familiar. Such a history would be less comprehensive and complete than the former [from the perspective of the historian's present]. It would also be more difficult to write, because historical imagination of this kind is rare and also because it is not easy to divest the past of its present estimate. Yet the imagination has that power and enables us to live again in retrospect what others have lived before us. [Ibid., p. 25]

In a review of Woodbridge's, *The Son of Apollo: Themes of Plato* (Boston: Houghton Mifflin Co., 1929), A. E. Taylor accused him of a lack of scholarly care:

> Why Professor Woodbridge could hardly expect to be very successful as an exponent of Plato will be clear to the readers of his introductory chapters on Plato's life and writings. He has not served his apprenticeship to the philological and historical studies without which no one can be competent in the subject. . . . [*Mind: A Quarterly Review of Psychology and Philosophy*, 39 (1930), 252.]

In this review, Professor Taylor was especially critical of what he claimed to be Woodbridge's misrepresentation of the "character of the age in which Plato lived" in that, according to Taylor, he took the dialogues where Socrates is the central figure as indicative of the age of Plato. Taylor concluded that to "forget the difference between the Athens of Socrates and the Athens of Plato would be like forgetting that the France of 1850 was separated from the France of 1750 by the Revolution . . ." (ibid., p. 253). If Woodbridge in *The Son of Apollo* was attempting to offer an accurate account of the life and times of Socrates and Plato from the perspective of *their* age, or to provide the historical data that would allow such an account to be presented, then (provided Professor Taylor is correct regarding the available scholarship) carelessness of the type Professor Taylor has claimed would be inexcusable. I do not believe, however, that this was Woodbridge's intent. Rather, in my opinion, he intended to use Plato in the development of a history of "human interests" and he was concerned with its relevance to contemporary moral concerns. He selected themes (e.g., love, death, and education) that he believed to be of perennial concern in human affairs and looked back from the perspective of his time to the Platonic dialogues for whatever understanding they might contribute to these themes. More precisely, he moved from beliefs and ideals illustrated in the human activities he experienced back to the *Dialogues* in order to clarify, through Plato's *dramatic* presentation of those holding comparable beliefs and ideals, their (fated) consequences in human living. Woodbridge believed Plato to be primarily a great, possibly the greatest, dramatist of the "life of reason"; as such, Plato was a historian of human interests.

Woodbridge understood why "scientific historians" like Taylor had no use for his scholarship; but what he could not understand is why they could not understand his dislike of their scholarship. For Woodbridge, the philosopher, not philosophy, is the primary subject-matter of the history of philosophy; therefore, his histories of philosophy were primarily histories of "human interests." In his classes, for instance, he did not teach the history of philosophy in their sense, but rather, he taught the history of philosophers whom history had kept alive because they still had something of human interest to say. As a student in Berlin (in 1893), he heard Ebbinghaus's lectures. After a thorough exposition of the work of a philosopher, Ebbinghaus would exclaim *"Was will der Mensch?"* (i.e., What is he driving at?). And, according to Woodbridge, Ebbinghaus's manner of presenting the great philosophers made a deep impression on him; so that he tried primarily to tell how and why those philosophers whom history has kept alive have something important to say (Woodbridge, *Nature and Mind,* p. 14).

For a discussion of Woodbridge's philosophy of the history of philosophy and a thorough presentation of his interpretation of Platonic thought, see Kathleen W. Harrington, "Frederick J. E. Woodbridge and The Naturalistic Interpretation of Plato" (Ph.D. dissertation, Emory University, 1971). See "Chapter 2: Woodbridge's Critical Examination of Other Philosophers" in William F. Jones' *F. J. E. Woodbridge's Theory of Man* (Ph.D. dissertation, Tulane University, 1976) for a discussion of Woodbridge's interpretation of Locke, Santayana, Spinoza, and Aristotle. His criticism of Dewey and the other pragmatists is given above in Chapter 5.

70. See Woodbridge, *Purpose of History,* p. 44.

71. Woodbridge, *An Essay on Nature,* p. 44.

72. Woodbridge, *Purpose of History,* pp. 42–43.

73. Ibid., p. 44.

74. For a more detailed presentation of his argument for "pluralism," see above "From History to Science of Existence," in Chapter 2.

75. Woodbridge, *Purpose of History,* pp. 49–50.

76. Ibid., p. 52.

77. Ibid.

78. Woodbridge says of these evolutionary theories in regard to reductive philosophies of education:

> Let it be that evolution has produced us, . . . we are then sent to school. How can we then cherish the faith that evolution is progressively working out our solution? How can we believe that education is growth or that the best system of education is that which removes those artificial restraints which limit the free and natural development of the individual? Is not education precisely something which does restrain and limit? Is not its proper business to convert us from products of evolution into controllers of it? What sense can there be in controlling it if it is itself the norm and guide of our purposes. [Woodbridge, "Contrasts in Education," p. 6]

> She has taken as much pains to produce our natural enemies as to produce ourselves; and if she has given us any advantage over them, it is solely the advantage we acquire by using the discovery of her forces to do battle with them. . . . It is not the forces of nature which have made us what we are, but the discovery and use of those forces. . . . Evolution has given us life; education has given us the kind of life we distinguish as human. [Ibid., p. 8]

79. Woodbridge, *Purpose of History,* pp. 53–54.

80. Ibid., pp. 46–47.

81. Ibid., p. 81.

82. Ibid., p. 65.

83. Ibid., pp. 63–64.

84. Ibid., p. 64.

85. Ibid., p. 4.

86. Ibid., pp. 66–67.

87. Woodbridge, *Purpose of History,* p. 67.

88. Ibid.

89. Ibid., pp. 69–70.

90. Ibid., pp. 71–72.

91. Woodbridge, "Contrasts in Education," pp. 34–35.

92. Although Dewey contributed indirectly to progressive education, it should be noted that Dewey himself was critical of and disavowed connection with what is commonly called 'progressive education.'

93. Woodbridge, "Contrasts in Education," pp. 46–47.

94. See above "The Moral Order," in Chapter 4 for a discussion of Woodbridge's distinction between *natural* goods and bads and *supernatural* moral standards and religious sanctions.

95. Woodbridge, *Purpose of History,* pp. 74–75. He makes it clear that the fact that natural histories have *progressive* natures, or careers, does not *per se* imply "progress." 'Progressive' as applied to *natural* histories means only "temporal."

> The career of things in time . . . is naturally purposeful. To call it progress adds nothing to the meaning of it unless a standard is introduced by which it can be measured. [Ibid., p. 76]

96. Ibid., pp. 76–78.

97. See, for example, ibid., p. 2.

98. Ibid., p. 79.

99. Ibid., pp. 86–87.

7

The Pursuit of Happiness and the "Supernatural"

> The pursuit of happiness leaves Nature, as I have phrased it, in suspense. She loses her self-sufficiency in the human view of her.[1]

> With Aristotle the conception of human life is perfectly sound, for with him everything ideal has a natural basis and everything natural an ideal fulfillment.[2]

Introduction

Woodbridge believes that all dualisms are unwarranted except one, Nature and the supernatural dimension of human living. Moreover, he believes that the fundamental difference between Nature and the supernatural is displayed in many kinds of human activities, but it is especially evident when man raises scientifically unanswerable questions and makes scientifically unverifiable statements. According to Woodbridge, the failure to acknowledge this one genuine dualism has contributed to the unwarranted belief philosophers have in other dualisms, in problematic epistemologies, and in nonrealistic, reductive metaphysics.

This chapter introduces Woodbridge's views regarding the supernatural, his reasons for distinguishing a supernatural realm from Nature, and his criticisms of philosophers who do not make this distinction. In addition, related conceptions, such as Woodbridge's views regarding the human "soul" and personality, moral sensitivities, religious experience, sacred literature, "faith," and the "life of reason," are presented.

163

Pursuit of Happiness

Since Woodbridge is emphatic in his claim that man's scientific activity must be distinguished from his "pursuit of happiness," he uses the terms 'soul' (*psyche*), 'spirit', and 'person' to identify the noncognitive activities or interests of man. Woodbridge emphasizes his belief in these important differences of human living at the end of *The Realm of Mind*:

> [Man] is inquisitive, social, moral, religious, creative. The universe he would have is not ultimately the universe which the metaphysician and others pick to bits and then put together again. He does that picking and putting in order that he may have another universe built upon that which he analyzes. He knows for a purpose. And were his knowledge complete, that purpose would still control his living. He would still go on building out of what he knew a different world to live in. This he does even with his little knowledge and this reveals *his essential nature*. He is easily snuffed out of existence, but *his life is a moral event* in the universe which the chemistry of *his body* and the logic of *his mind* support. And being a moral event, the quality of his life transmutes the uses of matter into something with which they are incomparable. [Italics mine][3]

Man's "moral" quality, which is also emotional, volitional, animating, and actuating, is distinguishable from both his body and his mind.

As a realist, Woodbridge accepted the principle that everything is somehow real. Accordingly, when he discovered men raising scientifically unanswerable questions and making scientifically unverifiable statements, he believed that he must somehow account for the reality of these actions. Man may ask, for example, Why do some men possess bodily health? or Why do some men have cancer? If in asking these questions he wants to know "how" — that is, what factors are sufficient to the possession of health or the having of cancer — then they are in principle answerable through scientific inquiry. If these are not "how" questions but, rather, *expressions* of man's search for answers to the question "why should" factors cooperate and thereby cause, for example, either health or cancer, then the questions are not genuinely scientific; for according to Woodbridge, they are not answerable in terms of Nature's cooperation of individuals.

> Men have persistently asked both questions. Their attempts to answer the first [e.g., Why is there health or cancer in the world?] have been increasingly successful and uniform, while their attempts to answer the second [e.g., Why *should* there be health or cancer in the world?] are no more successful and uniform today than they ever have been. . . . We increasingly discover why [or "how"] there is [health or cancer], but we do not discover at all why there should

be. This latter remains among what we call the riddles of existence. The difference between *is* and *should be,* as here illustrated, is ultimately a difference which is not wiped out by any discovery we make in the realm of the *is*. The *should be* drives us to quite a different realm and always has. Why should we be what we are, and being what we are why should we ask the questions which we ask, in themselves questions which have no discoverable answers like answers to the questions what we are.[4]

According to Woodbridge, the fact that natural science can answer man's "how" questions and cannot answer his "why should" ones indicates that, although Nature presents man with natural goods like bodily health and natural bads like cancer, she shows *no preferences* that would *justify* the existence of either. Moreover, although man's cooperation with the rest of Nature can yield knowledge, Nature does not indicate *why* man *should* seek knowledge; for she neither shows a preference for the pursuit of knowledge over other natural activities nor indicates any preference regarding what knowledge should be used to accomplish. "Nature exhibits no preference for one state of affairs as over against another."[5] Yet man in his "pursuit of happiness" continually seeks justification by raising and attempting to answer "why should" questions. Woodbridge claims that this fact of human experience shows that man is not only natural but also transcends Nature and, thereby, enters the realm of the "supernatural."

There are thus important questions which we ask and nature does not answer. We try to answer them none the less and being debarred from answering them in terms of nature, we turn to something else. Our answers are given in terms of the supernatural, in terms of something which nature neither proves nor disproves. Hereby the supernatural is identified. It can not be found by searching nature through and through. It rises to answer questions which we ask but nature does not answer.[6]

Man as perceiver, inquirer, and knower is a natural being, but in his search for justifying ideals and standards, he displays his supernaturalness.

The Supernatural Roots of Problematic Philosophies

Woodbridge believes that the failure to clearly distinguish scientific knowledge of Nature from the supernatural interests of man's "pursuit of happiness" was in part responsible for the development of problematic epistemologies and nonrealistic, reductive metaphysics. If the distinction is not acknowledged, then Nature's inability to answer the question of why man should seek knowledge would, in effect, encourage epistemologies that imply the erroneous belief in the unreliability or even the impossibility of knowledge. Indeed, Woodbridge claims that epistemologies perform a spiritual rather than a philosophical or scientific function.

> But if we ask what actual service this [epistemological] scrutiny performs, we seem compelled to answer that the service is not logical, but moral and spiritual. It does not modify knowledge. It modifies character. It does not give us new or increased information about our world whereby that world may be more effectively controlled. It gives us rather considerations the contemplation of which is more or less satisfying to the spirit.[7]

Likewise, the epistemologist's questioning of the general reliability of human experience springs from a failure to distinguish questions of justification from the evident fact of man's perception of his environment.

> I am pleading that we do not *deceive ourselves by confusing questions of existence with questions of justification.* Failure to justify the visible world for being what it is, failure to justify why it is that . . . failure to justify all that is wholly irrelevant to an interest in knowledge and in action guided by it. *To make that failure relevant is to be deceived.* Why should the stars be visible? I have never found any explanation of that, nor have I been able to invent one. That the stars are visible is not a matter of belief or disbelief, of certainty or uncertainty. *If I should admit that it is, I should also have to admit that the visibility of anything is in doubt; and that means that I am crying to have visibility justified.* It means that I am crying to be told *why* it *should* happen that with stars in the sky, with light in Nature, and with eyes on the earth, there *should* be astronomy. [Italics mine][8]

Moreover, when man begins to realize that Nature has no preferences and, therefore, that she offers no standards justifying human preferences, then man may seek to avoid this realization either by an unwarranted metaphysical projection of his supernatural ideals upon Nature or by a rejection of the genuineness of the supernatural dimension of human life. Instances of the former are metaphysical theories of preference such as those of the idealists who claim that there is a spiritual science, or those who interpret Nature as a phase in the evolution of the Absolute. Of natural theologians and cosmologists who are guilty of similar projections, Woodbridge says,

> Ideals and values . . . can be viewed as more important—even cosmically—than those processes [of living] themselves. It is thus congenial to spirit to

regard them as cosmological forces which determine existence to be what it is. Here we find the source and motivation of all ideal cosmologies. They are ideal. If they are taken to be true histories of existence in time and space, they become ridiculous and are sources of superstition and the belief in magic. When not thus perverted, spiritual cosmologies may become energizing and directive and transform life into something else than a worldly and mortal career. The spiritual interpretation of existence is not the discovery of the efficient causes of existence, but a revelation of its final causes.[9]

Against those who reject the genuineness of the supernatural dimension of human careers by, for example, a materialistic reduction of human history, Woodbridge says,

Neither astronomy nor geology affords good reasons for putting an end to human reverence and faith. If the stars have not begged man to worship them, he has begged them to be an inspiration to a steadfast purpose. It is in his history, not in theirs, that they have been divine. How stupid of him, therefore, and how traitorous to his own history, if he shames his capacity for reverence, when once has found that the stars have a different history from his own.

The inevitable failure of astronomy and geology to afford man gods suitable for his worship is not a recommendation that he should vigorously embrace the superstitions of his ancestors. . . . The counsel is rather that . . . [human] history can not be wholly resolved into physical processes nor the enterprises of men be construed solely as the by-product of material forces.[10]

Other philosophers, being aware that human life displays a radical distinction of some kind, misinterpreted its nature; they replaced the only genuine dualism, Nature and the supernatural, with unwarranted metaphysical dualisms such as the mind-body dichotomy: according to Woodbridge, "the roots of dualistic philosophies go down deep into the soil of moral struggle, so deep that the food that nourishes them is often forgotten."[11]

Faith and Devotion

My insistence that the natural, or Nature, is the only object of knowledge is not a stubborn clinging to a particular use of a word, but a recognition that the supernatural is something confessed that that the word "faith" suits it better than the word "knowledge." This is both orthodox knowledge and the confession that faith is a force. It is not a force which removes mountains, but one which gives to the pursuit of happiness a character beyond the moral order. The evidences of its power are abundant. . . .

Appeals to the supernatural neither explain nor justify Nature. They may explain a good deal about ourselves and confirm the doctrine that we, not Nature, are justified by faith.[12]

Since Nature constantly places man in situations of having to make choices and, therefore, of having to discriminate between the better and the worse without providing him with standards for evaluation, according to Woodbridge, Nature is a "moral order" and, as such, she provides the basis for her own human, moral or spiritual, transcendence. One response to Nature as a moral order is to attempt to avoid the moral responsibility that Nature places upon mankind through the development of problematic epistemologies or reductive and dualistic metaphysical theories. Another response is "faith" — to acknowledge the distinction between knowledge of Nature and the supernatural pursuit of happiness and to accept the responsibility for having to choose an ideal that will justify the search for knowledge to use in the pursuit of the happiness of realizing that ideal; therefore, according to Woodbridge, the life of faith is a life of commitment or devotion.

A devoted life, no matter to what it is devoted, only let it be deliberately devoted . . . is one that has, provisionally at least, solved the riddle of existence by flying to the supernatural. . . . Rob human life of the supernatural, of propositions which can not be understood or proved by natural logic or in nature's terms and you rob it of the thing which is most characteristic of it. . . . So long as the natural is grasped in the realm of knowledge, the supernatural will emerge in the realm of belief.[13]

Man has the capacity to establish through acts of commitment or devotion ideals and values that function for him in practical contexts as *absolute* standards. And since Nature is her spatial, temporal, and logical *relativity* of mutually conditioned and conditioning individuals, man's holding of *absolutes* shows his *super*naturalness or soul. Although man as body and as mind is a natural being, as a committed or devoted being, he is supernatural.

Although when we consider our genesis we find ourselves illustrating nature's orders, when we consider the quality of human life we find we are not illustrating it at all. It will not do to say that the quality of [human] life is as natural as anything else about it for that is to obliterate by words the precise distinction which the quality of life makes.[14]

Man's "soul" is his power to establish and to respond to ideal standards in light of which he justifies his life, judges his own worth and the worth of the rest of Nature, and is inspired to artistic transformation of himself and his world. Human beings are, therefore,

> creatures whose lot in life should be constantly to reach beyond themselves in order to live at all, whose whole existence should be a world-transformation and a self-transformation in the interest of what they would have prevail, who, while they must draw the materials of their work from what they could discover of Nature's constitution and their own, must none the less draw life's inspiration and motives, must get the mainspring of their activity and progress, not from what they are, but from what they might be. . . .[15]

In the context of his metaphysical science of mind, Woodbridge accounts for the individualization of mind in terms of what he calls the "insistence of bodily perspective";[16] and this explanation is an example of his belief that, in so far as science can explain the individuality of human existence, it does so in terms of the human body functioning within the context of Nature. Now, he acknowledges another, though nonscientific, principle for man's individualization as a personality or character: the human "soul."

> It is common to entertain the conviction that one has a soul, the possession of which distinguishes him from others by giving him his peculiar individuality. . . .
> . . . To be a person is to use the materials and machinery of life in the service of ideals.[17]

Accordingly, as a personality or character, man is, to a significant degree, what he holds to be of value; and personalities and characters differ primarily because human beings differ in their ideals.

During the process of realizing his soul's commitments, man appropriates many resources to the accomplishment of his values; and yet, since he knows that Nature shows no preferences, he must acknowledge that he has no more of an absolute claim to the use of materials when realizing his career than does any other career, whether human or not.[18] Given his need to justify this selfishness to himself and to others, he may be taken over by the values he had possessed; thereby, these ideal standards become his spiritual justification. Woodbridge believes that religious experience and activity give evidence of man's search for justification: "he knows religion. For his world . . . is, in spite of his property in it, a borrowed world, calling for payment, dust to dust or spirit to spirit."[19]

> [Human] beings find no permanent peace until they should commit themselves freely and wholly in complete self-surrender, to what their ideals reveal them to

be. . . . It is the truth of [human] experience, and in that truth our personality is disclosed.[20]

We want to be justified ultimately, not to Nature or even in our own eyes, but in the eyes of one to whom we might pray, "Thy will be done," and who might say in judgment, were speech possible, "Well done! Good and faithful servant." There the supernatural is acknowledged.[21]

Sacred Literature

The pursuit of happiness leaves Nature . . . in suspense. . . . But how shall that in which she is suspended be expressed when it is not available to the pursuit of knowledge? The expression is found in sacred literature. The embarrassment of that literature is its language, for that is the same as the secular. But it has an intonation of its own, whereby in religious doctrine the ultimate categories developed in the pursuit of knowledge are transmuted into categories of the divine.[22]

Woodbridge believes that the acknowledgment of man's supernaturalness encourages not only a more complete appreciation of the richness of language but also a clearer understanding as to the nature of its different uses. For, in addition to the communicative or informative function, there are the expressive and directive linguistic activities. Statements expressing man's supernaturalness are not claims in the sense that they have truth value, for any genuine claim can in principle be verified experimentally. How, for example, would the scientist approach the experimental verification of "The wages of sin are death"? According to Woodbridge, such a statement is not a scientific judgment regarding "how" the human organism dies, but rather the *expression* of the author's *devotion* to certain values, or his *directing* that others accept these ideals—an indication of his *faith* that these values will finally satisfy man's concern regarding "Why *should* man die?" It is the expression of man's commitment to judgments that *justifies* rather than explains life and death.

Such statements do not assert claims; according to Woodbridge, they express the *super*natural. Although human beings may use supernatural terms that appear to refer to Nature, this use of language cannot be taken literally without getting involved in confusion. Here language is used mythically.

We may now say that nature leads men to ask questions which are meaningless in terms of nature, but which they answer by constructing a supernatural world which in its turn borrows its terms from the natural. This makes the language of the supernatural logically a different sort of language from the language of the natural. In the latter language our propositions may intelligibly be said to be true or false, but in the former language this can not be said. If we ask in the language of nature what becomes of an individual after death we know precisely what we mean and where to look for an answer. All answers in terms of nature we can test as to their truth or falsity, for we can tell whether they answer the question or not. But ask the same question in the language of the supernatural—what does the question itself mean? What is "after death" if "after death" is not in the natural order. . . . Before and after are terms intelligible in the natural order but what intelligibility have they outside that order? . . . Strictly speaking, then, it would seem that propositions in the language of the supernatural are neither intelligibly true nor intelligibly false. The attempt to bring them under these categories renders them meaningless. . . .

. . . Ask him [the devotee] to formulate his belief and he must do so in terms borrowed from nature and by means of such terms he can be readily confounded. Then his only answer is: "In Thee have I trusted, let me never be confounded."[23]

[Moreover, it] . . . seems clear . . . that the effect produced by propositions in the language of the supernatural is not primarily a logical effect. . . . When Emerson exclaims "O my brother, God exists," the immediate effect on the reader is not likely to be curiosity as to whether God exists or not, but rather surprise, astonishment, confidence, hope, joy, fear, despair. Propositions in the language of the supernatural do something to those who utter or hear them quite different from awakening in them intellectual curiosity. They tend even to forbid such curiosity or to suppress it. They often make the plea to put all logical considerations aside, Only believe! But believe what? Believe that which by all the canons of natural logic and in all the terms of natural knowledge is quite unintelligible. . . .[24]

Although statements expressing the supernatural do not make claims whose truth value is contingent on existent fact, nonetheless, statements of faith can express what Woodbridge describes as "truths still in the making."[25] That is, if a statement of commitment or devotion is expressed by a person attempting to realize that ideal in existence, then his statement concerns a state of affairs that, as ideal, does not exist, but, as a possibility, may in the future become partially realized in existent fact; therefore, it is a "truth still in the making." More generally, while Nature-supernatural is a genuine metaphysical dualism, Woodbridge believes that this dichotomy is partially overcome through the faithful attempting to realize their ideals in Nature.

Now it is clear that the existence of the strength of the plank . . . remains the same whether anyone believes in it or not. Continual peace can exist at all only if we believe in it and act on our belief. Faith is thus much more than a matter of truth and falsity. It is a genuinely constructive process, entering, by our accepting it and acting upon it, into the structure of things, shaping them in some measure to be congenial to our desires and aspirations. . . . Faith is not only the substance of things hoped for; it is also an instrument for their attainment.

. . . It should not lead them [i.e., philosophers] to neglect the study and disinterested search for truths already made, but it should teach them to avoid the confusion attending the supposition that the personal consequences of faith prove the existence of faith's objects; and, what is more, it should teach them not to think of truths still in the making in terms of present truth or falsity, or to think lightly of those faiths whose significance is not to be true or false, but to be attained and sustaining possessions in the life of man.

Faith is thus a fact which testifies to the unfinished character of man's world and to the sense in which that character is unfinished. As just material, we may say that the world is never more or less; its properties and relations may be unchanged forever; it is a domain where fixed laws rule, and where care, concern, and desire find no place. But as a possibility and a promise it is a world with a future, a world of outlook and of prospect, of truths to be made and beliefs to be realized. It is an object of knowledge for those who would find out its structure. It is an enterprise of faith for those who would live its possibilities. . . .[26]

Nature, Society, and Social Institutions

In and of itself, the experience of natural goods or evils is not an exercise of man's soul until he is aware of the possibility of controlling either his desires (i.e., exercising prudence regarding their gratification) or his environment in a manner allowing satisfaction of these desires. For in such cases, he becomes aware of his freedom of choice in his selection of natural goods and evils; and such choices require that he hold an ideal standard relative to which goods and evils can be rank ordered along a scale from better to worse. Woodbridge holds, therefore, that man participates in the supernatural to the extent that he is aware of his freedom and the nature of his freedom.[27] In his behavior, man is not free to disobey Nature's laws. When he recognizes his supernaturalness, however, he is capable (with sufficient knowledge of these laws) to realize to some extent his ideals in Nature.

Here, I must think, is where we discover what freedom is. Nature relentlessly pursued seems to carry us at last to the recognition that, in reflection at least, our ultimate attitude is never by nature determined. The world we would have becomes ultimately the world of our choosing and our choice is made at our peril.[28]

To be free is not to be free from nature's order, but to act with the recognition that that order, while exhibiting no preference, is material for the exercise of preference. In short, freedom is deliberate choice, choice with an understanding of what choice ultimately is. It is action in view of the contingency of all existence.[29]

In relation to Nature, man is free to establish any ideal standard; however, according to Woodbridge, the choice of one ideal excludes other possible ideals. In choosing to attempt to realize an ideal, a man denies himself and, to some extent, others the opportunity to realize alternative ideals; his choices limit subsequent choices and, in so doing, limits are placed upon freedom of choice for everyone. Furthermore, since the relative value of natural goods and evils varies with the establishment of different ideal standards, the choice of an ideal determines which of several natural goods or evils is to be pursued or avoided to the exclusion of others. The only justification a man has for his preferences and their effect on himself and others is the ideals to which he is committed or devoted.

Nature never interferes with the operation of her own forces. She lets them run their own course inevitably to their own end no matter what happens. It is we who interfere—a part of nature, if you will, interfering with the rest of nature, but so interfering that responsibility is lodged wholly with the part for weal or woe. . . . It is we, not nature, who are discontented with what nature is, who insist on improving her and on interfering with the natural conditions of our existence. Our improvements result in limitations on our freedom. They put us under new restraints and obligations which we have to defend to one another. They create a state of things which increasingly robs each new child of the freedom it might claim as a child of nature. . . . There is profound truth in Rousseau's remark that man was born free, but is now everywhere in chains. They are, however, chains of his own forging. It is useless to cry: "Back to nature!" For nature is precisely the thing with which man is everlastingly discontented. He either prefers the chains of society or, when he breaks them forges new ones in their stead. Thus it is that by improving on nature we find ourselves under increasing responsibility for the kind of world into which we let new beings be born.[30]

Woodbridge thus recognizes that the social context plays a role in man's discoveries and in his exercise of the pursuit of happiness. Unlike Dewey and other naturalists, however, Woodbridge does not present an analysis of the social realm in order to discover what social factors, if any, condition the emergence of values or ideals. Accordingly, it is difficult to determine what he believes regarding the social aspects of the pursuit of happiness. Evidently, however, he does not believe that society is the basis for man's supernaturalness:

A precise definition [of morality] is never discovered by comparing the shifting laws, customs, rules of conduct, or religions which diversify mankind into alien groups the world over. These are what they are, instruments of administration and control or of edification and spirituality. They are brought to bear on the

moral situation in the interest of regulating or sanctifying it. But the moral situation is there first. . . . To be obliged to accept events, to work with them and
adjust them in order to live well, and to do this without being compelled to
accept a theory of their meaning and value, is something very real and very concrete, and something very different from having shifting opinions and beliefs,
or living up to a code or worshipping a god. It is this compulsion which makes
men make morals and which makes them religious. It is not the other way
around, as if this compulsion were the product of legislative authority or priestly
craft. Human history can not be adequately read in that fashion, for it is the
initial compulsion to morality in us all that gives the king and priest their
power.[31]

Even though Woodbridge did not engage in analysis of the social realm,
he believes that man comes to recognize himself as soul from within his
social setting. From his society and, especially, its institutions, man learns
of moral and religious possibilities.

And so I say that when we ask, How have the possibilities of man been made
available for his use in life? we get the answer, Through the moral ideals and
religious aspirations and beliefs of the race.[32]

Society preserves the memory of concrete examples of the possibilities for
human commitment or devotion in the form of traditional heroes and saints.

These persons are great, simply because they have actually shown to us . . .
what our moral possibilities are. For no other reason are they great. . . . To my
mind, it has not been the doctrine of the nature of Jesus of Nazareth, or of His
origin, that has succeeded in winning men to His side, but the fact that men
have seen revealed in Him, in a genuine human experience, what their moral
and spiritual possibilities are.[33]

As man discovers some of his possibilities for devotion, according to
Woodbridge, he must not overlook the distinction between his freedom to
choose ideal commitments and his lack of freedom to choose whether or not
he will conform to Nature's order. The supernatural, as it is being made
available through society and its moral and religious institutions, and the
natural, as it is being made available through science, must be distinguished.

How has it [the supernatural] been made available? The answer is, in the moral,
ideal, and religious aspirations and beliefs of the race. We read in their history

how man's possibilities have been revealed to him, how he has been inspired and helped toward their attainment. In such a ministry morality and religion have found their proper function. When they have been true to it, they have won men as their friends. Only when they have been false to it have they turned men into their enemies. And they are false to it when they set themselves up as explanations of the origin of things, or to formulate the laws of natural events. Lightning and tempest, plague, pestilence, and famine have indeed a moral significance for us and for our attitude toward life, but when we attempt to explain their occurrence through moral and religious causes, we do not only fail, but also subject morality and religion to ridicule and attack.[34]

Furthermore, unless the distinction between natural science and the supernatural interests of man's pursuit of happiness is maintained, scientific inquiry is liable to be biased and, therefore, science will not yield the reliable knowledge of Nature needed for the struggle to realize ideals in the world.

Inspiration and faith are nothing without knowledge. I may have the purest and loftiest purpose, but unless I am in some degree master of the machinery by which that purpose can be realized, I might as well not be inspired. On the other hand, if I have all knowledge and have not charity, I am nothing.[35]

Although man discovers ideal possibilities through society, Woodbridge does not believe that society determines the values to which the individual finally commits himself. Discovering within his society a range of possibilities, man can become aware of his freedom of choice and exercise it even by establishing a standard critical of his society.

The world may praise or blame him for what he does, but he knows that neither nature nor God ever will. . . . How he has lived is a matter of historical record. How he should live, rests with him. He will not expect either nature or God to tell him. He will look wearily at the advice of his fellows.[36]

The Life of Reason

Since every object of devotion is absolute within human experience, none as such is more worthy than any other. Yet Nature determines what results when man's ideal preferences are expressed in action. Since Nature's response can be captured in the suffering caused by natural evils or the enjoyment brought about by natural goods, although Nature does not determine man's commitments, she provides some guidance to him in his selection of ideals: "the world we would have becomes ultimately the world of our choosing and *our choice is made at our peril*" (italics mine).[37]

> She may suggest, as it were, ideals to the pursuer of happiness, because he finds her a moral order with pains and penalities interlocked, with the consequences of deeds overtaking the doer of them, . . . but she does not exhibit any preference for human life.[38]

Nature's response suggests that if man is prudent in his pursuit of happiness, he will establish ideals the pursuit of which will enable him to perform his natural functions with greater effectiveness and efficiency. But Woodbridge believes that, although natural prudence must somehow be included in any practical, viable ideal, it is never ultimately satisfying as the object of commitment or devotion. For even when man has secured himself against many natural evils and liberally acquired natural goods, he longs for something more that would perfect his life. Especially, he has the need to justify his pursuit of happiness.

> Material prosperity is provisional. To be well-housed, well-fed, well-clothed, and even to have friends and the opportunity for unlimited amusement, these things have never been permanently regarded as defining human happiness to the full. Having these things man is still curious to know what he will do. Material progress indicates mastery of the necessities of his existence in order that he may then be free to act. If no free act follows upon such mastery, life loses its savor, and pleasures grow stale. Material progress would thus seem to be a preliminary to living well, but would not be living well itself. . . .
>   . . . He begins then to wonder for what purpose and by what right his possessive attitude is warranted; for unless he suppresses his reflections or yields himself thoughtlessly to his instincts and emotions, he can not fail to observe that things are no more rightfully his than another's, and that to belong rightfully to any one there must be some warrant drawn from a world with which his soul could be congenial. . . . Reflection thus gives birth to a new kind of life. . . .[39]

Man's pursuit of happiness, therefore, becomes a life of faith. But what shall be the nature of this faith and the nature of its object of devotion? For Woodbridge, a paraphrase by Santayana of Aristotle acted as a catalyzing agent in bringing faith into focus: " 'Everything ideal has a natural basis and everything natural an ideal fulfillment'. . . ."[40] Woodbridge's conviction is that if man pursues happiness not only responsibly but also intelligently, then his pursuit will flower into a devotion to the "life of reason." Having learned the lesson of natural prudence, that is, that any workable ideal must be responsive to man's natural situation, the pursuer of the life of reason uses the content of his natural situation *as the material* for his quest—for example, his animal impulses and needs, his natural capacities, and his existing context of human relationships, such as social customs and institutions. Drawing upon Santayana's statement that "everything ideal has a natural basis," Woodbridge writes,

> In that one sentence . . . I found an acceptable standard of criticism, for it seemed to me that ideals are significant as they round out and complete some natural function.[41]

But the response given by the life of reason to man's natural situation essentially cannot be a prudence of any kind, whether hedonistic or utilitarian, for the pursuer of a life of reason has also learned the lesson of the emptiness of material progress as an ultimate justification for human effort. Woodbridge believes, therefore, that the object of devotion designed to sustain and justify man's attempt to remove conflicts and difficulties from the natural materials of his situation will be his vision of the harmonious perfection of human nature.[42]

> One of the major tasks of philosophy . . . [is] to exhibit the passage from the natural to the ideal; from common sense to reason; from animal love to ideal love; from gregarious association to free society; from practice and invention to liberal art; from mythology to enlightened religion, and from crude cosmologies to that impersonal objectivity found in science.[43]

Faith in the "life of reason" is, therefore, the pursuit of the realization in the world of the perfection of human nature—man and his natural and communal situation.[44] It is a faith that nurtures and, in turn, is nurtured by the hope expressed by Santayana: "everything natural has an ideal fulfillment."[45] Originally, in light of man's pursuit of happiness, Nature had shown her insufficiency. Now, however, man's hope in Nature's perfectibility and his faith that his pursuit of her perfection is his ultimate justification have given him another vision of Nature—a vision that inspires charity, or respect and care, towards man's natural and communal sources.[46] If man attains this charitable vision of his natural sources to the extent that his respect for, and care of, Nature is sufficient for him to transcend the distortions of his soul's personal preferences in his view of Nature, then man attains, however fleetingly, a vision of Nature like that of the Divine. Woodbridge calls this undistorted intellectual vision of Nature, "theory" (*theoria*).[47] Drawing upon the Greek etymology of "theory" in its cognate "theater," he says,

[For a Greek like Aristotle] a spectator at a play and the spectator of existence were kinsmen in attitude. Detached from what they beheld, they had a clearer and more comprehensive view of it than would be possible otherwise. Could a man see the spectacle of existence as he sees a play in a theater, he might understand what existence is, get the gist of it and in the moment of that beholding be like a god who sees the world wag, but keeps himself aloof.[48]

If a man could so control his living that he rises to those moments when his life can be viewed as a spectacle, and yet viewed with that freedom or purification which the theater can reveal, he would have controlled his life well. He would be a wise man, a philosopher. To get such moments is the supreme aim of human life. . . .[49]

For Woodbridge, the fulfillment of the faith and hope of the life of reason is a divinely charitable and, therefore, an undistorted intellectual vision of Nature, that is, a "natural piety" or a love "of the sources of one's being."[50] But, for man, this charity is not just a vision but also an inspiration to attempt artistically to realize in the world the perfections that the vision suggests.[51] Given his participation in the world and all the practical limitations this inevitably includes, man, unlike God, is not able continually to maintain this vision.[52] To the extent that man is able to practice this charitable vision, however, he is wise and his arts attempt to realize the perfections *appropriate to his natural materials*—both himself and his natural and communal situation—rather than exploiting Nature and manipulating himself and others for narrowly selfish interests.

[Men] can get on without the vision . . . , but it is unlikely that they will get on as well. Men may know how to run a city *as they want to, but they run it better if they understand what a city is.* Men can not help knowing nature because, like plants and animals, they live with it the whole course of their lives, but *they may* live better if they understand what nature is. [Italics mine][53]

[Philosophy] should be taught inspired by an ideal of human life which, like a vision, will reveal that labor, business, and education are good, because through them man comes nearer to what he calls divine. *And to be divine is not to conquer other men or even nature. It is to honor both.* [Italics mine][54]

Woodbridge says, therefore, of the life of reason:

History is . . . not only the conserving, the remembering, and the understanding of what has happened: it is also the completing of what has happened. And since in man history is consciously lived, the completing of what has happened is also the attempt to carry it to what he calls perfection. He looks at a wilderness, but, even as he looks, beholds a garden. For him, consequently, the purpose of history is not a secret he vainly tries to find, but a kind of life his reason enables him to live. As he lives it well, the fragments of existence are completed and illumined in the visions they reveal.[55]

Natural Science and the Supernatural Vision

Although the metaphysician must acknowledge the distinction between Nature and the supernatural, as a natural scientist, he cannot offer any explication of the supernatural dimension of human life. Moreover, the life-transforming vision of the life of reason, although intellectual, is not a scientific vision. For it is comprehensive and synthetic; whereas, according to Woodbridge, the subject matter of every science, even metaphysics, is specific and its method analytic. Yet, while the metaphysician is a scientist, he is also a human being and a philosopher; therefore, in addition to scientific knowledge, he seeks this vision ultimately to satisfy his pursuit of happiness. And, to the extent that he can attain it, Woodbridge believes that man will wisely be able to put into practice what he has learned from science in the service of Nature and mankind.

Mankind will have a new world. Its will is set upon this with increasing clearness and increasing power. But what kind of a new world? Shall philosophy sit still and leave mankind to be enticed by all sorts of administrative theories, theories which encourage the hope that, through their adoption, we shall automatically come to happiness and salvation? Shall philosophy not rather teach that no administration can be successful if it is not inspired by a consciousness . . . that human life is a commitment. . . .

What should we believe? . . . Consider our character and our destiny, and . . . believe that these can never be divorced from the character and destiny of nature at large. They go together; and in the hearty acceptance of their going together is to be found the quickening of the human spirit.[56]

Woodbridge was truly a philosopher—a lover rather than one who claimed the possession of wisdom. For he acknowledged that even the pursuer of the life of reason only occasionally and fleetingly attains the vision that is the basis for wisdom. But it was those momentary glimpses of supernatural vision that, for Woodbridge, provide the surest foundation for maintaining the realistic attitude of science and ultimately justify human practice.

Summary

As a realist, Woodbridge followed the lead of the subject matter, and, in his view, the subject matter of human living, especially the raising of scientifically unanswerable "why should" questions by man in his search for that justification not provided by Nature, shows that man is both a natural and a "supernatural" being; he is not only a body and a mind but also a "soul." Woodbridge claims that the failure to acknowledge this one genuine dualism within human living has contributed to an unwarranted philosophical belief in other dualisms, in problematic epistemologies, and in nonrealistic, reductive metaphysics.

According to Woodbridge, if man acknowledges that his life has both natural and supernatural dimensions and, therefore, accepts responsibility for his commitment to an ideal, which in turn justifies his search for knowledge used in pursuit of the happiness to be found in realizing that ideal, man lives a life of "faith."

Woodbridge's conviction is that if man responsibly and intelligently pursues justification, then his life of faith will be fulfilled in the "life of reason." Any workable ideal must be responsive to man's natural situation— for example, his animal impulses and needs, his natural capacities, and his existing social context—however, material progress of itself is not an adequate justification for human effort. Woodbridge believes, therefore, that the object of devotion that will sustain and justify man's attempt to remove conflicts and difficulties from the natural materials of his situation will be man's vision of the harmonious perfection of human nature and his communal situation. The life of reason leads its pursuer to attain a fleeting, but undistorted, intellectual vision of Nature: "theory." Once attained, theory inspires man to attempt to realize, without selfish interests or manipulation, the perfections appropriate to his natural materials—not only to realize himself but also society and the rest of Nature. According to Woodbridge, it is the momentary glimpses of theoretic vision within the life of reason that provide the surest foundation for maintaining the realistic attitude of science and ultimately justify human practice.

In 1922, Irwin Edman, a colleague of Woodbridge, wrote a sonnet that begins:

They do not live who choose the middle way

Edman knew it would tease Woodbridge; he may have had Woodbridge in mind when he wrote it. In any case, upon presenting it to Woodbridge, the emotional response was: "Give me a little time and you'll have a sonnet." On November 26, 1922, Edman was handed the following sonnet expressing Woodbridge's conviction that man's supernatural interests should be harmonized with his natural situation in pursuit of a life of reason:

Mark how the living still desire to live
By some excess of effort, pleasure, pain,
Reluctant measuredly to take and give,
Or find their due in balanced loss and gain.
O, measureless abundance! Dare we taste
The sweet without the bitter; sorrow leave
For soaring on unanchored clouds; or haste,
When joy's delayed, luxuriously to grieve?
Blest they who see the stars yet walk the earth,
In anguish keep the torch of hope aglow,
Share equably life's sorrow and life's mirth,
Hold beauty chaste and yet love's rapture know.
    Soul one with body, neither cloud nor clay,
    They only live who choose the middle way.[57]

NOTES

1. Frederick J. E. Woodbridge, *An Essay on Nature* (New York: Columbia University Press, 1940), p. 328.

2. Frederick J. E. Woodbridge, *Nature and Mind: Selected Essays of Frederick J. E. Woodbridge* (New York: Columbia University Press, 1937; reprint ed., New York: Russell and Russell, 1965), p. 4. Here he quotes Santayana's *Life of Reason,* which is, in turn, a paraphrase of Aristotle. Of Santayana's paraphrase, Woodbridge writes,

[*The Life of Reason*'s] controlling theme is simple and understandable. It can be condensed into a simple sentence as Santayana himself has condensed it in a sentence of great power, modestly attributing the idea of it to Aristotle, but expressing it in words which exhibit that idea in a manner which Aristotle never matched. . . . [Frederick J. E. Woodbridge, "Papers, 1884–1940" (Woodbridge's unpublished correspondences, diaries, essays, and lecture and reading notes, Columbia University, Special Collection), paper entitled: "Santayana's Philosophy," undated, p. 3.]

Santayana's *Life of Reason* was a source of inspiration for Woodbridge. Woodbridge writes, for example:

If I may use a chemical figure, the rending of Santayana has acted upon my own thoughts like a catalyzing agent, dissolving them and recombining them in ways better suited to my own satisfaction at least. [*Nature and Mind,* p. 4]

Woodbridge, however, believes that Santayana's development of the theme of the life of reason was problematic. In his reviews of Volumes I, II, and V of *The Life of Reason,* Woodbridge criticizes primarily Santayana's denying thought any efficacy within the domain of physical Nature. He reviewed the first two volumes of Santayana's *The Life of Reason* (i.e., *Reason in Common Sense* and *Reason in Society*) in the *New York Evening Post*, July 1, 1905, p. 6. A year later (March 10, 1906) he reviewed the fifth volume, *Reason in Science*, in the same publication (p. 7.)

3. Frederick J. E. Woodbridge, *The Realm of Mind* (New York: Columbia University Press, 1926), pp. 138–139. Nonetheless, elsewhere, he says,

> When the soul thinks, it is mind; when the mind feels, it is soul. To love with all one's heart, with all one's soul, with all one's mind, and with all one's strength is not to set up four compartments in which love may be exercised. [*Essay on Nature*, p. 301]

4. Woodbridge, "Papers, 1884–1940," essay entitled: "Easter Day, 1928," p. 11.

5. Woodbridge, "Papers, 1884–1940," essay entitled: "Platonism and the Spiritual Life," undated, p. 5. In this essay Woodbridge critically discussed ideas he believed were developed in Santayana's "Platonism and the Spiritual Life." This passage, however, and the others quoted hereafter from Woodbridge's essay reflect Woodbridge's own views.

6. Ibid., "Easter Day, 1928," p. 5.

7. Woodbridge, *Nature and Mind*, p. 358.

8. Woodbridge, *Essay on Nature*, p. 71.

9. Woodbridge, "Papers, 1884–1940," "Platonism and the Spiritual Life," p. 16.

10. Frederick J. E. Woodbridge, *The Purpose of History* (New York: Columbia University Press, 1916; reissued, Port Washington, New York: Kennikat Press, 1965), pp. 54–55.

11. Woodbridge, *Essay on Nature*, pp. 88–89. Furthermore, he says, "a dualism of the natural and the supernatural arises. . . . All other dualisms impress me as variants of that one" (ibid., p. 333).

12. Ibid., p. 280.

13. Woodbridge, "Papers, 1884–1940," essay entitled: "N. Y. Times April 8/28," pp. 4–5. For previous discussion of Nature as a "moral order," see *The Moral Order* in Chapter 4.

14. Ibid., "Easter Day, 1928," p. 5.

15. Woodbridge, *Nature and Mind*, p. 306. Here he anticipates a prevailing theme within the writings of existential philosophers: man is his projects; he is self-transcendence.

16. See Woodbridge, *Realm of Mind*, p. 92; also see above, Chapter 4, *The Human Mind as It Functions in the Human Organism and Person*, and especially, n. 50.

17. Woodbridge, *Nature and Mind*, pp. 299, 305–06.

18. See, for example, Woodbridge, *Realm of Mind*, p. 135.

19. Ibid., pp. 135–36; see also, *Essay on Nature*, p. 291.

20. Woodbridge, *Nature and Mind*, p. 306.

21. Woodbridge, *Essay on Nature*, p. 281.

22. Ibid., p. 330.

23. Woodbridge, "Papers, 1884–1940," "N. Y. Times," pp. 1–2, 4.

24. Ibid., pp. 2–3.

25. F. J. E. Woodbridge, "Faith and Pragmatism," *Chronicle*, 14 (1914), 322.

26. Ibid., 322–23.

27. Since Nature places man in a position of having to exercise choice, his freedom is not a freedom from choice. Rather, it is a freedom of choice of ideals or standards. Even here, however, his choices are limited by, for example, his knowledge, intelligence, and social situation.

28. Woodbridge, "Papers, 1884–1940," "Platonism and the Spiritual Life," p. 5.

29. Ibid., p. 8.

30. Frederick J. E. Woodbridge, "Contrasts in Education," three lectures given under the provisions of the Julius and Rose Sachs Endowment Fund, Bureau of Publications, Teachers College, Columbia University, 1929, pp. 18–19.

31. Woodbridge, *Nature and Mind*, p. 476. Possibly here Woodbridge is denying that any specific social or cultural tradition is constitutive of man's supernaturalness; nonetheless, even though Woodbridge did not offer any clarifying analysis, I believe that he held that man's being a social being is somehow basic to man's supernaturalness. Probably because he believes that social matters are too complex to allow for experimental scientific inquiry, Woodbridge writes,

> The social subjects . . . hardly can be taught without bias. Those subjects are not yet a science. A body of fundamental facts and principles is available in very few, if any, of them. [Paul A. Wolfe, "Conversations with the Old Man," *American Scholar,* 14, No. 1 (January 1945), 35.]

32. Woodbridge, *Nature and Mind*, p. 304.

33. Ibid., p. 305.

34. Ibid., pp. 303–04.

35. Ibid., p. 304.

36. Woodbridge, "Papers, 1884–1940," "Platonism and the Spiritual Life," p. 15.

37. Ibid., p. 5.

38. Woodbridge, *Essay on Nature*, pp. 336–37.

39. Woodbridge, *Purpose of History*, pp. 83–85.

40. Woodbridge, *Nature and Mind*, p. 4; see above, n. 2.

41. Ibid., p. 4.

42. See, for example, *Purpose of History*, pp. 79, 86–87, and 89. Of Aristotle, whose view greatly influenced his ideal of the "life of reason," Woodbridge says,

> So the theory of pleasure must be turned into a theory of the pleasant.
>
> But this, thinks Aristotle, is the complete abandonment of the hedonistic theory. The moment we turn to the pleasant as distinct from pleasure, we find that every free and unimpeded natural activity is pleasant. . . . For men, the good is the pleasant . . . but the pleasant in connection with that activity which characterizes and distinguishes man. [Frederick J. E. Woodbridge, *Aristotle's Vision of Nature,* (edited and intro. by John Herman Randall, Jr. New York: Columbia University Press, 1965), p. 97.]

Regarding Woodbridge's claim that the "life of reason" is *not* a utilitarianism, see, for example, his "Pluralism," p. 69. For other discussion, see "Chapter VI" ("A Note on Woodbridge's Ethical Theory") in Hae Soo Pyun, *Nature Intelligibility, and*

Metaphysics: Studies in the Philosophy of F. J. E. Woodbridge (Amsterdam: B. R. Grüner, 1971), pp. 195–104.

43. Woodbridge, *Nature and Mind,* p. 4.

44. Like other pursuits of happiness and of faiths in its attemp to realize an ideal in the world, the life of reason is not a science; rather, it is a "practical reason." It is artistic activity (*techné*) that, as such, applies scientific knowledge but is not itself a science. Woodbridge, therefore, distinguishes between "the rational" of science and the "reasonable" of practical reason:

> The rational is rigorous, impersonal, and averse to compromise; the reasonable is yielding, personal, and makes compromise a virtue. The rational entertains causes, the reasonable seeks consequences, so that a man is not rational unless he is reasonable or reasonable unless he is rational. (*Essay on Nature,* p. 302.)

Moreover, Woodbridge believes that, although scientific inquiry must be realistic in order to realize its goal of knowledge, the ideals and standards men seek to realize alone *justify* scientific inquiry. "We pursue knowledge for the sake of happiness and . . . if the pursuit of knowledge is to be effective it must be disinterested" (ibid., p. 277).

45. Woodbridge, *Nature and Mind,* p. 4.

46. Although, insofar as I know, Woodbridge only referred to charity or charitable love once (ibid., p. 304), and even there he did not use it precisely as I have used it, nonetheless, I believe that, following the suggestiveness of his comments regarding "theory" and of other textual materials (for example, see ibid., pp. 258–63), my interpretation is faithful to his vision of the "life of reason."

47. Woodbridge, *Nature and Mind,* p. 272.

48. Ibid.

49. Woodbridge, *Aristotle's Vision of Nature,* p. 91. Furthermore, he says,

> the consequent awakening in him of the suspicion that his life is committed, committed to possibilities which reach far beyond his daily joys and sorrows, hopes and fears—*he can see that it is this kind of seeing that makes him a man, and reveals to him what it really means to live with other men and to live with nature.* . . . Spiritual experience is also an experience of nature, and it is this experience alone which quickens and inspires living. [*Nature and Mind,* p. 260 (italics mine)]

50. See Herbert Schneider's *Ways of Being: Elements of Analytic Ontology* for a brief discussion of "natural piety" (New York: Columbia University Press, 1962), p. 68.

51. In his unpublished essay *Platonism and the Spiritual Life* Woodbridge argues against Santayana's view that, once spirit attains the freedom of an intellectual and contemplative vision, spirit is subsequently free from moral involvement in the world.

> It is not clear that the spiritual life, so essentially intellectual as he conceives it, should bear fruit of the kind he describes. A purely intellectual attitude may be attained reflecting in this insistent world, but it can not be sustained practically.

One must at least breathe and holding one's breath soon become a fleshly burden. The truth seems to be that the intellectual *attitude* attained is not entitled to be considered as a finality which defines an exercise in its own terms. . . . [It] is followed by something else than an intellectual exercise. If one could intellectually behold all things without refraction by his human self, . . . ultimately that attitude is bound to be followed by practical consequences of one sort or another. . . . the intellectual attitude once attained is followed by a suffusion of the self which can hardly be described otherwise than as an emotional commitment of its attitude toward existence. The self may then refract as it never refracted before. . . . A man is bound to become in some way more consciously and significantly a man than he ever was before. . . . The life he then chooses to lead will be no mere sustaining of the intellectual attitude but a commitment to some form of temporal and human existence. ["Papers, 1884–1940," pp. 12–13]

52. He notes,

The Greeks, in spite of an abundant egotism, did not normally forget their humanity. . . . The moment of divine aloofness [of *theoria*] with its cleansing of laughter and tears or of pity and fear is followed by a return to existence shared with others. *Only God can keep his isolation intact and serene.* Man must work, get on with one another, and manage cities. Perhaps they can do all this better after they have had the theoretical vision. At least they ought to understand better what they are about and *be wise about it instead of foolish.* [*Nature and Mind,* p. 273 (italics mine)]

53. Ibid.
54. Ibid., p. 262. Woodbridge, therefore, believes that the only surety against natural, social, and political abuse and exploitation is the development of wise characters in our leaders and citizenry. Although wise leaders and citizens will seek to forge the best administrative tools possible, they are more liable to maintain, for example, social justice, even with poor administrative instruments than are the corrupt with the best of tools.

Has the modern world a vision . . . which can inspire men even when they depart from it and sin against it? Perhaps some will say yes. There is democracy, there is socialism, there is communism, there is capitalism, there is fascism. But what do these names name? Surely not ideals of human life, but different methods of administration. There is no doubt that our happiness and well-being are bound up with methods of administration, but there is also no doubt that the successful carrying through of any method depends, not on its character, but on the character of its administrators. Communism as well as capitalism can ruin mankind. . . . Mankind always suffers when it has neither a religion nor a philosophy to quicken and inspire. . . . who can be so foolish as to believe that any administration can be invented which will automatically free men once for all from suffering? . . . Human salvation lies in inspiration, in a conception of the nature of man, which rises above his daily life to become its ideal and its judge. [ibid., pp. 259–60]

Woodbridge's conviction that it is the human wisdom of an enlightened soul which alone can insure mankind and Nature against exploitation and ruin is basic to his skepticism regarding the social sciences being scientific. Given the complexity of human social life, probably in most instances the social disciplines are not sciences in the sense of experimental science. If they are not scientific and yet make declarations in the name of science, then they may be using the title 'science' as a warrant for what is genuinely their expression of personal preferences or even biases (Wolfe, "Conversations with the Old Man," p. 35). More important, however, is Woodbridge's concern that social subject-matter rendered scientifically would encourage the belief that social reality is *determined* in such a way that the attempt to perfect human character would be futile.

"The only kind of world in which [genuine] democracy has any meaning is a world in which men are not cogs in a machine but separate themselves from their circumstances, to rise above their prejudices and their passions, to act justly, mercifully, fairly. The faith that inspired democracy was the faith that believed this reasonable soul of man could be saved and redeemed. Man's sin could be forgiven, his wickedness could be transformed, biased men could become judicious, and unjust men could become just . . .

. . . our ancestors could have a democracy because they could entrust men with responsibility. . . . they believed it was possible in a moral world for both men and courts to rise above prejudice and bias." [ibid., pp. 43–44]

55. Woodbridge, *Purpose of History*, p. 89.
56. Woodbridge, *Nature and Mind*, pp. 262–63.
57. Herbert Schneider provided both the sonnet and the information regarding the circumstances of Woodbridge's writing it. The interpretation of the sonnet's meaning is my own.

Woodbridge and his architect son, Fred, designed the stone together and the Greek inscription, expressive of Woodbridge's philosophy and life, is his adaptation of I Corinthians 15:46.

Selected Bibliography

Works by F. J. E. Woodbridge

Books

Woodbridge, Frederick J. E. *An Essay on Nature.* New York: Columbia University Press, 1940.

———. *Aristotle's Vision of Nature.* Edited with an introduction by John H. Randall, Jr. New York: Columbia University Press, 1965.

———. *Nature and Mind: Selected Essays of Frederick J. E. Woodbridge.* New York: Columbia University Press, 1937; reprint ed., New York: Russell and Russell, 1965. (See comprehensive bibliography of Woodbridge's writings, pp. 487–495.)

———. *The Purpose of History.* New York: Columbia University Press, 1916; reprint ed., Port Washington, New York: Kennikat Press, Inc., 1965.

———. *The Realm of Mind.* New York: Columbia University Press, 1926.

———. *The Son of Apollo: Themes of Plato.* Boston: Houghton Mifflin Company, 1929.

Articles

Woodbridge, F. J. E. "Berkeley's Realism." In *Studies in the History of Ideas,* Vol. I. New York: Columbia University Press, 1918, pp. 188–215.

———. "Consciousness and Meaning." *Psychological Review,* 15 (1908): 297-298.

———. "Ethics and Education." *A Cyclopedia of Education,* 2 (1911): 442–444.

————. "Faith and Pragmatism." *Chronicle,* 14 (1914): 319–323.

————. "John Locke." *A Cyclopedia of Education,* 4 (1912): 58–59.

————. "Locke's Essay." In *Studies in the History of Ideas,* Vol. III, edited by Columbia University Department of Philosophy. New York: Columbia University Press, 1935, pp. 243–251.

————. "Philosophy." In *Greek Literature.* New York: Columbia University Press, 1912, pp. 209–228.

————. "Philosophy and Modern Life." In *The Creative Intelligence and Modern Life.* University of Colorado Press, 1928, pp. 35–67.

————. "Pluralism." *Encyclopedia of Religion and Ethics,* 10 (1919): 66–70.

————. "Pragmatism and Education." *Educational Review,* 34 (1907): 227–240.

————. Review of *The Life of Reason,* Vol. V: *Reason in Science,* by George Santayana in *New York Evening Post,* March 10, 1906, p. 7.

————. "Santayana's Philosophy of Reason." Review of *The Life of Reason,* by George Santayana. Vol. I: *Reason in Common Sense* and Vol. II: *Reason in Society.* In *New York Evening Post,* July 1, 1905, p. 6.

————. "Some Implications of Locke's Procedure." In *Essays in Honor of John Dewey.* New York: Henry, Holt and Company, 1929, pp. 414–425.

————. "Spinoza." Lecture given at Columbia University and later published in *Columbia University Quarterly,* 25 (1932): 107–119.

————. "The Dominant Conception of the Earliest Greek Philosophy." *Philosophical Review,* 10 (1901): 359–374.

————. "The Importance of Philosophy." *Columbia University Quarterly,* 19 (1917): 367–383.

————. "The Moral Aspect of Pragmatism." *Church Congress Journal* (1913): 200–205.

————. "The Study of Philosophy." *Columbia University Quarterly,* 13 (1910): 39–45.

————. "The University and the Public." *Educational Review,* 49 (1915): 109–125.

Unpublished Materials

Woodbridge, F. J. E. "Contrasts in Education." Three lectures given under the provisions of the Julius and Rosa Sachs Endowment Fund. New York: Bureau of Publications, Teachers College, Columbia University, 1929.

————. "Opuscula." Essays, articles, and addresses bound for the Butler Library of Philosophy, Columbia University, New York.

————. "Papers, 1884–1940." Manuscript collection of Woodbridge's unpublished correspondences, diaries, essays, lecture notes, and notes on reading. Located in the Special Collections of the Columbia University Library, New York. Especially noted are the following:

"Ethics," I. Lecture and reading notes, 1894–1899, 198 pp.

"Ethics," II. Lecture and reading notes, 1894–1899, 127 pp.

"Child Study." 1894–1899, 15 pp.

"The Doctrine of Creation in the Old Testament." 1894–1899, 30 pp.

"The Idealism of Spinoza." 1894–1899, 10 pp.

"Interest and Will in their Relation to Education." 1894–1899, 65 pp.

"Logic." Lecture and reading notes, 1894–1899, 154 pp.

"Metaphysics." Lecture notes, 1894–1899, 29 pp.

"Psychology." Lectures, 1894–1899, 14 pp.

"The Two Aspects of Experience." 1894–1899, 4 pp.

"Pleasure and Morality." Essay, July 1896, 15 pp.

"Character." Commencement address, 1896, 22 pp.

"Religion: Preliminaries." Lecture, 5 pp.

"Skepticism." Lecture, 13 pp.

"Metaphysics." 1908, 26 pp.

"Time and Space." About 1910, 7 pp.

"The Concepts of Physics." About 1925.

"Greek Philosophy (1927–28)," 14 pp.

"Aristotle." Barnard Lecture, 1928, 11 pp.

"Supernatural." April 9, 1928, 9 pp.

"Lectures on Metaphysics, Spring, 1928–29," 133 pp.

"Plato and Aristotle." Lectures, 1929–1930, 63 pp.

"The Genetic Method." Notes, about 1930, 13 pp.

Notes on James, December 15, 1936, 23 pp.

"The Claims of Science." 111 pp.

Dewey's Reply to Nagel, Notes, 19 pp.

"Failures in Intelligence." Notes, 13 pp.

"Ideology." 34 pp.

"Language." Phi Beta Kappa lecture, 9 pp.

Santayana, "Discovery of Natural Objects." 20 pp.

"Santayana's Philosophy." 4 pp.

"Easter Day, 1928," 10 pp.

"Platonism and the Spiritual Life." 14 pp.

"Metaphysics 1932–33," 66 pp.

"*N. Y. Times,* April 9/28," 8 pp.

"Nature Beheld," 3 pp.

Works by Other Authors

Books

Delaney, C. F. *Mind and Nature: A Study of the Naturalistic Philosophy of Cohen, Woodbridge, and Sellars.* Notre Dame Press, 1969.

Krikorian, Yervant H., ed., *Naturalism and the Human Spirit*. New York: Columbia University Press, 1944.

Lamprecht, Sterling P. *The Metaphysics of Naturalism*. New York: Appleton-Century-Crofts, Inc., 1967.

Nagel, Ernest. *Logic Without Metaphysics*. Glencoe, Ill.: Free Press, 1957.

Pyun, Hae Soo. *Nature, Intelligibility, and Metaphysics: Studies in the Philosophy of F. J. E. Woodbridge*. Amsterdam: B. R. Grüner, 1971.

Articles

Costello, Harry Todd. "The Naturalism of Woodbridge." In *Naturalism and the Human Spirit,* edited by Y. H. Krikorian. New York: Columbia University Press, 1944, pp. 295–318.

Randall, John Herman, Jr. "Dean Woodbridge." *Columbia University Quarterly,* 32 (December, 1940): 324–331.

————. "Epilogue: The Nature of Naturalism." In *Naturalism and the Human Spirit,* edited by Y. H. Krikorian. New York: Columbia University Press, 1944, pp. 354–382.

————. "Introduction" and "The Department of Philosophy." In *A History of the Faculty of Philosophy, Columbia University*. New York: Columbia University Press, 1957, pp. 308.

Taylor, A. E. Review of *The Son of Apollo: Themes of Plato,* by F. J. E. Woodbridge. *Mind: A Quarterly Review of Psychology and Philosophy,* 39 (1930): 252.

Wolfe, Paul A. "Conversations with the Old Man," *American Scholar,* 14 (January 1945): 33–44.

Unpublished Materials

Columbia University. Minutes of the Faculty of Philosophy Upon the Death of Professor Frederick J. E. Woodbridge, June 1, 1940.

Harrington, Kathleen W. "Frederick J. E. Woodbridge and the Naturalistic Interpretation of Plato." Ph.D. dissertation, Emory University, 1971.

Heuser, Patricia A. "Woodbridge, Critic of Modern Philosophy." Ph.D. dissertation, Columbia University, 1950.

Jones, William F. "F. J. E. Woodbridge's Theory of Man." Ph.D. dissertation, Tulane University, 1976.

Pyun, Hae Soo. "On the Metaphysics of F. J. E. Woodbridge." Ph.D. dissertation, Columbia University, 1966.

Ross, H. Gordon, and Schneider, Herbert W., conversations.

Index

191